"*To every man his chance, to every man, regardless of his birth, his shining golden opportunity—to every man the right to live, to work, to be himself, and to become whatever thing his manhood and his vision can combine to make him—this, seeker, is the promise of America.*"

THOMAS WOLFE

NORTH
CAROLINA
AND
THE NEGRO

Editors

CAPUS M. WAYNICK
SPECIAL CONSULTANT TO THE GOVERNOR
ON RACE RELATIONS

JOHN C. BROOKS
ADMINISTRATOR
NORTH CAROLINA MAYORS' CO-OPERATING COMMITTEE

ELSIE W. PITTS
RECORDING SECRETARY
NORTH CAROLINA MAYORS' CO-OPERATING COMMITTEE

Published by the North Carolina Mayors' Co-operating Committee
Raleigh, 1964

Library of Congress Catalog Card Number: 64-23203

The State College Print Shop, Raleigh, North Carolina

R. Wensell Grabarek

David Schenck

Mayors' Co-operating Committee

O. O. Allsbrook

Stanford R. Brookshire
Chairman

J. Harper Beall, Jr.

M. C. Benton, Jr.

Wilbur Clark

Levin B. Culpepper

Earl W. Eller

William B. Harrison

Floyd D. Mehan

James W. Reid

25063

iii

PREFACE

This publication reports the experiences of cities and towns in North Carolina when they were confronted by the organized revolt of Negroes against segregation which denied them citizenship equality. The sponsor of this is the Mayors' Co-operating Committee, composed of the mayors of 12 cities and towns, which came into being on the initiative of the Greensboro Conference of Mayors held on July 5, 1963. That meeting was called by Governor Sanford at a time when Negro demonstrations were in progress in many communities.

Governor Sanford indicated that he thought the handling of the race problem should rest largely with local government and businessmen. He urged cities and counties to organize groups to be allied with the State Good Neighbor Council which he had established. He also encouraged the formation of local biracial organizations throughout the State.

The Greensboro meeting endorsed Governor Sanford's position and authorized our Committee to work closely with him and with local government throughout the State in maintaining law and order while opening communications with Negro leadership calculated to promote adjustment of racial differences.

The extension of citizenship rights and equal opportunities can, the Committee believes, lift the level of responsible citizenship in all our communities by making more of our citizens self-supporting, self-respecting, and contributing members of society.

Before the book could be published as an aid to local government, The Civil Rights Act of 1964 was enacted, changing the conditions under which the work in this State was proceeding. The Committee still believes that there is value in recounting the history of the Negro movement and the way that it was handled at the state level and in the cities and towns in North Carolina.

Chairman
North Carolina Mayors' Co-operating Committee

Terry Sanford, *Governor*, 1961-   .

FOREWORD

The decision of the Mayors' Co-operating Committee to publish this book has my approval and, with that approval, go my thanks for the diligence with which that Committee has proceeded with its support of programs based in good will and justice.

At the beginning of this century a great governor came to power in this State in a bitter campaign for white supremacy. Despite disfranchisement of many Negro voters, in that campaign, Governor Aycock advocated "universal education" and said emphatically that he meant the education of all children alike. I quote from a statement Governor Aycock made while in office: "If I had the power and the wealth to put a public school house in every district in North Carolina, I would enter into a guarantee that no child, white or black, in ten years from now, should reach the age of twelve without being able to read and write."

In elaboration of his position, Governor Aycock said: *"As a white man, I am afraid of but one thing for my race and that is we shall become afraid to give the Negro a fair chance. The white man in the south can never attain to his fullest growth until he does absolute justice to the Negro race."* Now, some 64 years later, as Governor, I affirm my own confidence in the philosophy of Aycock and I am pleased with the evidence that local government in this State is taking a lead in promoting justice for our Negro citizens.

I hope that the guidelines, explicit and implicit, in this book, will be helpful to encourage the continuation of a program based in good will and fair play so implemented as to improve the status of the one-fourth of our people who are of the Negro race. It is encouraging to me that not one of the Municipal Reports capsuled in this book indicates anything less than recognition of the need for action to assure even-handed justice and the full utilization of the Negroes' potential for good citizenship.

Raleigh, North Carolina
1964

Governor

ACKNOWLEDGMENTS

A book does not just happen. It requires the contribution of many talents in varying proportions. The Governor, the Mayors' Co-operating Committee, and the Editors thank the following for their valuable assistance:

Editorial Consultant: Mrs. Elizabeth W. Wilborn, State Department of Archives and History, whose professional assistance was invaluable and extraordinary.

Composition Analysts: David K. E. Wilborn and Noble J. Tolbert, State Department of Archives and History, whose aid in proofreading and indexing was comprehensive.

Source material: The Mayors, Chairmen of biracial organizations, and civic leaders, whose co-operation generated community progress reports and declarations.

Guest Authors: W. C. Chadwick, *Chairman,* Biracial Committee of New Bern; D. S. Coltrane, *Chairman,* North Carolina Good Neighbor Council; Dr. Eli Ginzberg, *Director,* Columbia University's Conservation of Human Resources Project; and Ralph Moody, *Deputy Attorney General,* whose contributions provided depth.

Bibliography: Roger B. Foushee, whose ingenuity bore a helpful addition.

Research: Nancy Katherine Williams, North Carolina State Library, whose deliberateness expedited fact determination.

General Support: Colonel David T. Lambert and the State Highway Patrol, whose multiple services assisted production.

Typing: Mrs. Rebecca S. Burgess, Sara Jo Gault, Mrs. Lois R. Haswell, Mrs. Rena Jean Long, June F. Sears, Mrs. Anna P. Stallings, Mrs. Ann L. P. Sterling, Mrs. Mary Kate Tarleton, and Mrs. Marie H. Wiley, whose patience and expertise facilitated recordation.

Mimeographing: J. Edward Massenburg and William L. Montague, whose services aided distribution of drafts.

Management: Mrs. Claire E. Nickels and Mrs. Mattie R. Keys, whose help furnished supplies.

Photography: Charles Clark, Conservation and Development; Mrs. Madlin M. Futrell, Archives and History; and Harold L. Powell, Highway Department, whose skill contributed pictorially.

Artists: Bill H. Ballard and Margaret E. Johnson, whose talent added interest and beauty.

Printing: Graham S. Fulghum and A. Wilton Kelly, whose knowledge and experience gave guidance.

Illustrations: The pictures on the following pages were furnished by: Dr. Albert Amon—36, 40, 42, 48; State Department of Archives and History—4, 228, 234, (by Madlin Futrell)—254; Fabian Bachrach—*iii;* Mrs. Agnew H. Bahnson, Jr. (by State Art Museum)—*Frontispiece* and End sheet; Bill H. Ballard—*Cover;* Burnie Batchelor—228; Dr. Andrew A. Best (by Fred Robertson)—98; Robert Blanchard (from *Great American Scientists and Inventors*)—13; Department of Community Colleges—218; Department of Conservation and Development (by Charles Clark)—6, 167; Coppedge Photography, Inc.—*iii;* Ellis Corbett—258, 268; *Equal Protection of the Laws in North Carolina*—8, 196; *High Point Enterprise* (by Art Richardson)— 108, (by Dick Swaim)—118; Margaret E. Johnson—16, 222; Killebrew Studio —*iii;* Kugler's, Inc.—190; Martin's Studio—*iii;* Floyd B. McKissick (by Purefoy's Foto)—26, 62, 65, 75, 126, 264, (by Service Printing Company)—241; Reverend Jack Piephoff—21; Sheep's Studio—*iii;* James N. Smith (by *Goldsboro News-Argus*)—86; Snow Studio and Camera Shop—*iii;* Southeastern Engraving Company—*iii;* Jim Thornton—*iii;* Jim Wallace—14, 28, 30, 32, 34, 38, 39, 44, 50, 68, 90, 102, 136, 142, 150, 158, 170, 173, 188, 202, 203, 204, 212, 226, 252, 270, 288; Bob Welsh Studio—*iii.*

INTRODUCTION

Nearly all of the material published herein was written, assembled, and in type before the Civil Rights Statute surmounted the hurdle of opposition in the Senate and moved on to final enactment. Despite the effect that the federal law will have on the problem of Negro discontent, it cannot solve it, and full discussion of that problem will continue.

When this report was initiated, progress towards alleviation of conditions in North Carolina about which Negroes complained was being made by representatives of city governments and of private businesses, who were convinced that conditions should be changed. Governor Terry Sanford encouraged these representatives in their approach. Early in 1963 he established the Good Neighbor Council to promote racial co-operation at the State level while local governments were trying to maintain order and institute reforms in the face of spreading Negro "demonstrations."

The brunt of the Negro movement was felt at the local level and many of the cities and towns had to deal with it largely without state aid except for occasional reinforcement of police by the State Highway Patrol. Recognizing the need for increased concert of effort, the Governor called a meeting of North Carolina mayors. Invitations were sent to some 350 mayors and a meeting was held in Greensboro July 5, 1963, to hear the Governor. Out of that meeting came the Mayors' Co-operating Committee, with members volunteering to work with the Governor and with their fellow mayors as helpfully as possible in racial matters. That Committee sponsors the publication of this report.

Governor Sanford believed that justice could be promoted without new laws, and this book was prepared while the chances seemed good that the problem would be left to the several states and to private businesses. Now conditions have been changed by enactment of the Federal Statute and its impairment of the theory that businessmen have the right to choose whom they would serve. Assuming that the new Federal Act will be upheld under prompt testing of its constitutionality, it must be recognized that the approach to racial peace will be changed.

The law will not resolve the problem of racial discrimination. It will have some effect on employment practices, but it alone cannot extend greatly the Negro's precarious beachhead in our economic system. Work of the kind that the local governments and the State Good Neighbor Council were doing remains essential, and this report reflects long standing and somewhat general willingness of white citizens to aid the Negroes in substantial improvement of their lot in North Carolina.

The Governor contemplated more than mere pacification of people who pleaded for citizenship equality. The Governor acted in the belief that measures should be taken to give the Negroes substantial aid in their aspirations towards better income and better homes. Many city governments recognized that the limitations on work opportunities for Negroes establish and maintain an unjust disparity between their economic status and that of their white fellow citizens, and these governments have been working to reduce these limitations in co-operation with the State Good Neighbor Council.

The subsidence of Negro demonstrations in North Carolina was due in large part to the Governor's actions in opening channels for interracial communications and keeping them open. At no time did he indicate tolerance of "civil disobedience"; but the Negro leaders gradually manifested their confidence in his will to promote fair and full consideration of their grievances, and thus tension was reduced.

The 55 municipal reports herein show that efforts have been largely directed toward accomplishing by negotiation most of the reforms that the new Federal Statute seeks to compel. The brief history of the movement in the State during the past several years, together with an authoritative analysis of the laws under which segregation existed, are in this book for consideration in connection with these municipal reports. Declarations pertinent to the race problem in the State are also included.

Southern efforts to find a basis on which Negroes and whites could co-operate were being exerted well before the development of the so-called Negro revolution. Thoughtful southern leaders of both races were seeking friendly rapprochement. In October, 1942, a meeting of southern Negro leaders was held in Durham. Out of that meeting came a manifesto of interesting character. The Negro conference declared:

All men who believe in justice, who love peace and who believe in the meaning of this country are under the necessity of working together to draw off from the body of human society the poison of racial antagonism. This is one of the disruptive forces which, unless checked, will ultimately disturb and threaten the stability of the nation. Either to deny or to ignore the increased tension between the white and colored races would be a gesture of insincerity.

The Durham Negro conference 22 years ago declared its optimism by saying:

That there are acute and intricate problems associated with two races living side by side in the South cannot be denied. But these problems can be solved and will ultimately disappear if they are brought out into an atmosphere of justice and good will. If we approach them with contempt in one group and with resentment in the other group, then we work on hopeless terms. The solution to these problems can be found only in men of both races who are known to be men of determined good will. The ultimate solution will be found in evolutionary methods and not in ill-founded revolutionary movements which promise immediate solutions.

The Negroes in the Durham conference stated a profound economic truth, saying that "if we cannot plan for a well-trained, well-employed and prosperous Negro population, the economic future of the South is hopeless."

A subsequent meeting of whites in Atlanta referred to this Negro manifesto saying in part, "Their statement is so frank and courageous, so free from any suggestion of threat and ultimatum, and at the same time shows such good will that we gladly agree to co-operate."

This promising racial co-operation in solution of the problems of the two races living side by side in the southern states, where the Negroes are one-third of the whole population, possibly appeared to some as too slow since only limited action followed noble statements. At any rate, some Negro leadership became impatient and precipitated the so-called "revolution" which has resulted in Congressional action.

The mayors who form the Committee sponsoring publication of this report believe that the good work that has been done in the interest of racial co-operation must be continued. They have observed the increase of crime throughout the country and believe that its control must depend largely upon the close co-operation of good citizens of all races. The importance of establishing conditions under which there will be no barriers to that kind of co-operation can hardly be exaggerated. In this faith, local governments and State government have worked diligently and the Mayors' Co-operating Committee hopes that there will be no break in the continuity of that kind of effort to build a greater State through the full use of the inherent power of all its people.

The Bibliography published herein points to a vast volume of literature pertinent to the case of the American Negro. Interest in his case is not merely regional or national—it is world-wide.

His determined drive for citizenship equality in our own democracy is one of the most dramatic and most important movements of our times.

All of us need to understand the Negro's position. The reading suggested in the Bibliography presents various views and it is fairly comprehensive. In the years ahead all of us will be working on the problem of racial discontent or will be a part of that problem. Informative reading can be helpful in reaching the right kind of judgment, or in guiding our action.

Adjustment of human relations to preserve the rights of the majority, as well as those of any minority, is essential to a great society, or even a good one, and something stronger than tolerance is needed. Courtesy and kindness—a liberal use of the Golden Rule—may help us make that adjustment.

THE EDITORS

TABLE OF CONTENTS

LIST OF ILLUSTRATIONS

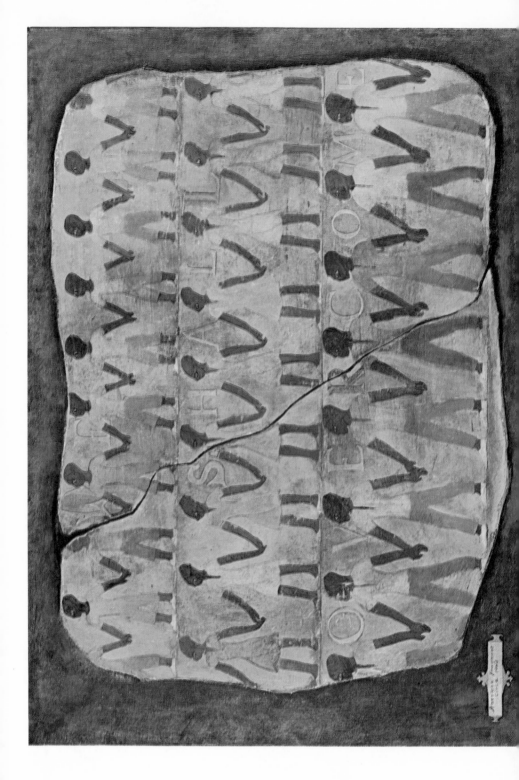

I

The Negro Protest Movement

The Negro leaders of the protest movement in behalf of equal civil rights date the beginning of massive demonstrations from 1946. An incident involving a "Jim Crowed" Negro passenger on a bus in Montgomery, Alabama, sparked the national movement which spread through the South in which Negroes marched and insistently demanded citizenship equality. The first of the "freedom rides" which passed through parts of North Carolina occurred in 1946. The riders passed through Chapel Hill, stopped there briefly, and proceeded westward to Asheville. They went on into Tennessee and disbanded this particular bus group at Knoxville.

For many years, the NAACP (National Association for Advancement of Colored People) had been active in the defense of civil rights claims in the courts where Negroes were involved, but it did not take charge of the vigorous protest movement which resulted in group demonstrations, sit-ins, and marching singers. A new organization, the Congress of Racial Equality, commonly known as CORE, did take the leadership and increased the tempo of the protest movement.

In August, 1960, following many demonstrations in February and March, some Negro leaders called a meeting at Shaw University at Raleigh with a view to setting up a permanent organization of southern student leaders. Those most active in calling this meeting included Reverend Douglas Moore, Floyd B. Mc-Kissick, both of Durham, and Gordon Carey, a field worker from New York. All these men were active in CORE. Probably this Raleigh meeting inspired the more complete organization in Nashville, Tennessee, of the Student Non-violent Co-ordinating Committee.

"AMERICAN FRAGMENT" BY MRS. PEGGY DODGE OF ASHEVILLE. USED WITH PERMISSION OF ITS OWNER, MRS. AGNEW H. BAHNSON, JR., OF WINSTON-SALEM.

With the younger leaders, many of whom were college students, becoming active, "sit-ins" were started in Durham in 1953 and somewhat later they were employed in Greensboro. In some parts of the State, particularly in the eastern part, the Southern Christian Leadership Conference, an organization which grew out of the leadership of the Reverend Martin Luther King, became active.

Songs were written expressing race aspirations, leaders were identified and cohesiveness developed among the different groups conducting demonstrations in various parts of the State. Many Negro ministers became leaders of the movement, abandoning their usual role as preachers of resignation and contentment. All advocated nonviolence. Passive resistence to customs and policies regarded as unjust was the usual order of the day.

The pressure of the marches and the picketing placed extraordinary burdens on municipal police forces, the sheriff's departments, and the State Highway Patrol. Municipal budgets were impaired by the unusual police demand. Public irritation resulted in a few outbreaks of violence. One white man was killed at Lexington.

Business was impeded. In some cases the demonstrators blocked streets or entrances to buildings by sitting down or lying down and ignoring police orders. The jails of some communities were crowded with Negroes arrested on charges of trespass, disorderly conduct, inciting to riot, or, in many cases, of marching without a permit. Old statutes and ordinances requiring permits to march were invoked. New ordinances designed to control the demonstrations were adopted by some municipalities and were challenged by Negroes as invasions of their constitutional rights to assemble peaceably and to petition for redress of grievances.

The white citizens reacted with less violence than they did in some other states. Both Governor Luther H. Hodges and Governor Terry Sanford counseled moderation. Governor Sanford dealt considerately with the Negro leadership, openly recognizing the need for change in traditional treatment of their race. He called for educational efforts and peaceful negotiations as alternatives to street marches and picketing. He made known his belief that neither federal nor state laws should be needed to bring about just reforms. While holding that the problem is primarily for local government and private enterprise to handle,

2

the Governor offered special counseling for communities that requested it, setting up an office for the purpose with Capus Waynick of High Point as his aide and consultant. A Mayors' Co-operating Committee resulted from a convocation of mayors held at Greensboro and addressed by Governor Sanford. The Governor also set up a State Good Neighbor Council to deal practically with the economic aspects of the race problem, and urged cities and counties to form chapters to be allied with that State Council.

Some of the cities in the State examined critically the conditions against which the Negroes protested and officially recognized that adjustments should be made to promote citizenship equality. Emergency biracial committees were formed, followed in some cases by human relations commissions, intended to be permanent. The experiences which are dealt with in this book reflect action by municipal government and private citizens to make changes by voluntary action. No community in the State has enacted laws to require opening public accommodations by private businesses, as requested by some Negro leaders. An ordinance to cover this request was introduced at Chapel Hill in the City Council, but was not passed.

This publication emphasizes developments during the administration of Governor Terry Sanford, who is serving the last of his 1961-1965 term. Actually, three governors have had to deal with the problem. The United States Supreme Court decision of May, 1954, calling for public school integration caused Governor William B. Umstead to name a committee to study the problem. This committee reported in December to Governor Luther H. Hodges, who became Chief Executive at Umstead's death, November 9, 1954.

Something of the roles played by all three Governors will be discussed briefly herein, but the report deals principally with what has happened since the inauguration of Governor Sanford in January, 1961.

Guidelines for action must be sought in the experiences of the State and its cities rather than in any formula the Mayors' Co-operating Committee has developed. There have been variations in the methods of the cities and towns in naming biracial groups and in the methods the groups have employed in dealing with the problem. These are presented herein for information and evaluation.

WHERE THE AMERICAN NEGROES LIVE

Living in North Carolina is about 6 per cent of the Negro population in the United States of 18,871,831. The state with the largest total Negro population is New York. North Carolina stands fourth among all the states in the number of its Negro people. Texas and Georgia have larger numbers and several of the deep south states which are having maximum trouble in meeting the Negro petition for civil rights have fewer Negroes than does this State. The North Carolina Negro population numbers 1,116,021 and constitutes 24.8 per cent of the total population of the State.

THE NEGRO EXODUS FROM NORTH CAROLINA, SCENE AT A RAILWAY STATION. COPY FROM *FRANK LESLIE'S NEWSPAPER*, FEBRUARY 15, 1890.

During the days of Negro slavery, a number of other southern states had larger Negro populations than did North Carolina. Slave ownership in this State was never as massive as in some of the deep south states, such as South Carolina, Mississippi, Louisiana, and Georgia. In 1860 there were 3,953,760 slaves and a large number of freemen among the Negro population of the South. Incidentally, many of the freemen had accumulated considerable wealth. It has been estimated that the Negro property owners—and some of their property was in terms of Negro slaves—concentrated around New Orleans and Charleston had taxable wealth of twelve to fifteen million dollars.

The 1960 census of the United States showed the following distribution of the Negro people:

Alabama	980,271	Missouri	390,853
Alaska	6,771	Montana	1,467
Arizona	43,403	Nebraska	29,262
Arkansas	388,787	Nevada	13,484
California	883,861	New Hampshire	1,903
Colorado	39,992	New Jersey	514,875
Connecticut	107,449	New Mexico	17,063
District of Columbia	411,737	New York	1,417,511
Delaware	60,688	North Carolina	1,116,021
Florida	880,186	North Dakota	777
Georgia	1,122,596	Ohio	786,097
Hawaii	4,943	Oklahoma	153,084
Idaho	1,502	Oregon	18,133
Illinois	1,037,470	Pennsylvania	852,750
Indiana	269,275	Rhode Island	18,332
Iowa	25,354	South Carolina	829,291
Kansas	91,445	South Dakota	1,114
Kentucky	215,949	Tennessee	586,876
Louisiana	1,039,207	Texas	1,187,125
Maine	3,318	Utah	4,148
Maryland	518,410	Vermont	519
Massachusetts	111,842	Virginia	816,258
Michigan	717,581	Washington	48,738
Minnesota	22,263	West Virginia	89,378
Mississippi	915,743	Wisconsin	74,546
		Wyoming	2,183

WHO IS THE NORTH CAROLINA NEGRO?

While the Negro is descended from Africans imported forcibly and sold into slavery, few of the race are pure-blooded. An infusion of white blood has occurred, affecting his inherited abilities and his attitudes. His characteristics derive from blood strains of masterful men of other races, perhaps as much as from his African origin.

Even in early Colonial days, a few Negro planters became slave-owners themselves. The first appeal to the courts to establish property rights to a Negro slave was made by a Virginia Negro planter in 1654—just three hundred years before the outlawing by the United States Supreme Court of the practice of "separate but equal" school facilities.

The first entry of Negro slaves in the Virginia Colony—North Carolina then was part of Virginia—occurred in 1619 when 20 arrived at Jamestown in one group. Most of the Negroes imported to the American colonies came from an area on the West Coast of Africa extending from the Niger River Valley nearly 1,000 miles southward. This coastal frontage was some 500 miles north of the Equator and about an equal distance south of it. Only a few more than 1,000 were imported from the far eastern part of Africa—almost altogether from Mozambique and the island of Madagascar—and very few came from the interior of the African continent.

The plantation system of the South lent itself well to distribution of the Negroes in such fashion as to break down their family life and their tribal loyalties, and to weaken the memory of their religions and African customs. This system also made slave rebellion more difficult than it might have been had the Negroes been concentrated in some area and possessed of a common language. Generally, they adopted the religion of their masters and many became members of Christian churches, especially Baptist and Methodist.

Despite their wide distribution there were Negro revolts in some southern states and many individual escapes of Negroes, as they found it possible to make their way into nonslaveholding territory following the establishment of the Republic.

It is interesting to bear in mind that the first American who lost his life in the Revolution against England was a Negro. As has been stated, the free Negroes in the United States, including

7

CONCENTRATION OF NEGRO POPULATION, 1960.

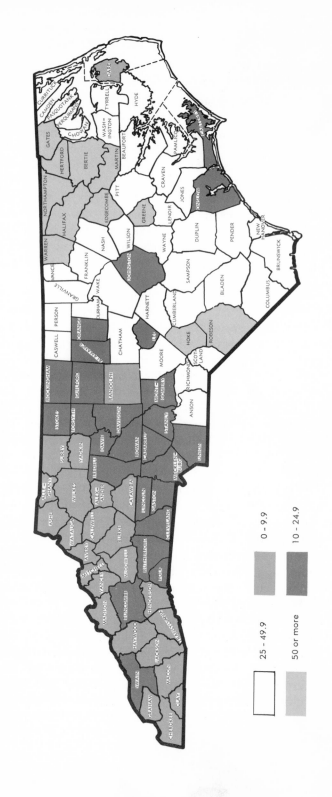

0 - 9.9

10 - 24.9

25 - 49.9

50 or more

many in the South, accumulated substantial wealth and many of them were prosperous in the years before the Civil War.

At the time of the outbreak of the Civil War many white southerners recognized both the evils of slavery and its economic burden for both white and Negro. Out of no love for the Negro, whom he would have deported, Hinton Rowan Helper of this State wrote a book against the slave system, *The Impending Crisis,* about 1859. The author was burned in effigy on a street in High Point.

In slavery the Negro acquired Christianity and some thoughtful members of the race now ascribe his long peaceful acceptance of discrimination as due in part to his faith in a reward hereafter for his patience and his kindness on earth.

After the Negro was freed from slavery, and following a brief exercise of equal political rights, he was reduced by both law and customs to limited expressions of his citizenship. Recently, he began speculating as to whether he should wait for rewards in the hereafter or attempt to change his earthly lot. Lacking both political power and great wealth, he gravitated to offering his body in passive resistance to injustice.

He has developed a pride in his own race and education has given him personal dignity and power. It has given him also a burning awareness of the injustice of discrimination because of his race and color. The discrimination is not because of his *creed.* His creed is the creed of his white neighbor. He usually has firm faith in the God his white neighbor worships, and is his white neighbor's equal in loyalty to the American political creed.

He is descended from black men and women, many of whom remained faithful to ties of friendship with white people formed in bondage—even when invading armies came to the State to end Negro enslavement.

In the slave era, Negroes in North Carolina taught white children in some cases, and some planned and built manor houses for their masters. Many were talented and superior individuals.

The past century has marked the rapid rise of the Negro in North Carolina. The record is impressive—in the arts, in sports, in education, in public and private administration. Competent teachers, notable diplomats and high-principled and capable public officials, and outstanding businessmen, have risen to attest the high quality of the North Carolina Negro. Wake Forest

College at Winston-Salem this year for the first time is recognizing the athletic potential of the State's Negroes by inviting several to matriculate and try out for the college's very able football and basketball teams.

The Negro is 25 per cent of human North Carolina—one-fourth of the building blocks with which the future must be constructed. With whites and Negroes co-operating in good will, he is an important and admirable asset; with them working at cross-purposes in hostility and hatred, he can be a tragic liability. Can this nation justify the great investment which it is making in promoting African and other alien peoples to first-class citizenship while denying these, its own people, liberation from indignities that create hate and handicap constructive co-operation? The fundamental question is not whether unjust discrimination is Christian, but whether it is sane.

WHAT THE PETITIONERS WANT

1. *Freedom NOW.*
   Their marching songs emphasize the complaint that a century after *Emancipation*, the Negro is denied essential American freedom.

2. *Complete INTEGRATION.*
   They insist on complete integration of the public schools and institutions of higher learning; and they protest restrictions on use of theaters, playgrounds, swimming pools, bowling alleys and places of public acommodation operated by private enterprise. They ask for "every right" the white man enjoys.

3. *They protest segregated housing.*
   The Negro denounces restrictions in real estate deeds codifying the aversion of his white neighbors to his entry into areas where white dwellings predominate or any interfering with the Negro's choice of a home or a community in which to establish one.

4. *His right to vote.*
   He charges that the small registration of the Negro is due to manipulation of political machinery to retard and discourage the Negro in his efforts to qualify.

5. *Discrimination in work opportunities.*

The Negro alleges frustration of the skilled and talented of his race because of the kinds of jobs available to them. He demands elimination of discrimination in public employment and pleads for its elimination in private employment. He asks for full equality in work opportunities.

6. *Equal treatment in hospitals.*

The Negro specifically demands that the institutions for the treatment of human ills, mental and physical, especially those constructed wholly or in part with tax funds, be open to both patients and staff, without racial discrimination.

7. *Religious freedom.*

He deplores the closing of white churches to him as worshiper or member. He asks for the elimination of these barriers.

8. *Total freedom.*

One of the principal Negro leaders says his race seeks "total freedom" as outlined in the Constitution, the right to do anything that any white person has the right to do. He maintains that the system of segregation as practiced in the South in the legislative, judicial, and administrative branches of the government, denies the Negro citizenship equality and a fair deal. He adds that the Negro seeks a change of values as well as a change of laws, and he charges that from the lowest court to the highest court in the State, racial discrimination is in practice.

WHAT MANY CITIZENS BELIEVE IS A CONSTRUCTIVE CREED

— that North Carolina should deal with the petition of the Negro citizen for civil rights in a spirit of sympathy and good will.

— that the Negro has the ability to make a great contribution to the future of the State.

— that North Carolina must use the constructive potential of all of its people to become the powerful State it should be.

— that many of the changes which the Negro is asking for should be granted in order that he may be relieved of the psychological burden imposed upon him by the daily indignities of discrimination.

— that it is impossible for the Negro to do his full part to control delinquency and crime while obsessed with a sense of unjust treatment and that there is an increasing need for the co-operation of all to reverse a dangerous trend towards hatred and disorder.

— that North Carolina should recognize the right of every citizen, regardless of race or color, to full equality before the law and that every person of good character and behavior should be treated without discrimination because of race, color, or creed in places of public accommodation, including hotels, motels, restaurants, theaters, and other places of licensed business engaged in the sale of goods or services to the general public.

— that visible traces of racial segregation should be eliminated from all branches of government and public business establishments in the State.

— that public playgrounds and areas or institutions for recreation financed by taxation should be opened to all of good behavior, regardless of race or color.

— that public health services should be administered without racial discrimination.

— that the State should accept the decision of the United States Supreme Court that the public schools be integrated, and handle the registration of all children generally in accordance with clearly defined school district lines.

— that all institutions of higher learning should be open to qualified applicants without regard to race or color.

— that the need should be recognized for special efforts to upgrade Negro skills and vocational opportunities in the belief that an approach to economic parity for the Negro is essential not only to justice but to a rich and happy State.

— that the Negro citizen should be encouraged to register for the exercise of suffrage to an extent proportionate to the registration by the whites.

— that a program or programs should be promoted for radical improvement of the housing of Negroes in full recognition of the relationship of hovel housing to human frustration and delinquency.

— that the right should be recognized of people to choose their own friends and social companions and to form their private clubs by the customary practice of selection, in the belief that an individual's true integration with the society in which he lives, or even in his own home, must depend not on law, but on the individual's personality and conduct.

GEORGE WASHINGTON CARVER, BY ROBERT BLANCHARD, ARTIST. FROM *GREAT AMERICAN SCIENTISTS AND INVENTORS*, BY MONROE HEATH, WITH PERMISSION OF PACIFIC COAST PUBLISHERS.

13

II

Municipal Response to the Challenge

". . . I appointed a biracial committee, composed of eleven members to come to grips with what we in Durham no longer call a problem—but an opportunity."

R. Wensell Grabarek
Mayor of Durham

Negro demonstrations did not create the race problem but they revealed its present intensity and brought it to crisis. The white North Carolinian has lived in the comfortable conviction that the Negro was content with his lot and was making satisfactory progress.

The Negroes' insistence on a fuller measure of "freedom" has brought before the State the fact of their great discontent. They are asking for full citizenship rights and privileges and they have raised an issue which many city governments recognize as just and importunate. They have revealed a state of mind which they complain and many cities plan effective adjustments that compels the white majority to examine the conditions about to correct some of these conditions.

These cities and towns recognize that justice and common sense demand action to relieve the psychological and some of the physical conditions of the Negro people. If they never marched again nor established another picket line, the State still is considered to be challenged to develop a program for their relief.

The response of North Carolina owners of private businesses to the Negro petitioning has been varied. Much of the pressure

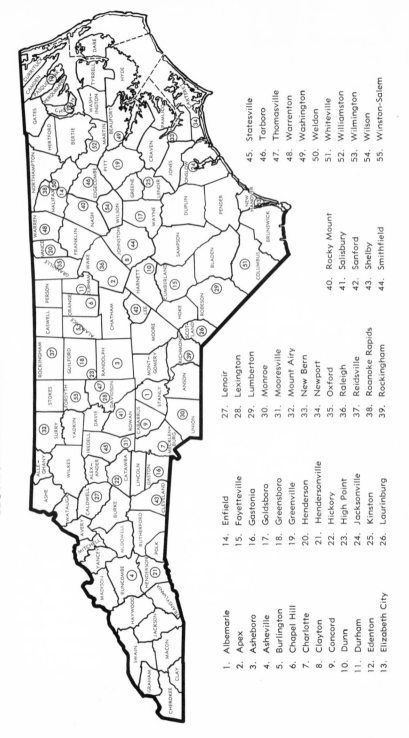

1. Albemarle
2. Apex
3. Asheboro
4. Asheville
5. Burlington
6. Chapel Hill
7. Charlotte
8. Clayton
9. Concord
10. Dunn
11. Durham
12. Edenton
13. Elizabeth City

14. Enfield
15. Fayetteville
16. Gastonia
17. Goldsboro
18. Greensboro
19. Greenville
20. Henderson
21. Hendersonville
22. Hickory
23. High Point
24. Jacksonville
25. Kinston
26. Laurinburg

27. Lenoir
28. Lexington
29. Lumberton
30. Monroe
31. Mooresville
32. Mount Airy
33. New Bern
34. Newport
35. Oxford
36. Raleigh
37. Reidsville
38. Roanoke Rapids
39. Rockingham

40. Rocky Mount
41. Salisbury
42. Sanford
43. Shelby
44. Smithfield

45. Statesville
46. Tarboro
47. Thomasville
48. Warrenton
49. Washington
50. Weldon
51. Whiteville
52. Williamston
53. Wilmington
54. Wilson
55. Winston-Salem

exerted by the Negro petitioners has been applied against operators of theaters and other places of amusement, hotels, motels, and restaurants. Biracial committees uniformly have indicated their belief that important revision of traditional practices should occur. This has resulted in definite community efforts to open places of recreation and public accommodation to the Negro—with many white citizens encouraging the committees. Most old segregation signs are disappearing, practically all of those which were up in tax-supported institutions.

These groups are acting upon the assumption that the operator of a business has the legal right to pick and choose whom he shall serve and the committees are attempting by negotiation to liberalize the customs and policies of private businesses. They are insisting that the Negro is entitled to citizenship equality, the extension of which need not and should not impair any person's right to choose his own friends and associates.

These efforts by groups formed to deal with the Negro complaints have been notably successful in several North Carolina cities and they have bogged down without much progress in others. This book comprises a brief report of what has been done at the State level under the direction of the Governor and by a number of municipalities. It will be distributed as information about methods used and progress attained. Published herein, in alphabetical order, are 55 "municipal reports." If Congress enacts into law the Civil Rights Bill now in the Senate, of course the privilege of customer discrimination will be impaired and the problem changed; but with or without Federal law what North Carolina seeks is progress in both justice and constructive interracial harmony.

The foregoing statement is left unchanged despite the enactment of The Civil Rights Act of 1964 by Congress. Many questions are now raised about the enforcement of this statute and about what effect the new law will have on the State's policy. No effort will be made in this book to deal with the changes that the federal statute will occasion. No doubt there will be a period during which test cases will reach the courts on the constitutionality of the statute. That question has been so thoroughly threshed over by the Senators who strongly opposed the legislation that it seems unlikely that any new angles on the issue will be developed. Judicial decision probably will not be delayed to the extent that it frequently is delayed when basic constitutional questions are raised.

ALBEMARLE

Population: 12,261; 12.6 per cent Negro

Mayor: Dwight Stokes—Office: 248 South First Street; Home: 916 North Tenth Street; Telephone: Office: 982-5213; Home: 982-1526

Biracial Organization: Stanly County Biracial Committee

Chairman: Henry L. Harris—Office: President, Home Savings and Loan Association, 108 East North Street; Home: 330 North Ninth Street; Telephone: Office: 982-1615; Home: 982-5947

Negro Action: There has been no Negro action as of May 1, 1964.

Municipal Reaction:

At the suggestion of the interdenominational desegregated Ministerial Association, the Chamber of Commerce sponsored the establishment of the City's and County's Biracial Committee. The Chamber of Commerce appointed the Chairman and then with the co-operation of the Chairman chose the membership of the Committee. There are ten members on the Committee in addition to the Chairman, five Negroes and five whites. This was organized in the latter part of June, 1963, and began functioning in July. The Committee has met twice a month since that time.

Adjustments:

Two drugstore lunch counters and two luncheonettes and several restaurants have desegregated, as well as two drive-ins. The single theater is closed, and the hotels and motels have not established policies of desegregation. The recreational program of the City is segregated, although the public library and its branches are desegregated. The Chamber of Commerce and the Merchants' Association are segregated.

There has been no school desegregation prior to this year and none this year thus far, although some is contemplated for next fall.

The hospital is a county hospital and it has a Negro section in the hospital and otherwise it is segregated.

The downtown hotel lunchroom is open to Negroes.

APEX

Population: 1,368; 26.3 per cent Negro

Mayor: Richard K. Helmold—Office: North Salem Street; Home: Pearson Street; Telephone: Office: 354-2301; Home: 354-6219

Biracial Organization: None

Negro Action:
There have been no demonstrations. A threat of demonstrations by the local committee of the NAACP was made, but other local Negro leaders dissuaded the committee from the threatened action.

Municipal Reaction:
The Mayor personally sought community adjustments from businessmen. The Mayor adopted the philosophy that although there were few public accommodations, facilities, or services in Apex that could become involved in a desegregation program, he would nevertheless undertake to encourage the local businesses and services to consider adjustments in their employment and operational practices.

Adjustments:
Upon the request of the Mayor, Roxanne Bathing Suit Company agreed to desegregate its labor force in September, 1963, when full production was resumed. Roxanne did inaugurate "equal employment" and has reviewed 50 to 60 Negro applicants from whom 12 have been employed. The Company intended to hire about ten Negroes during the first month and it hopes to have close to 40 Negro employees by the fall. The Scheffelin and Company plant will open in Apex about August 1, 1964. It will employ altogether on the basis of qualifications, without regard to race.

The "white only" signs have been removed from the front of all businesses except one in response to the Mayor's personal request. No white restaurant is serving Negroes.

The public library is in the Negro section of Apex and is being used solely by the Negroes.

The swimming pool in Apex is privately owned and the Negroes recognize that it will not be open to them.

Water and sewage facilities were put in areas of Negro homes that needed them.

ASHEBORO

Population: 9,449; 15.1 per cent Negro

Mayor: R. L. Reese—Office: 251 Ross Street; Home: 625 Holly Street; Telephone: Office: 625-2195; Home: 625-2374

Biracial Organization: Human Relations Committee

Chairman: Reverend Zachary T. Piephoff—Office: First Presbyterian Church, 420 West Walker Street; Home: 804 South Park Street; Telephone: Office: 625-3227; Home: 625-5650

Negro Action:

The first Negro demonstrations occurred in Asheboro August 3 and 4, 1963, under the sponsorship of the NAACP's Youth Council.

On January 15, 1964, after several months of inaction, two groups of young Negroes (five in one group and nine in another) went to various places of business asking proprietors why they did not serve Negroes. The group finally went to the City Manager and submitted to him a list of things including cafes, hotels, motels, hospitals, and jobs in the city of Asheboro, which they wanted to see desegregated. They stated that if something had not been done by January 19, they were going to demonstrate or promote pressure.

The NAACP Adult Branch, the NAACP Youth Council, and the Community Co-ordinating Committee of Asheboro submitted the following petition on January 14, 1964:

"Recommended to the City Council of Asheboro, North Carolina: (1) Biracial committee be appointed to investigate, to discourage, and dissolve racial discrimination in the City of Asheboro; (2) All restaurants in the City and those that serve the City on the outskirts of the City—open to all citizens; (3) That the city government refuse to sell licenses to eating establishments and other business that discriminate because of race, color, or creed; (4) That Negroes be given equal opportunities for employment in the city government, such as clerks, water department, fire department, recreation, etc.; (5) All recreational facilities become desegregated immediately; (6) City Hospital become desegregated; (7) That more and better lights be installed in the Negro community; (8) That the City enforce the law to eliminate unsanitary conditions in public housing." The Negroes also re-

THE ASHEBORO HUMAN RELATIONS COMMITTEE DISCUSSES ITS CURRENT PROGRAM. APPEARING FROM *LEFT TO RIGHT*: REVEREND J. W. JONES, W. R. GREY III, MRS. ELIZABETH JONES, MRS. MAMIE WILLIAMS, MISS ELDORA EWING, REVEREND ZACHARY T. PIEPHOFF, JR., *CHAIRMAN*, MRS. BETTYE TAYLOR, MRS. W. F. REDDING, JR., REVEREND DONALD WOOLLY, W. M. WATTS, AND W. F. VAN HOY.

quested that a private swimming pool be opened. On Saturday, January 19, 1964, demonstrations were resumed through the use of a silent march. Most of the participants were teen-agers in this march and there were over 100 participants. The purpose of the demonstration was said to be "toward total integration." The demonstrations occurred again on January 20, 21, and 22. On January 25, sit-ins were held and there were, as a consequence, mass arrests. Demonstrations occurred again on January 28 and 29, and on February 1, 4, 12, and 15. On February 15, there were again sit-ins and mass arrests.

Municipal Reaction:

Several years ago the community established what was known as the Negro Affairs Committee. This Committee was organized so that Negroes could bring grievances which they might have to the City through the Negro citizens serving on the Negro Affairs Committee. The Mayor considered the Negro Affairs Committee to be equivalent to a biracial committee because on occasions when it had matters to present to the City Council, it met with the all-white Asheboro City Council.

In reaction to the demonstrations which occurred on August 3 and 4, Asheboro adopted on August 6, two ordinances regulating "obstructions" and "disturbing the peace." Reverend Ron Hall was approached as Chairman of the Ministerial Association and was asked if he would be willing to ask the Ministerial Association to sponsor a biracial committee for Asheboro. He accepted the challenge and undertook to establish a biracial committee which became known as the Human Relations Committee. The appointments were made January 29, 1964. The Human Relations Committee is composed of 16 members, eight white and eight Negroes, including two youths, one from each race. The first meeting of the Human Relations Committee occurred on February 3, 1964. The Human Relations Committee was established without any agreement that demonstrations by the protesting Negro group would cease, but with encouragement that they be discontinued. Three subcommittees were established within the Human Relations Committee: one on accommodations, another for housing, and a third for job opportunities.

Adjustments:

On July 29, 1963, the Mayor announced that municipal "jobs would be available to all persons on a qualification basis." One Negro policeman has been hired.

On August 3, 1963, some of the restaurants and motels assured the Mayor that if they had small groups of Negroes who desired to be served, that these establishments would serve such Negroes in the same manner that they served whites. At a subsequent open meeting of merchants, the merchants aired their views on desegregation and a proposal was made, but not adopted, that if the merchants could desegregate their establishments at the same time that there could be little objection from the Asheboro public.

One merchant indicated that he was seriously considering hiring two Negro salesclerks.

Both theaters desegregated, but after a near riot resulted one Saturday evening in August (August 3 or 4, 1963), the theater without a balcony in which to seat Negroes reverted to a segregated practice.

Five restaurants have served Negroes.

The Memorial Park swimming pool is privately owned and remains segregated.

The Mayor announced July 29, 1963, that the new library under construction would be opened to Negroes as well as to whites. A municipally owned golf course and a privately owned bowling alley are open to both Negroes and whites.

The superintendent of public schools declared that the school board would review all applications for transfer of assignment upon the merits of each.

The Mayor personally undertook to bring about adjustments through visiting the merchants of Asheboro until the Human Relations Committee was appointed.

ASHEVILLE

Population: 60,192; 19.0 per cent Negro

Mayor: Earl W. Eller—Office: 202 City Hall, Court Plaza; Home: 18 Windsor Road; Telephone: Office: 253-3611; Home: 252-4709

Biracial Organization: Asheville Area Council on Human Relations

Chairman: William E. Greene—Office: 311 Jackson Building; Home: 27 Robin Hood Road; Telephone: Office: 253-3661

Negro Action:

The active Negro organizations are the local chapter of the NAACP, the Asheville-Buncombe County Citizen's Organization, and the Asheville Student Committee on Racial Equality (ASCORE). CORE held a mass meeting in Asheville in August, 1963, as the last lap of the Human-Freedom Highways Project.

Asheville's only demonstration occurred in late 1962 when CORE representatives marched in front of a local grocery store. This march was not publicized by any news medium. CORE's demand was for the immediate employment of Negroes in higher positions (primarily as cash register operators) without physical and mental examinations, company requirements. After several weeks, CORE and the grocery store requested that the Asheville Area Council on Human Relations hear this matter.

Municipal Reaction:

The Council heard both sides fully and took no action because of CORE's untenable position. The Council's position was supported by the Negro members of the Council. Negro leaders say that a chain of highway restaurants desegregated 30 days after and as a result of the August mass meeting.

The Asheville Area Council on Human Relations has been in existence since 1956. It was conceived and initiated by the Right Reverend Bishop Henry of the Episcopal Church and white and Negro leaders and did not result in response to demonstrations. It is presently composed of 60 to 70 whites and Negroes with no prescribed membership ratio. The Council is representative of a cross section of the City. From the beginning there was an agreement between the Council and the press, radio, and television not to publicize actions of the Council or results accomplished. This policy was considered a major contributing factor to the success of the Council. Since June, 1963, news media have reported the Council's actions.

Adjustments:

Several stores have voluntarily employed Negro salesmen and clerks without any contact from the Council on Human Relations. In a few instances this has resulted in an elevator operator being moved up to a sales position by his employer rather than being discharged when the elevator was mechanized.

Dime stores opened their lunch counters in 1962. Drugstores followed suit after observing the dime and variety stores' experience of suffering no losses from this procedure. The method of approach in this case and in the case of restaurants and theaters was that the Council worked out an agreement with the proprietor of each store that two or four Negroes who were leading citizens of the community (doctors, lawyers, dentists, etc.) would approach the lunch counter at a relatively non-rush hour and be served. Then they would move the time to a more congested time of day and proceed to increase the number attending until gradually the counter was open to as many Negroes as would like to be served at any time of the day.

Motel restaurants have been open for some time. Practically all drive-ins have also been opened. All local cafeterias as well as the restaurants on Tunnel Road have desegregated with practically no exceptions. These were opened through the process of proprietors meeting with the full Council to discuss their desegregation. Members of the Council seldom went out and talked to individual proprietors.

Both hotels have been desegregated since 1958. All large and most small motels are desegregated.

Both theaters in Asheville are desegregated.

The public library and its three branches are desegregated.

There are some 60 Negroes in the junior high school and the Asheville schools have been largely desegregated from the first through the eighth grades. A gradual program of desegregation was worked out for both city and county schools. A lawsuit to test the validity of the county plan is now pending in the local United States District Court.

Asheville-Biltmore College receives qualified Negroes. There have been many demands that Negroes be admitted to business colleges where they could acquire the skills needed to better their job positions. The business colleges have responded that they are members of a State organization which follows a policy of excluding Negroes. The Council was assured that the subject would be brought up at the State organization's meeting on May 16, 1964.

Both hospitals have been desegregated. The City owns two swimming pools. Both are desegregated, although the tendency is still for the whites to use the previously white pool and the Negroes to use the previously Negro pool.

The municipally owned recreational park is desegregated and it contains rides and a zoo. The municipal golf course has been desegregated for ten years. The Buncombe County Bar Association, the Chamber of Commerce, and the Ministerial Association are desegregated.

All segregation laws have been repealed.

The Council on Human Relations and the City Council in a public statement have declared Asheville totally desegregated.

BURLINGTON

Population: 33,199; 9.8 per cent Negro

Mayor: John H. Alley—Office: 2017 Shirley Drive; Home: 1215 Rockwood Avenue; Telephone: Office: 227-3658; Home: 226-2061

Biracial Organization: Alamance County Good Neighbor Council

Chairman: Reverend Coy Bovender—Office: Shiloh Presbyterian Church; Home: 2634 Alamance Road; Telephone: Office: 226-7664; Home: 226-3103

Negro Action:
The active Negro organizations are the Alamance Voters League, the NAACP, CORE, and the Alamance County Committee of Civic Affairs. Voter registration and job training are the primary activities of these groups.

There have been no demonstrations in Burlington.

Municipal Reaction:
The Alamance County Good Neighbor Council was founded by the county government at the suggestion of the Ministerial Association. Men of influence in industry are among the members of the Good Neighbor Council. The Council is hopeful of expanding into a full Human Relations Council for the entire community. Presently the Council operates with three subcommittees. The personal contact of members of the Council with merchants to discuss adjustments has been the primary method of operation.

Adjustments:
Thus far there are few tangible results. The dime store lunch counters are now open and there are Negro students attending the first four grades of the Burlington public school system. This system will extend its desegregation through the sixth grade for the 1964-1965 school year. The Alamance County Board of Education will desegregate the first four grades of its system for the 1964-1965 school year.

The Burlington Board of Education has a Negro member and several Negroes are serving on other city commissions.

"White Only" signs remain in many downtown stores.

Negroes have been employed as salesclerks in variety stores. The Ministerial Association has been interracial for 20 years.

PETITION FOR EQUAL EMPLOYMENT OPPORTUNITIES.

UNITED STATES P ST OFFICE
CHAPEL HILL NORTH CAROLINA
CORE
CURED
FREEDOM LETTERS
FOR
CIVIL RIGHTS
NOW!

CHAPEL HILL

Population: 12,573; 10.7 per cent Negro

Mayor: Sandy McClamroch, Jr.—Office: Radio Station WCHL, Durham Road; Home: 815 Greenwood Road; Telephone: Office: 968-4484; Home; 968-5963

Biracial Organization: Human Relations Committee

Chairman: Mrs. George Taylor—Home: Kings Mill Road; Telephone: 942-2376

Negro Action:
Desegregation demonstrations began in Chapel Hill early in 1960, and an "open theater" movement was conducted during the 1961-1962 school year.

On February 26, 1963, the University of North Carolina chapter of the NAACP voted to co-operate with the Durham NAACP youth chapter in their picket against a segregated Durham theater beginning March 1, 1963.

Friday, April 5, 1963, the Student Peace Union began picketing a segregated cafe on Franklin Street in support of the Union's resolution instituting a boycott of 13 Chapel Hill businesses which practiced racial discrimination. Patrick Cusick, chairman of the local chapter of the Student Peace Union, said in regard to the picketing: "The continuation of racial discrimination in Chapel Hill is an insult to the spirit of a free university and to the fundamental precepts of human dignity and freedom." John Dunne, a member of the Student Peace Union's steering committee, added this: "The problems of world peace and the problems of civil rights and human freedom are not separate, but are both a part of the Student Peace Union's concern for the human community as a whole."

April 7, 1963, the University chapter of the NAACP marched from South Building to the North Carolina Memorial Hospital in protest of the limited segregation within the hospital. Other groups supported this demonstration. Among these were the staff of *Reflection Magazine,* local high school students, the adult chapter of the NAACP in Chapel Hill, the Durham NAACP-CORE chapter, the Student Peace Union, and various congregations of Negro churches in Carrboro and Chapel Hill.

The history of the local efforts to desegregate North Carolina Memorial Hospital goes back to the 1961-1962 school year when the University chapter of the NAACP sent a negotiating committee to the director of the hospital to urge him to take steps to end segregation there. Two meetings were held with the director in which there were discussions of the removal of signs denoting racial segregation in rest rooms and of the ending of segregation in wards and private rooms. During these discussions, the director indicated that he was receptive to the idea of removing the "Colored" and "White" signs from the rest rooms, but he indicated that the signs would have to be removed over a period of time, and that they would have to be removed during the night so that their removal would be inconspicuous. The director refused to hear any arguments in favor of desegregating bed facilities at the hospital.

Picketing of a downtown cafe by the Student Peace Union continued April 25, 1963.

The Committee for Open Business (COB) grew out of the Student Peace Union boycott of 13 local segregated restaurants. The new group was designed to co-ordinate efforts by students and townspeople to end segregation at the local restaurants. This organization first met on Friday, May 3, 1963, at the St.

DEMONSTRATORS SIT-IN AT THE MERCHANTS' ASSOCIATION.

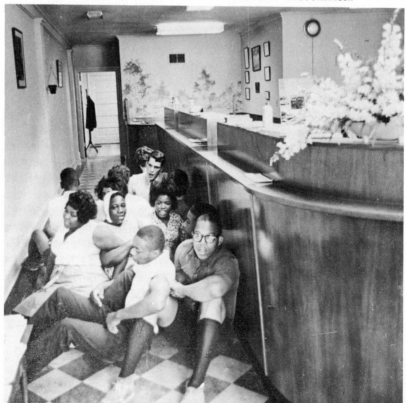

Joseph Methodist Church on West Rosemary Street. Harold Foster, editor of *Campus Echo,* the student newspaper of North Carolina College, and Father Clarence Parker, retired Episcopal minister, were elected co-chairmen of the new organization. The Committee for Open Business was composed primarily of whites from the University of North Carolina and young Negro adults from the Chapel Hill area.

The executive committee of the Committee for Open Business was 50 per cent Negro and 50 per cent white. All meetings and workshops sponsored by this group were held in Negro churches. Nonviolence workshops were conducted each night until civil disobedience occurred. On July 12, 1963, the Committee proposed to the Mayor and the Merchants' Association an agreement by which the Merchants' Association would secure the desegregation of three businesses each week and all demonstrations would be ceased. This proposal was rejected by the Merchants' Association.

CORE assigned Vivian McCoy and Quinton Baker to work with the Negro protest movement in Chapel Hill during the week of July 14-21, 1963, and to work with the Committee for Open Business. This action contributed to the momentum of the 13 weeks of demonstrations conducted in Chapel Hill during the remainder of the summer of 1963. Several of these demonstrations had as many as 500 participants.

A silent march was held in the downtown area on July 13, 1963. Singing was conducted at one segregated business.

The Committee sponsored a sit-in at the office of the Merchants' Association on July 19 because this organization, which favored the desegregation of businesses, had publicly opposed the adoption of the proposed public accommodations law. Thirty-five persons were arrested as a result of these demonstrations.

On July 21 a meeting was called by the Human Relations Committee for July 22 of all business leaders and civic leaders in the community to make suggestions on ways to resolve the racial difficulties. At the meeting the businessmen agreed with the Committee for Open Business and Reverend Loren Mead, Chairman of the Human Relations Committee, to discuss the desegregation of the remaining segregated establishments with these establishments' proprietors and to report to the Human Relations Committee on Sunday, July 28. The group set up terms for the discontinuation of demonstrations on August 1, 1963.

DURHAM TO CHAPEL HILL
WALK FOR FREEDOM

The Human Relations Committee held an open meeting at which the Merchants' Association was to issue a public report on Sunday, July 28. No one appeared to represent the Merchants' Association and, thus, there was no report. After adjournment of this meeting, the nonviolence workshops were resumed with the intention of continuing them until a satisfactory report was forthcoming from the Merchants' Association.

The Merchants' Association requested that all charges be dropped against those who were arrested for their participation in the sit-in in the Merchants' Bureau. The solicitor of Chapel Hill reported July 29 his unwillingness to drop any charges against demonstrators, even though he had been requested to do so by the Mayor and other civic leaders.

The Committee for Open Business requested the NAACP to furnish an attorney to represent them at the August 6 judicial hearing. Throughout the summer of 1963, the anti-segregation group was the Committee for Open Business, which sponsored marches, picketing, and sit-ins. At the end of the summer, the Committee for Open Business was replaced by Citizens' United for Racial Equality and Dignity (CURED) and at the beginning of the school year, October 2, 1963, the local chapter of CORE was established.

Citizens' United for Racial Equality and Dignity was only a local organization while CORE is a member of one of the largest national civil rights groups. The Committee for Open Business was disbanded because many of its members believed their work to be ineffective and desired new tactics that were contrary to the beliefs of many members.

One representative of the Negro movement said: "Citizens' United for Racial Equality and Dignity encompasses all those who are willing to make certain contributions, but not go so far as to go to jail. CORE's members are ready for anything."

CORE and the NAACP began a new wave of sit-ins Sunday, December 15, 1963.

Quinton Baker, a student at North Carolina College and head of the State Youth Program for the NAACP, was carried from a restaurant December 15 and 16 during sit-ins, and nine persons were arrested in the December 16 restaurant sit-in.

From December 19, 1963, through January 7, 1964, some 133 arrests were made on charges of trespass and obstructing sidewalks. January 7 seven persons were treated for first-degree

SUNDAY AFTERNOON WALK FROM DURHAM TO CHAPEL HILL.

CHAPEL HILL

burns at North Carolina Memorial Hospital after being doused with ammonia and bleach water during a sit-in.

Anti-segregation protests resumed on January 11 after a five-day lull with picketing at five segregated businesses. No arrests were reported.

On Sunday, January 12, 1964, the day before the Chapel Hill Board of Aldermen had scheduled a vote on the proposed public accommodations ordinance, which had been pending before it since June, 1963, chapters of CORE and the NAACP sponsored a march in support of the proposed ordinance from the Duke University and North Carolina College campuses in Durham to the University of North Carolina at Chapel Hill. Nearly 200 Negroes and whites walked in the rain the 12 miles from Durham to the Negro First Baptist Church in Chapel Hill where James Farmer of New York, national director of CORE, spoke to a terminal rally of more than 500 persons. He expressed the opinion that if Chapel Hill would take the lead in passing a public accommodations ordinance, it would enable CORE to secure a similar one in a Tennessee city and it might be the spearhead for a breakthrough in many other communities.

Upon the Board of Aldermen's circumvention of a vote on the proposed public accommodations ordinance at its meeting Monday evening, January 12, 1964, 45 Negroes and whites spent the remainder of the night inside the Town Hall in protest of the Board's action.

The following day James Farmer delivered an ultimatum giving Chapel Hill 16 days to completely desegregate all places of public accommodations or face massive demonstrations at the instigation of the national office of CORE. He told newsmen in Durham, "Unless Chapel Hill is an open city by February 1, it will become the focal point of all our efforts. All our resources, staff, funds, and non-violent training will be centered there after D Day." Farmer added that the date was also the anniversary of the nation's first sit-ins in Greensboro in 1960.

Governor Sanford immediately responded January 15 by offering his complete support to Chapel Hill officials in dealing with the town's racial problem with the issuance of a stern warning to CORE. Governor Sanford said: "We cannot and will not allow any group to coerce public officials with threats or ultimatums, no matter how meritorious they believe their cause to be." He pledged his full support to the Chapel Hill Board of Aldermen

JAMES FARMER, NATIONAL EXECUTIVE DIRECTOR OF CORE, MEETS WITH CHAPEL HILL LEADERS TO DISCUSS DESEGREGATION PROGRESS. PICTURED FROM *LEFT TO RIGHT:* WILBUR JONES, FLOYD B. MCKISSICK, REVEREND CHARLES M. JONES, FARMER, C. A. MCDOUGLE, HUBERT ROBINSON, JAMES BRITTEN, JOHN D. DUNNE, AND QUINTON BAKER.

for any stand it might take against a continuance of demonstrations. The Governor further said: "Chapel Hill will be given complete and absolute support by me with every resource at my command."

On January 25, 1964, some 70 persons marched peacefully through Chapel Hill requesting enactment of an ordinance banning racial discrimination in places of public accommodation. Since demonstrations were resumed December 13, 1963, 260 persons, including students from Duke University, North Carolina College, and the University of North Carolina, had been arrested for acts rising out of the demonstrations.

The transfer of 18 cases January 29 from the Municipal Court to the Orange County Superior Court brought to 185 the number of civil rights cases sent to the county court for jury trials.

Further demonstrations—lie-ins and sit-ins—and arrests occurred January 28 and 29. Sixty demonstrators sat-in at the Town Hall courtroom following a meeting of the Board of Aldermen January 28.

February 1, "D Day," arrived without there being a public accommodations ordinance in Chapel Hill.

During the afternoon, some 300 desegregation demonstrators marched, on the sidewalk, two abreast from a church toward the center of town. The group was led by persons carrying placards saying: "Black is not a vice." "Segregation is not a virtue." "Chapel Hill's reputation is a fraud." A demonstration was held downtown where 22 marchers were taken into custody. After the arrests, the marchers proceeded to the Town Hall where they sang and waved the placards bearing anti-segregation slogans.

Later in the day 53 demonstrators were arrested for trespassing and resisting arrest when they sat in front of two segregated restaurants on U. S. Highway 15-501 between Chapel Hill and Durham, just outside the Chapel Hill city limits. These arrests brought the number of arrests since demonstrations were resumed on December 13, 1963, to 363.

The following week, beginning Sunday, February 2, 1964, was filled with activity. Thirty-four demonstrators were arrested Monday night in a downtown drugstore as protests continued. Tuesday morning 22 civil rights cases were transferred to the Orange County Superior Court for jury trial. That evening 50 members of the Freedom Movement staged a march through downtown Chapel Hill. No arrests were made.

Thursday evening, Mike Lawler, president of the University of North Carolina student body, requested a complete student boycott of all segregated businesses in a message before the student legislature. He said: "I urge that this student body withdraw its support from those establishments which do not and will not serve us all. . . . We are not only a commuity of scholars; we are also a community of men and women, citizens. And as such, we are obliged to reflect upon our society and to involve ourselves in its progress." Mr. Lawler suggested student activity in job retraining and employment, voter registration, tutoring and educational opportunities.

On Saturday the NAACP-CORE, the Student Non-violent Coordinating Committee (SNCC), the Student Peace Union (SPU) and the Southern Conference Educational Fund (SCEF) organized three sets of demonstrations. At 3:30 P.M. 110 silent demonstrators marched in double file from the Church of God on Franklin Street in Carrboro to the corner of Franklin and Columbia Streets where they sat down in the intersection. Floyd McKissick, national chairman of CORE, and the first Negro

DEMONSTRATORS BLOCK FRANKLIN STREET IN DOWNTOWN CHAPEL HILL.

student to attend the University of North Carolina, led the march. Demonstrators were arrested for blocking traffic.

At 4:15 P.M. demonstrators simultaneously tied up four major traffic arteries out of Chapel Hill while others staged sit-downs in two downtown streets, choked with heavy traffic of the afternoon UNC-Wake Forest basketball game. More demonstrators were arrested for blocking traffic. The two afternoon demonstrations resulted in 48 arrests. Fifty more resulted from an evening sit-down in the middle of the town's busiest intersection from which the demonstrators refused to move. These arrests during the week boosted the total number since December from 363 to 534.

Sunday night, February 9, 180 demonstrators paraded single file down Chapel Hill's main street. No arrests were made. The following night police arrested 50 Negro and white protesters when they sat down in a downtown intersection, blocking four-way traffic, while the Board of Aldermen met to determine how to cope with the racial situation.

The Board of Aldermen voted four to three to amend the town's picketing ordinance by restricting parading and picketing to the hours between 7:00 A.M. and 7:00 P.M. Mayor Mc-Clamroch cast the "first reading" tie-breaking vote.

On Tuesday morning 82 additional civil rights cases were transferred to the Orange County Superior Court in Hillsboro for jury trials. "The Committee of 100," a new organization, began considering a judicial test of the Monday night amendment to the town's picketing ordinance. That evening 35 faculty members of the University of North Carolina and Duke University, members of the Committee, marched down Franklin Street carrying signs saying: "Constitutional rights apply 24 hours a day."

The University student legislature, in special session Tuesday evening, adopted by a vote of 22 to 11 a resolution urging its constituents to boycott segregated businesses in Chapel Hill.

Eight persons demonstrated against the 12-hour picketing ordinance on Wednesday.

Two days later 70 students at the all-Negro Lincoln High School staged a walk-out in protest of what they called "inferior and segregated facilities." Some 60 of the 300 students remained absent the following day from classes held to make up a day missed because of a winter snow.

DEMONSTRATORS STOP SATURDAY BASKETBALL TRAFFIC IN MIDTOWN.

SIGNS DROP FROM STICKS IN SHOW OF NON-VIOLENT COMMITMENT AS DEMONSTRATORS PETITION FOR THE PASSAGE OF A PUBLIC ACCOMMODATIONS ORDINANCE.

PICKET LINE IS ORGANIZED OUTSIDE CITY HALL AS SHOW OF SYMPATHY WITH DEMONSTRATORS SITTING IN BOARD OF ALDERMEN COUNCIL ROOM IN PROTEST TO TABLING OF PUBLIC ACCOMMODATIONS ORDINANCE.

Anti-segregation leaders called a six-day moratorium on their civil disobedience tactics on Saturday, February 15, but declared that protest visits to segregated businesses would continue. This announcement concluded two weeks of stepped-up racial demonstrations which had resulted in a massive number of arrests and which had focused national attention on Chapel Hill. During the afternoon, 14 members of the Chapel Hill Freedom Committee were arrested during a hit-and-run sit-in at a suburban restaurant. The following evening members of the Wesley Foundation, Methodist student group, picketed the same restaurant, where a sorority was holding an initiation banquet.

Over the week end University of North Carolina philosophy professor, Dr. E. Maynard Adams, proposed a long-range plan to eliminate racial discrimination in Chapel Hill through the establishment of a permanent full-time local agency responsible for dealing with racial problems and for making a variety of efforts to improve the situation of the Negro. The proposal was made at a special session of the Human Relations Committee meeting with members of the Chapel Hill School Board, the Mayor's Mediation Committee, the Chapel Hill Board of Aldermen, the Orange County Board of Commissioners, and the Inter-Church Council. Those present unanimously agreed that a committee from the group should draw up a polished proposal, investigate the mechanics of putting the proposal into effect, and present the proposal and the means of implementing it to the Board of Aldermen for approval.

On Wednesday evening, February 19, members of the Wesley Foundation again picketed a suburban restaurant, this time while a fraternity was having a banquet.

At the same time a "third force" in Chapel Hill's racial picture showed the first signs of moving out of its embryonic state when it met, remanned itself, elected a chairman, and elaborated on its goal. The organization, composed of some 100 persons, had been in existence for three weeks under the name of the Committee of 100. The group renamed itself the "Committee of Concerned Citizens" and undertook a program of picketing of four local segregated establishments. It subsequently raised $400 to pay the hospital expenses of demonstrators injured during the first three months of 1964.

On Friday, February 21, the Chapel Hill Freedom Committee,

FIVE MEMBERS OF FREEDOM COMMITTEE FAST ON LAWN OF POST OFFICE PRIOR TO EASTER. *LEFT TO RIGHT*: PATRICK CUSICK, REVEREND LAVERT TAYLOR, MELODY DICKINSON, JAMES FOUSHEE, AND JOHN DUNNE.

announced that it was extending its declared moratorium on civil disobedience until February 28.

During the first week of March, 150 University of North Carolina faculty members signed a petition vowing not to patronize segregated businesses in Chapel Hill.

The Chapel Hill Freedom Committee announced on Saturday, March 21, that five of its members, two Negroes and three whites, would fast for eight days on the grounds of the Chapel Hill Post Office, beginning at sunrise Sunday, March 22. This fast proceeded as scheduled and the participants only consumed water during the week.

A rally of the Ku Klux Klan was held Saturday night, during the week of the fast, near Chapel Hill, after which a scuffle broke out at the scene of the fast in front of the Post Office. Some 600 persons attended the Klan rally.

The fast ended Sunday, March 29, with the participants' consumption of soup. A street march downtown was followed by 200 persons attending a 3:00 P.M. rally at the First Baptist Church at which Williamston desegregation leader, Golden Frinks, spoke.

Saturday, May 2, the second civil rights demonstration since the April 24 adjournment of the five-week special session of the Orange County Superior Court took place at 1:30 P.M. The march downtown from St. Joseph Methodist Church on West Rosemary Street was designed as a protest against the "harsh" sentences given demonstrators by the judge in the Orange County Superior Court during the special criminal term. Twelve members of the local civil rights movement were given active jail terms ranging from four months to a full year.

Municipal Reaction:

The Board of Aldermen adopted a resolution in November, 1958, establishing a Human Relations Committee. The Mayor, Oliver K. Cornwell, appointed members to the Committee in the spring of 1959. The original membership of 11 included no merchants. The group primarily served as an advisory board to the Mayor and Board of Aldermen.

Reverend Loren Mead was appointed chairman of the Committee in July, 1963. After street demonstrations began in the spring of 1963, the Committee sent teams of white and Negro members to consult with merchants to determine which had discriminatory employment policies.

The Committee of six whites and five Negroes recommended to the Board of Aldermen the organization of a "Mayor's Committee on Integration." A 25-member Mayor's Committee on Integration was appointed in early June, 1963, with Mayor McClamroch serving as chairman. This Committee recommended to the Board of Aldermen the passage of a public accommodations ordinance. The proposal was formally presented to the Board of Aldermen by the Human Relations Committee. The Board tabled the proposal in order to determine the legality of its adopting such an ordinance. The Mayor's Committee on Integration dissolved.

The public accommodations ordinance, which had been before the Chapel Hill Board of Aldermen for seven months, was scheduled for consideration by the Board at its regular meeting Monday night, January 13, 1964. The Board had tabled the proposal after the State Attorney General's office said in an informal opinion that the Board of Aldermen lacked the legal authority to enact such an ordinance.

On Sunday, January 12, 1964, some 1,800 persons signed an advertisement stating "We, the persons whose names appear be-

CHAPEL HILL'S BOARD OF ALDERMEN MEETS TO ACT UPON A PUBLIC ACCOMMODATIONS ORDINANCE. SEATED AROUND THE TABLE FROM *LEFT TO RIGHT*: HUBERT ROBINSON, SR.; ROLAND GIDUZ, AND GENE STROWD, BOARD MEMBERS; ROBERT H. PECK, CITY MANAGER; SANDY McCLAMROCH, MAYOR; DAVID B. ROBERTS, TOWN CLERK; AND MRS. HAROLD W. WALTERS, DR. PAUL W. WAGER, AND JOE PAGE, BOARD MEMBERS.

low, urge the passage of a public accommodations ordinance in Chapel Hill that will forbid discrimination." This advertisement was arranged by the Ministerial Association through the efforts of some 80 persons who conducted a telephone campaign for the endorsements.

The ordinance was also recommended by the Mayor's Human Relations Committee. The proposed public accommodations ordinance read as follows:

ORDINANCE: To amend the Ordinances of the Town of Chapel Hill by addition of new subchapter_____to be entitled "Discrimination in Places of Public Accommodation."

It is hereby declared to be the public policy of the Town of Chapel Hill, North Carolina, that discrimination in places of public accommodation against any person on account of race, color, religion, ancestry or national origin is contrary to the morals, ethics, and purposes of a free, democratic society; is injurious to and threatens the peace and good government of this Town; is injurious to and threatens the health, safety and welfare of persons within this Town; and is illegal and should be abolished.

Scope of Ordinance: This Ordinance applies to discriminatory practices in places of public accommodation within the territorial limits of the Town of Chapel Hill and shall apply and be applicable to every place of public accommodation, resort, or amusement of any kind in the Town of Chapel Hill, North Carolina, whose facilities, accommodations, services, commodities, or use are offered to or enjoyed by the general public either with or without charge, and shall include, but not be limited to, the following types of places, among others: all restaurants, soda fountains and eating or drinking places, and all places where food is sold for consumption either on or off the premises; all inns, hotels, and motels, whether serving temporary or permanent patrons; all retail stores and service establishments; all hospitals and clinics; all motion picture, stage and other theaters, and music, concert or meeting halls; all sports arenas and fields, amusement and recreation parks, picnic grounds, fairs, bowling alleys, golf courses, gymnasiums, shooting galleries, billiard and pool rooms, and swimming pools, and all places of public assembly and entertainment of every kind.

Prohibited Acts: It shall be unlawful for any owner, lessee, operator, manager, agent, or employee of any place of public accommodation, resort or amusement within the Town of Chapel Hill, North Carolina, to make any distinction with respect to any person based on race, color, religion, ancestry or national origin in connection with admission to, service or sales in, or price, quality, or use of any facility, or service of, any place of public accommodation, or amusement in the Town of Chapel Hill, North Carolina.

Commission on Human Relations: There shall be duly constituted a Commission on Human Relations for the Town of Chapel Hill, empowered to hear and negotiate in regard to all cases arising under this ordinance. Prosecutions when necessary shall be brought by the Town only after the case has been heard by this Commission.

In a legal memorandum prepared by George H. Esser, Jr., of the Institute of Government and addressed to the Mayor and Board of Aldermen of Chapel Hill, Mr. Esser wrote in part:

Municipalities, or municipal corporations, are creatures of the State and possess only those powers delegated to them by the State. In North Carolina, powers are delegated to municipal corporations through general laws (applying to all municipal corporations or a class of municipal corporations) and through special laws applying to single municipal corporations. Such special laws are generally part of the "charter" of the municipal corporation. Taken together, police powers granted from both sources do not add up to the total of the "police power" held by the State.

. . . .

The Town of Chapel Hill has inquired as to its power to enact a "public accommodations ordinance," which would make it unlawful for any proprietor of a place providing food, lodging, or other services to the general public to deny service to any well-behaved person on the basis of color, race, religion, or creed.

. . . .

In short, although general welfare clauses are worded very broadly, there is no common rule of interpretation that would assure any municipality that it had the authority to enact a regulatory ordinance on the basis of this authority alone. Whether or not authority is properly delegated through such provision . . . is a question of interpretation for the courts, once an ordinance has been adopted and its validity challenged.

The conclusion states:

This report could go on indefinitely in terms of case analysis and application to the issue involved. No amount of analysis will make any positive addition to the opinion of the Attorney General to the Mayor of Chapel Hill on this subject:

"It is our official opinion that in North Carolina this is an open question and that no one can advise you with any degree of legal certainty what the Supreme Court of North Carolina would rule in such a situation."

This opinion does not mention the town's charter power to regulate all businesses, a power which seems to make the Kansas City case (*Marshall v. Kansas City, Missouri* 335 S.W. 2d 877 [1962]) a much stronger precedent for the validity of an ordinance in Chapel Hill. Taken alone, the general welfare clauses grant *prima facie* power, but the cases generally do not give assurance that such clauses will be broadly interpreted. The general power to regulate all businesses, however, is a more specific power and would seem to provide the legislative authority needed to enact an ordinance defining those persons entitled to be served by businesses offering public accommodations. There is a possibility, of course, that the courts would apply a more limited interpretation to this section.

The executive committee of the North Carolina Council of Human Rights, a voluntary organization, adopted a resolution urging the Chapel Hill Board of Aldermen to pass this public accommodations ordinance. Dr. T. Franklin Williams, Chairman of the Council, read the statement at the Monday night, January 13, Board of Aldermen meeting.

The Board voted four to two to by-pass consideration of the public accommodations law and for adoption of a substitute motion to create a new nine-member committee, to be headed by the Mayor, to try to iron out Chapel Hill's racial problems. An overflow crowd of more than 100 townspeople and students with divided sympathies, attended the town meeting.

In response to the new resolution Mayor Sandy McClamroch appointed a Mediation Committee of eight persons, two each from the Ministerial Association, the Merchants' Association, the Chamber of Commerce, and the University of North Carolina faculty. The first meeting of this Mediation Committee was closed to the public and was held Wednesday evening, January 22.

The Mediation Committee met with segregated businesses in an effort to end discriminatory policies. The Committee was charged with a second function, the hearing of complaints about racial discrimination. It met Wednesday night, January 29, to hear such complaints. There have been weekly meetings since that time.

The Human Relations Committee called upon the Board of Aldermen to forego passage of a proposed restriction-on-picketing ordinance on its required second reading. At its February 24 meeting the Aldermen passed up their opportunity to adopt the ordinance.

Civil disobedience cases resulting from the arrests of anti-segregation demonstrators were presented to the grand jury for indictments when the first of five special one-week criminal terms of the Orange County Superior Court was convened in Hillsboro on February 24, 1964.

Attorneys for the civil rights demonstrators, in a surprise move, petitioned the Orange County Superior Court on Monday,

SIT-IN IS HELD IN BOARD OF ALDERMEN COUNCIL ROOM IN PROTEST TO TABLING OF PUBLIC ACCOMMODATIONS ORDINANCE.

March 2, 1964, for the removal of 932 cases to the United States District Court of the Middle District of North Carolina. Upon presentation of the petition to the clerk, the cases were automatically transferred to the federal court until such time as that court might decide to remand the cases to the Orange County Superior Court.

On Tuesday, March 3, an assistant professor of psychology at the University of North Carolina went on trial on charges stemming from a sit-in demonstration on January 3, 1964, at a suburban restaurant. The assistant professor was one of five college faculty members arrested at that time. He was found guilty of trespassing by a jury which included two Negroes. The superior court judge sentenced him to a 90-day road term. The case was appealed.

Three members of the Duke University faculty were also tried and convicted of trespassing. The judge sentenced one to a 90-day road term and another to a 60-day road term and levied a $50.00 fine on the third. These cases were appealed.

The judge of the United States District Court, Middle District, ruled on March 20 that the Orange County Superior Court rather than the United States District Court had jurisdiction over the 932 civil disobedience cases involving 217 persons which had been removed to the federal court.

The same superior court judge who presided over the first special term returned to the Orange County Superior Court bench on April 13, 1964, for a special three-week criminal term to deal with the nearly 1,000 cases stemming from Chapel Hill's racial demonstrations.

Another Duke University professor, the last of the five faculty members arrested on January 3, 1964, to be tried on trespass charges, was sentenced by the judge on Friday, April 17, to 90 days at hard labor and court costs. The case was appealed.

Nine students were also tried on counts of resisting arrest and obstructing traffic on February 1 and 8. All pleaded *nolo contendere* to the resisting arrest charge and eight pleaded *nolo contendere* to the charge of obstructing traffic. Three of the nine defendants were sentenced to two months of hard labor and court costs, suspended upon agreement to certain conditions set forth by the judge. These conditions included that the defendants pay costs and agree not to engage in or be a part of civil rights demonstrations in any way for a three-year period. Six-month sentences to hard labor were given to two students, suspended upon agreement to these same conditions for a period of four years. Prayer for judgment was continued for four defendants.

Two leaders of the local civil rights movement were sentenced to prison by the judge on April 23. Patrick Cusick and Quinton Baker were given active sentences of one year and six months respectively, after being convicted of blocking traffic and resisting arrest during racial demonstrations during February. Mr. Cusick received a two-year suspended sentence in addition to his active term. He was also put on probation for five years. Mr. Baker also received a $100.00 fine. Another 47 demonstrators received sentences from the judge in Hillsboro, but all were suspended. Arthur Simmons received a 12-month suspended sentence and a fine of $100.00. William Robert Bullard III, a junior at the University of North Carolina, was sentenced to 12 months in prison, fined $100.00, and charged costs. The prison term was suspended for five years. Tucker Clark was sentenced to prison for 60 days and charged costs. The prison sentence was suspended for three years on the provisions that the defendant pay costs by 10:00 A.M., and partici-

pate in no demonstrations during the three-year suspension.

On April 25, John D. Dunne, Joseph "Buddy" Tieger, and J. V. Henry, more leaders of the local civil rights movement, were given active one-year sentences by the judge. Miss Rosemary Ezra, a participant in street and courtroom sit-ins, was given an active six-month term by the judge. One hundred other defendants received suspended sentences which can be activated if the defendants violate any law or become involved in racial demonstrations during the next three to five years. The Friday session brought to a close the last of five special weeks of the Orange County Superior Court, called for the trial of civil disobedience cases stemming from the Chapel Hill racial movement.

Adjustments:

Twenty-five per cent of 116 businesses surveyed by *The Daily Tar Heel,* University of North Carolina student newspaper, indicated that they have some form of segregation.

On May 27, 1963, the Board of Aldermen made a public statement that the policy of this community is equal service for all citizens in places of public accommodations.

Thirty-two per cent of the local restaurants maintain discriminatory policies of some type. The discrimination ranges from stand-up or back-door service to complete refusal of Negro customers. One of these restaurants noted that they would serve Negroes who are University students. Of nine establishments which serve beer and ale, five do not serve Negroes.

Only one of 21 grocery stores denies Negroes permission to make purchases. Two of 37 service stations have different rest rooms for whites and Negroes.

Of nine barber shops, eight do not serve Negroes and the other caters to Negroes, but accepts white customers.

Three of Chapel Hill's five motels do not lodge Negroes. The other two are predominantly Negro, but permit white patronage. The University's inn is desegregated.

One billiard parlor has a separate annex for Negro customers. The other is desegregated; although it is primarily patronized by Negroes.

One ice cream parlor is segregated and the other is not. The frozen custard drive-in serves Negroes only at its rear window.

Both theaters and the bowling alley are desegregated. The

51

Jaycee recreation center is operated as a desegregated unit of the city recreational program.

The municipal library is open to all and is used extensively by Negroes. The public schools are tokenly desegregated.

The University has had Negro students since before the 1954 United States Supreme Court decision in *Brown v. Board of Education.* As of December 23, 1963, the University had 61 Negro students.

On January 31, 1964, the director of the North Carolina Memorial Hospital announced that racial discrimination was not a policy of the hospital in either admissions, the treatment of patients, or the employment of personnel. Forty-six per cent of the hospital's non-academic employees are Negroes. Thirty Negroes serve in supervisory positions.

The Ministerial Association is desegregated and one civic club is considering adopting a policy of nondiscrimination in membership.

CHARLOTTE

Population: 209,551; 27.3 per cent Negro

Mayor: Stanford R. Brookshire—Office: 200 City Hall, 600 East Trade Street; Home: 900 Huntington Park; Telephone: Office: 334-6968; 376-0731; Home: 366-0531

Biracial Organization: Mayor's Committee on Community Relations

Chairman: Reverend John R. Cunningham—Office: 1004 Wachovia Bank Building; Home: 1207 Belgrade Place; Telephone: Office: 375-6667; Home: 377-3373

Negro Action:

Charlotte's first sustained desegregation demonstrations were organized in 1960 by students from Johnson C. Smith University in protest against segregated downtown variety store lunch counters.

Several of these demonstrations were led by a Negro dentist and political leader. Following the demonstrations, former Mayor James S. Smith, named a biracial Friendly Relations Committee to serve as arbiter. Within a month of this appointment the variety stores opened their lunch counters to Negroes.

Demonstrations were again organized and sponsored over a period of weeks in the spring of 1961 against segregated downtown restaurants and theaters. These were again carried on for a few days in the late summer of 1961 without resulting in policy adjustments by the segregated establishments.

Sporadic demonstrations were conducted in 1962 against segregated hotels, motels, restaurants, and theaters. These also failed to gain adjustments. A few arrests were made on charges of trespassing, but these were later dropped.

Demonstrations were threatened during April, 1963, against segregation at the Trade Fair. These did not materialize.

There was a peaceful desegregation march of about 75 Negroes on May 20, 1963.

Municipal Reaction:

When Mayor Brookshire took office in May, 1961, he named a new 27-member biracial Committee on Community Relations, one-third of whom were Negroes. Dr. John R. Cunningham, former chairman of the Friendly Relations Committee, was named chairman of the new Committee. The roster of the Committee included doctors, lawyers, preachers, teachers, and businessmen and women of both races, all carefully selected from top leaders. The Negro members were militant, but reasonable and were very carefully selected for their leadership qualities. Extremists were left off the Committee, the Mayor explaining that he did not wish the Committee to be bargaining among its own members.

In his charge to the Committee the Mayor asked that it look for solutions to the racial problems currently plaguing the nation and approach both the problems and solutions in a constructive manner, giving careful study to the educational, health, and employment needs of the disadvantaged minority group.

The Committee has met in regular monthly sessions, with subcommittees reporting on both problems and progress.

Because of the splendid work of this Committee, demonstrations in both number and size have been minimal and peaceful.

Student demonstrations and the work of the Mayor's Committee on Community Relations succeeded in getting the two large department stores to eliminate discrimination in their dining rooms in 1962. Since that time, these and other merchants have hired Negro sales personnel.

Negotiations continued in a climate of understanding, good will, and co-operation, with major breakthroughs in June, 1963.

The City of Charlotte co-operated with the Mayor's Committee by rescinding all ordinances which made any reference to race or color, and adopted a merit employment policy.

Adjustments:

Racial discrimination has now been largely eliminated in the community life of Charlotte.

Soon after World War II the segregated seating on city buses was abandoned. In the middle 1950's the new auditorium and coliseum were built and opened on a non-segregated basis. Soon thereafter, the public libraries and parks were desegregated and a number of Negro policemen were employed.

Job opportunities for Negroes are opening up more rapidly than persons qualified to fill the positions are found. There is demand for clerks, sales personnel, and bank tellers.

Douglas Aircraft Company, employer of 1,700 persons, adheres to its national policy which guarantees equal opportunity to all. Negroes are employed in personnel, clerical, planning, drafting, and graduate engineering jobs.

The municipal parks, including three swimming pools, and the public library are desegregated. The library with 13 branches has been extensively used by Negroes.

A number of Negroes were admitted to previously all-white schools in the late 1950's and their number has been steadily increasing.

The Charlotte-Mecklenburg Ministerial Association and the Chamber of Commerce are desegregated and there are now about 60 Negro members in the Chamber of Commerce. A Negro minister is currently president of the Ministerial Association.

The Medical Association has desegregated to some extent. Staff and patient discrimination has been eliminated at the four hospitals operated by the Charlotte-Mecklenburg Hospital Authority.

The adjustments which have been made were the result of the work of both the Chamber of Commerce and the Mayor's Committee on Community Relations.

Many of Charlotte's public accommodations operators quietly desegregated through a highly organized plan, few details of which were released to the press, an account of which follows.

The president of the Chamber of Commerce, at the request of the Mayor, called a meeting of the executive committee of the Charlotte Chamber of Commerce to discuss what adjustments could be made in opening accommodations—hotels, motels, restaurants, and theaters—to the Negroes. This was in May, 1963. The meeting was called without a planned agenda and without the chairman having used anyone for a sounding board. The chairman went around the room requesting each member to express how he felt about opening accommodations. The expressions were unanimous that accommodations should be opened. One member asked: "Why don't we go ahead and do it?" Three members were asked to write a brief resolution for the consideration of the full board of directors.

The Mayor asked the executive vice-president of the Chamber to invite a representative group of hotel, motel, theater, and restaurant owners and managers to a meeting at the Chamber. They were not told what the subject for discussion would be, but rather they were invited to come to discuss a matter of vital concern to the City and its development.

Immediately prior to the scheduled meeting of accommodation facility representatives, the 39-member Board of Directors of the Chamber of Commerce met and unanimously adopted the report of the resolution committee. The resolution read: "We, the directors of the Charlotte Chamber of Commerce, recommend that all businesses in this community catering to the general public be opened immediately to all customers without regard to race, creed, or color." With the passage of this resolution public sessions were ended.

It is, of course, one thing to pass a resolution and something else again to sit down in a private dining room with men who own businesses and begin the task of discussion, persuading—to begin to make the actual adjustments. There were about 30 representatives of the accommodation businesses present at the Chamber's called meeting. In addition, there were four ministers present—invited because "we wanted to know that the business leadership of this community felt that this was the right thing to do."

The Chairman told the businessmen simply that he thought it was "the right thing to do." He spoke of the economic consequences of not making a change. But he emphasized the moral obligations.

He told them the Chamber was not trying to tell them what to do, but that it was assuring them that the business leadership would be behind them "one hundred per cent if they should decide to do it."

Birmingham and Little Rock were mentioned. One participant said, "There are hard choices, but this is too good a town to have it ruined. We won't have it. I think the time is right. The community is ready." Every participant voiced his opinion that adjustments should be made.

No one seemed to know how, but all agreed that they would be willing. However, no one was willing to make adjustments alone. There was economic fear. The operators seemed afraid to act alone because they did not want to be criticized individually. Neither did they want to risk letting a competitor have any sort of advantage.

At that same session it was decided that businessmen would meet in groups of their own types of business to see if specific plans could be made.

The Chamber officials committed themselves to participate in the desegregation personally. A restaurant representative had asked: "If I desegregate, will you come to my place and bring a Negro guest?" The chairman, the Mayor, a councilman, an editor, a minister, and a banker all said, "Yes." Representatives of the Mayor's Committee on Community Relations participated throughout as plans were formulated and they assumed responsibility for most of the arrangements.

There was subsequently a meeting of 40 hotel and motel men. There was hesitancy on the part of some, but others were ready to go. Concern about the possible loss of white customers and concern about a possible incident seemed to be the delaying factors. Eight decided to desegregate. The others would wait. Within a week the others moved. Adjustment was made, completed, and announced. The hotel men agreed to desegregate their dining rooms first. On three successive days the white directors of the Chamber of Commerce and several other leading business, civic, and government leaders went to lunch with Negroes as guests. In groups of two, four, and six, they went by appointment. There was no publicity. On one occasion when an out-of-town newsman sought to take pictures for national television, the appointment was switched to another restaurant in order that the agreement not to take pictures would remain unbroken.

So well did that phase of the effort go that the day after the three-day test period, the names of the hotels whose restaurants had desegregated were announced. Further, their rooms and those of three motels were also announced to be desegregated.

So rapidly had the Chamber moved that there had been little co-ordination between the Chamber and the already existing and functioning Mayor's Committee on Community Relations. The Mayor's Committee, however, had set a good climate for progress.

The theaters came next. However, for the theaters most of this discussion was done by half a dozen Negroes, all members of the Mayor's Committee, and the theater owners. Those participating in the planning of the adjustments had thought the gravest problem would be here. The themes of some movies create tensions and emotions that are quite different from those encountered in a restaurant during lunch. Like the hotel and restaurant man, the theater man wanted no publicity. They agreed to accept Negro patrons, by appointment and reservation, for a limited time to see how it worked.

It took a couple of meetings to work out a plan for the beginning. Whereas the hotels and motels had announced their doors were open to all only nine days after the Chamber's resolution, the theaters took their first Negro patrons 19 days after the adoption of the resolution. The trial period ran nearly three weeks. Now, all major indoor theaters are following a policy of admitting Negroes who choose to come. A couple of neighborhood theaters are not included in the agreement, nor are any of the half-dozen or so drive-in theaters.

Negroes, at first, were admitted only by reservation, by name. At the end of the first week, some of the theater managers were letting in a few Negroes who did not have reservations.

Altogether, 30 to 50 Negroes a day were formally attending the eight all-white theaters. Usually they arrived in twos and fours.

Restaurants presented another situation. There was no effective organization in which to work with restaurant operators. Only one restaurant was represented at the Chamber's called meeting for accommodation facility representatives. Within a few days following this meeting contact was made with 15 or 20 restaurant owners. In general, they said the same thing: "We will desegregate when Frank O. Sherrill desegregates the S and W Cafeterias."

After more telephone calls, 20 restaurant operators gave their assurances that they would desegregate. A meeting with the operators to make specific plans to act together appeared to be impossible. A typical situation: Seven operators said that they had no objection to a public announcement of their accepting Negroes immediately, whereas three others wanted no publicity, but simply agreed not to turn Negroes away if they came.

It became apparent that if all restaurants were to desegregate at one time it would take quite a long time to do the necessary organizing. A break came about two weeks after the Chamber's resolution, when Mr. Sherrill of the S and W announced the desegregation of his chain as fast as individual community problems could be worked out. Working without an effective organization, eight leading restaurants said that they would take Negroes under the previously used control plan for three days to see how it worked. The plan went into effect. It worked, just as it had with the theaters, hotels, and motels.

Attention was turned, then, to drive-in restaurants. Meetings and telephone calls brought an agreement for 18 drive-ins to begin accepting Negroes, two groups each night, for three nights, beginning June 24. After that, it was hoped, general desegregation would be announced. However, something that can never be predicted or planned for happened over an intervening week end. There was a big social affair that involved several restaurant owners. Some of the dining room owners chided some of the drive-in owners about their plans to desegregate. By Monday several of them had changed their minds. When the Negro groups showed up Monday night, they were turned away at 11 of the 18 places.

Another effort was made by the Chamber to hold a large meeting of restaurant owners. A total of 130 owners were invited. Seven came. It was decided that a list of the desegregated restaurants would be drawn up and mailed with a letter to all restaurant owners and operators in the County, asking about their policy, requesting that they consider desegregating, and requesting a reply in writing to the Committee.

Gradually more and more restaurants have adopted a desegregation policy. At the end of 1963 only a few remained segregated. Credit for Charlotte's progress must be shared widely among both the white and Negro leadership. The citizens at large have accepted and supported the progressive steps taken to preserve racial harmony and make human progress.

CLAYTON

Population: 3,302; 17.8 per cent Negro

Mayor: R. L. Cooper—Office: 410 East Main Street; Telephone: Office: 922-7111

Biracial Organization: Mayor's Co-operating Committee

Chairman: To be appointed at the first meeting which is called for action on any complaint.

Negro Action: There have been no demonstrations by Negroes nor have any petitions been presented to the City Council or Mayor.

Municipal Reaction:

The Mayor attended the Governor's conference of Mayors on July 5, 1963, in Greensboro and subsequently appointed an 18-member committee to assist him in his efforts to resolve equitably any racial problems. The Committee is composed of five Negroes and eight whites who have lived in Clayton most of their lives, and five whites who have lived in integrated cities of the North. This Committee has never had occasion to meet. It is composed of representatives of all segments of the community, and in particular, those who have strong views, pro and con, on racial issues.

It is the Mayor's intention that when the Committee meets, it will select a chairman. The Mayor has asked that all requests for any sort of desegregation in the community be taken before the Committee. There has been no request of any kind and the Mayor does not foresee any soon.

Adjustments:

There are no desegregated facilities in the town. The Negro school principal, a member of the Committee, is reported to have stated that in his opinion there are no Negro children qualified to participate in white schools at the present time.

CONCORD

Population: 17,799; 22.1 per cent Negro

Mayor: James G. McCachern—Office: City Hall, 66 South Union Street; Home: 169 West Corban Street; Telephone: Office: 782-3215; Home: 782-5318

Biracial Organization: The Mayor's Biracial Committee

Chairman: James G. McCachern, Mayor

Negro Action:

There were four or five demonstrations held during the spring and summer of 1963.

Municipal Reaction:

Upon the request of the Chamber of Commerce, the Mayor appointed a seven-member Mayor's Biracial Committee with four white and three Negro members. This Committee was created upon the understanding between the white and Negro communities that it would seek to make adjustments so long as there were no demonstrations. Therefore, a demonstration which was held six weeks after the appointment of the Committee resulted in the dissolution of this Committee. A new biracial committee is being organized.

Adjustments:

One department store has hired a part-time Negro salesclerk. Many Negroes are employed by industry.

No attempts were made to discuss desegregation with the hotel and motel proprietors. The lunch counter in a major department store has been desegregated for several years.

Seventeen restaurants and drugstore lunch counters agreed with members of the Committee to serve Negroes who presented themselves for regular service. It was agreed that the names of these businesses would not be published until the package agreement had been fully settled upon.

There are two theaters in the town and the Committee negotiated with these without reaching an agreement.

The City operates recreational facilities, including two swimming pools. These were desegregated in 1963. Attendance at the previously all-white pool declined approximately 75 per cent during the remainder of the summer season.

The City operates libraries for both the white and Negro communities; however, Negroes are permitted to use the white library. There are no Negroes attending any of the city or county white schools.

The hospital does have segregated services.

The Ministerial Association is desegregated. There are no Negro members in the Chamber of Commerce or Merchants' Association.

DUNN

Population: 7,566; 38.3 per cent Negro

Mayor: George F. Blalock—Home: 1004 West Divine Street; Telephone: Home: 892-3967

Biracial Organization: Dunn Human Relations Committee

Chairman: Reverend Thomas M. Freeman—Office: First Baptist Church; Home: 110 South Layton Avenue; Telephone: Office: 892-6161; Home: 892-7953

Negro Action:

There have been demonstrations on several occasions in Dunn, and the Citizens Co-ordinating Committee of Negroes in Dunn has made several requests to municipal bodies for adjustments in the conditions in Dunn. The NAACP is the formal Negro organization functioning in Dunn.

Municipal Reaction:

The Mayor appointed the Dunn Human Relations Committee during the summer of 1963. The Committee consists of ten members, five white and five Negroes. The major portion of the work of the Committee has been in the area of employment opportunities, but future work will extend to other areas where grievances have been expressed.

Adjustments:

On September 30, 1963, 11 department and variety stores adopted an employment policy based upon merit alone. In addition, five grocery stores have agreed to upgrade Negro employees and to hire without regard to race. City officials have declared that municipal employment will offer equal opportunities to both races.

The drugstore lunch counters and the other lunch counter have been desegregated; a restaurant has also desegregated.

The municipal library is desegregated. There are no Negroes attending the white schools, although there are some Indians enrolled.

The hospital, city parks, and privately owned recreational facilities are segregated. There are plans to build a new hospital with Hill-Burton Fund help.

DURHAM

Population: 78,302; 36.3 per cent Negro

Mayor: R. Wensell Grabarek—Office: 111 North Corcoran Road, Room 505; Home: 1412 Ward Street; Telephone: Office: Mayor-682-8370; Office: 682-2525; Home: 489-5279

Biracial Organization: Committee on Community Relations

Chairman: George Watts Hill, Jr.—Office: 505 Chapel Hill Road; Home: 1212 Hill Street; Telephone: Office: 682-6024; Home: 684-7031

Negro Action:

The Negro desegregation movement in Durham was organized and directed by NAACP-CORE Chapters at North Carolina College and in the City. In 1960 NAACP-CORE submitted a memorandum to the City Council, which resulted in the city's tennis courts being desegregated. Chapters of the NAACP-CORE first conducted large-scale demonstrations in Durham on May 18, 1963, on the night of the Mayor's election. Of the 425 demonstrators, 130 Negroes were arrested after staging sit-ins at six downtown eating establishments. Hundreds flocked to the Courthouse and to City Hall to demonstrate in support of those who were arrested. The crowds, comprised of both white and Negro students —mostly from North Carolina College and all-Negro Hillside High School—sang, clapped their hands, and cheered at the Courthouse as integrationists entered police headquarters in the same building. The assault on at least six Durham eating establishments came after an opening rally staged in front of City Hall. From there the sign-carrying demonstrators weaved through downtown traffic across Five Points and down Main and Chapel Hill Streets. All those arrested were booked and released without bond.

On Sunday, May 19, the following day, it was obvious that an all-out drive for desegregation had begun. Hundreds upon hundreds of youthful Negroes taunted by hundreds of whites, staged more Courthouse demonstrations while some 700 Negroes were being booked on trespass charges as a result of a Howard Johnson's sit-down outside the City, where more than 4,000 Negroes were conducting a mass meeting in front of the restaurant.

NAACP-CORE members mapped strategy for the mass rallies during a meeting Friday night, May 17, at North Carolina College.

Typical of the sit-ins was a pattern followed by more than 60 demonstrators who entered the Oriental Restaurant shortly before 5:00 P.M. All sat quietly at tables or in booths while a leader talked with the manager. After learning that the students would not be served, the leader announced that any of the students were free to leave.

Some 800 college students staged a sympathy demonstration behind the Administration Building at North Carolina College Saturday night, May 18.

NAACP-CORE announced that 30 consecutive days of mass demonstrations would begin in Durham on Monday, May 20. On that day the crisis reached its peak. Thousands of Negroes marched on City Hall only a few hours after Mayor Grabarek had taken the oath of office. This was his mandate to act and act quickly. Several hundred demonstrators were arrested. Most of the white demonstrators were from Duke University. All of those arrested were released without bond after being booked on trespass charges.

The East End Betterment League, a 15-year-old Negro clinic association in North Durham, voted unanimously on the evening of May 21 to continue its boycott of the unburned unit of East End School where classes were being held on a split-shift basis. The boycott continued until school closed in the summer, at which time that part of the school which burned in April, 1963, was rebuilt.

Student NAACP-CORE leaders gave the City Council a petition at its meeting on May 21 which asked for fair employment in city jobs and for a law which would require all businesses licensed by the public to serve each member of the public without discrimination. This public accommodations ordinance for the City of Durham was submitted to the City Council in writing in draft form for its adoption on May 30, 1963.

MEETING OF SPECIAL COMMITTEE WITH MAYOR R. WENSELL GRABAREK. FROM *LEFT TO RIGHT:* REVEREND MELVIN C. SWANN, MISS JOYCE WARE, FLOYD B. MCKISSICK, REVEREND J. A. BROWN, PRESIDENT OF DURHAM NAACP, AND GRABAREK.

Mayor Grabarek met with the leaders for more than an hour later in the day following his noon swearing-in. Upon obtaining an uneasy truce, leaders from the NAACP-CORE thanked the Mayor for his efforts and in the same breath warned, "Unless noticeable progress is made on a daily basis, we cannot promise that mass demonstrations will not resume at any time."

The demonstrations have not been resumed.

On May 24 a seven-item petition was sent to and presented to the Mayor's Interim Committee.

On September 11, 1963, the executive committee of the Durham Youth and College Chapters of the NAACP-CORE responded in writing to the final report of the Durham Interim Committee which had been submitted to it on July 12, 1963. In its reply, signed by the committee's co-chairmen, Floyd B. McKissick and Joyce Ware, the executive committee suggested that a public accommodations law and a fair employment practices act would do more for guaranteeing the implementation of a person's natural and civil rights than would other labors of a biracial committee. The committee pointed out that fair employment laws have been extremely useful as prods to employers who preferred to continue to discriminate, and that they have been equally useful to employers who wished to stop discriminating, but who were warned by their foremen or their union that there would be trouble in the labor ranks if they did. The committee recommended that in the absence of a fair employment practices act in the City and County of Durham, that a Job Talent Center should be established in one of the existing local governmental offices to be certain that both the potential employee and employer could be in friendly communication. The committee suggested that the Mayor and the Board of County Commissioners should instruct the superintendents of the Durham City and County Schools of the advisability for continuing the desegregation of these schools on a free-assignment basis. In the absence of a public accommodations law, the committee suggested that a list of open facilities should be made available to potential Negro patrons, since Negroes had been refused admittance to certain theaters, restaurants, and motels which had previously declared a policy of desegregation before the preparation of the final report of the Durham Interim Committee. The committee suggested that its analysis revealed that some of the subcommittees' reports were merely citations of previous accomplishments and not investigations into broader and more meaningful solutions of the racial problems of the City and County of Durham. As a final recommendation the committee suggested that the Mayor appoint a permanent "Implementation Committee."

Municipal Reaction:

A Mayor's Committee on Human Relations had been established in Durham many years ago to serve as a link in interracial communications. When demonstrations began in May of 1963, Asa T. Spaulding, the chairman of the Mayor's Committee on Human Relations noted the Committee's concern over the grave situation in the community and offered the committee's services to the Mayor and the Negro protesters. On Sunday afternoon, May 19, the Mayor-elect visited the scene of the mass Negro rally at the Courthouse.

Monday, May 20, the new Mayor met with the leaders of NAACP-CORE for more than an hour, later in the day following his noon swearing-in. At this meeting the Mayor heard the Negroes' grievances.

Adding to the drama of the day, the United States Supreme Court (*Avent v. North Carolina*, 373 U.S. 375, May 20, 1963) voided a Durham trespass case of 1960, wherein five young Negroes and two white Duke University students were charged with trespass when they refused to leave the Kress Store lunch counter on May 6, 1960. The defendants in the case were among 80 sit-down demonstrators who were arrested by police. Charges against the remaining 73 defendants were dropped by the Court on August 2, 1960, when Kress and several other downtown stores opened their lunch counters to Negroes.

Chief Justice Earl Warren of the United States Supreme Court (*Peterson v. Greenville*, 373 U.S. 244, May 20, 1963), declared that "When a state agency passes a law compelling persons to discriminate against another person because of race, and the State's criminal processes are employed in a way which enforces the discrimination mandated by that law, such a palpable violation of the Fourteenth Amendment cannot be saved by attempting to separate the mental urges of discriminators."

On Tuesday, May 21, Mayor Grabarek obtained a promise from desegregation leaders to suspend mass demonstrations "for the time being" on the reciprocal promise that he would continue efforts to resolve major grievances of the Negro protest movement. News of the truce was announced at a mass meeting Tuesday night of students and other participants in the demonstrations which was held at St. Joseph AME Church. The meeting attracted a crowd estimated at more than 1,000 persons. The Mayor spoke briefly at the session.

During the day, seven eating places, including three drive-ins and two cafes, agreed to drop their racial barriers while the Durham Restaurant Association, in an afternoon meeting, voted to continue its practice of segregation.

On Wednesday afternoon, May 23, the Mayor named an 11-member Durham Interim Committee, composed of nine white and two Negro civic leaders. The Mayor's assignment was: "Seek the highest possible level of understanding on a totally voluntary basis acceptable to all parties concerned." The Committee was designed to "resolve and reconcile" racial differences. The Mayor requested the group to hold its organizational meeting the afternoon of its appointment. The group itself selected George Watts Carr, Jr., the Mayor's political opponent in the city election whom he had appointed to the Committee, as its chairman.

The Durham Interim Committee was divided into four subcommittees which invited persons who were involved in the areas

DURHAM

of their concern to meet with them to discuss the racial situation.

On May 28, the Durham Industrial Education Center announced that it was ready to make available to "qualified" Negroes training in retail distribution and marketing, beginning during the summer session.

The Durham City Schools took their first step towards complete desegregation of classrooms by assigning two all-Negro eighth grades to predominantly white junior high schools. Sixty Negro eighth-grade students were assigned to predominantly white schools for the 1963-1964 term and all first-grade pupils were assigned to the elementary schools located in the attendance area in which the pupils resided for the 1963-1964 term. The assignment of the first-grade pupils resulted from the United States District Court decision to permit the free assignment of Negro pupils to schools of their choice.

On June 1, it was announced that the subcommittee of the Durham Interim Committee working with food service businesses had been in contact with all parties responsible for establishing policies regarding their restaurants in the Durham area. The Committee requested the parties directly concerned to re-examine voluntarily their existing policies in the light of the present conditions and circumstances. They requested the food service businesses to adopt the following resolution:

We the undersigned food service establishments of Durham agree to open our places of business to the public.

It is understood and agreed that as operators of a private business we reserve the right to select our customers, regardless of race— white or Negro. We would be expected to serve bona fide customers who come to us in proper spirit but we would not be expected to admit those who come in large groups, who come as test teams, or who are not normally suitable customers in our place of business.

On June 1, the City Council, meeting in committee-of-the-whole, voluntarily voted to open the city's swimming pools on a desegregated basis for the first time in Durham's history, before the Council had received any specific demands for such action to be taken by either desegregation leaders or the courts. Desegregation proceeded peacefully.

On June 2, "A Pledge of Support to Our Durham Merchants" appeared in the *Durham Morning Herald* over more than 600 names.

TOP: FLOYD B. McKISSICK SPEAKS TO FREEDOM RALLY.
BOTTOM: MAYOR R. WENSELL GRABAREK SPEAKS TO FREEDOM RALLY.

We of the community strongly believe that it is in the best interest of Durham for theaters, stores, hotels, motels, restaurants and other enterprises to adopt a policy of equal treatment for all without regard to race. We urge our merchants to take this honorable and progressive action. To do so now would be of great credit to you, and a benefit to our city and all its residents.

You, the merchants, are entitled to reassurance that such a decision will be supported by the community. Accordingly, we the undersigned hereby pledge our full support and patronage to those merchants who serve the public and employ help without regard to race.

On June 4, 1,400 trespass charges against Negro demonstrators arrested during the desegregation attempts on May 18, 19, and 20 were nol prossed upon the advice of North Carolina Assistant Attorney General Ralph Moody.

Recorder's Court Judge A. R. Wilson declared that Mr. Moody was of the opinion that the demonstrators were arrested under a city ordinance similar to the one under which trespassing cases had been discharged by the United States Supreme Court in the case of *Peterson v. City of Greenville* (S.C.). That ordinance required that on hotel, restaurant, or cafe furnish meals to white persons and colored persons in the same room or at the same table, or at the same counter. The ordinance said that white persons and colored persons could be served in the same establishment where separate facilities were furnished, and this meant separate eating utensils, separate tables, counters or booths, and a distance of 25 feet between the area where white and colored persons were served. "It was required that a separate facility be maintained and used for the cleaning of eating utensils and dishes furnished the two races."

Mr. Moody was of the opinion that "as long as this obsolete and unconstitutional ordinance is in the Code of the City of Durham it attaints, infects, pervades, and destroys the legal efficacy of the Trespass Statute."

On June 4, the Durham Interim Committee published a report in which it reviewed the status of the Durham desegregation program. Durham had been a community with a pattern of society which identified it as a southern city with longstanding traditions. The Committee's report noted that in the scarcely three weeks since the first Negro demonstration that motels, hotels, and restaurants had opened their doors. Fifty-seven restaurants and lunch counters were serving persons of all races. Another 46 retail establishments had announced their intention to begin their own "fair employment practices" program. The report concluded with recognition that merchants were still enjoying good retail sales.

On July 12, 1963, the Durham Interim Committee submitted a final written report to the Mayor and requested the Mayor to discharge it.

The report summarized the work of the Durham Interim Committee's four subcommittees: the Fair Employment Practice Subcommittee, the Education Subcommittee, the Subcommittee on Hotels, Motels, and Restaurants, and the Subcommittee on Miscellaneous Items.

On Friday, May 24, 1963, the Negro demonstration leaders presented a series of requests to the Durham Interim Committee. In the list of requests submitted was an item relating to employment practices in the City and County of Durham. The specific request was, "We seek a fair employment practices act prohibiting employers, unions, and schools from discriminating against applicants, employers, members, or students because of their race, color, religion, or national origin."

The Fair Employment Practices Subcommittee addressed itself primarily to the determination of community attitudes toward voluntary acceptance of this aspect of the race problems in the community. Commercial, institutional, industrial, and governmental employees were invited to attend one or more of a series of meetings devoted to discussion of this problem.

Item number seven in the list of requests, dealt with educational subjects and read as follows:

That this committee investigate the practices of segregation existing in the City School System and the County School System and demand that such practices be discontinued immediately and that the County Board of Education be directed to present a plan of desegregation of County Schools forthwith and that the City Schools comply with the order of the Court.

In subsequent discussions with Negro leaders, additional items of concern were presented, such as alleged "Acts of Discrimination and Unfair Treatment" of Negro students attending predominantly white schools in the Durham City School System, joint teachers' meetings, location of supervisors and questions of school organizations, and use of bond funds in the County School system.

The full membership of the Durham Interim Committee instructed the Education Subcommittee to refer questions of school administration to the appropriate school board for action. The Subcommittee did this with regard to each subject covered by the demonstrator's request.

The Subcommittee on Miscellaneous Items addressed itself to the request by integration leaders falling in the categories of public accommodations ordinances and fair employment practices acts.

The Subcommittee held numerous discussions on the matter of the city's and county's employment policies. It also did considerable research on this subject and the manner which other municipal units have approached it. As a result of its study, it recommended that the City Council and County Commissioners give serious consideration to passage of a resolution establishing a policy of hiring and upgrading employees without respect to race or color. A similar resolution, passed by the City Council of Richmond, Virginia, on May 28, 1962, was attached to its recommendation and appears as follows:

BE IT RESOLVED BY THE COUNCIL OF THE CITY OF RICHMOND:

That the Council hereby declares it to be a policy of the City of Richmond that applicants for employment by the City should be employed, and employees of the City should be promoted, solely on the basis of merit and fitness for the particular position for which they are employed.

BE IT FURTHER RESOLVED BY THE COUNCIL OF THE CITY OF RICHMOND:

That the Council favors the adoption of a rule by the Personnel Board to the effect that the employment of applicants for positions in the City's service and the promotion of employees shall not be refused solely on the basis of race, creed, or color or arbitrary maximum age limits. That the City Manager is hereby directed to cause to be submitted to the Personnel Board for adoption in form of a rule the foregoing provisions of this resolution.

It is the further opinion of the Council that the Personnel Board should adopt the rule as submitted.

The Committee also addressed itself to the matter of a "public accommodations" ordinance prohibiting discrimination based upon race, at hotels, motels, restaurants, and similar establishments.

After extensive research the Subcommittee discussed the wisdom of recommending the immediate enactment of a Public Accommodations Ordinance. Acknowledging the fact that this is basically a moral issue with overtones of economic impact, the Committee sought an answer to this important question, namely:

Will the purposes sought be better served by the passage of and administration of law, or by continuing, for the present, to develop and encourage the voluntary acceptance of the nondiscriminating principle?

The members of the Subcommittee reflected the Committee's varied opinions in answer to such a question. The dilemma was stated as follows:

Are laws indicated in the wake of the failure of voluntary moral responsibility or do they serve to buttress and make secure moral positions which have been achieved by free choice? In the present situation two relevant points of view emerge. One point of view is that laws would serve to protect those voluntarily adopting nondiscriminating practices against competitors not adopting such principles in like manner. Another point of view is that the passage of such law would serve to antagonize those voluntarily accepting nondiscriminatory practices and that the gains reflected under the voluntary program might be substantially dissipated.

Faced with the resolution of such a fundamental issue, the Subcommittee felt that its comparatively short tenure as a part of the Durham Interim Committee provided it with insufficient time and opportunity for it to arrive at the best conclusion. It recommended that succeeding biracial organizations give attention to this issue and to the material which it had assembled.

The Durham Interim Committee concluded its report with this recommendation:

In the days to come, there will undoubtedly be misunderstandings to be resolved and other associated problems calling for the existence of some permanent organization through which these may be handled. We, therefore, wish to recommend the establishment at once of a permanent committee with properly delegated power and authority to succeed the Interim Committee. Serious thought should be given to the creation of a county-wide committee.

On April 7, 1964, Mayor Grabarek announced to the City Council the appointment of a 15-member committee designed "to establish the maximum level of understanding possible" between the races in the City of Durham. The new Committee on Community Relations includes four local Negro leaders. The membership is composed of classes of five, staggered for three-year terms. George Watts Hill, Jr., was named chairman of the new Committee. The Mayor announced that "the purpose of the Committee is to assist and to advise the Mayor and the City Council of Durham as deemed necessary and appropriate to help provide our citizens with a self-respecting, peaceful, harmonious, and tranquil community."

Adjustments:

Forty-one members of the retail community pledged themselves to hiring practices based on qualifications for the job available without regard to race, color, creed, or national origin. Admitting that few Negroes had the opportunity to gain required experience, these merchants further pledged to work with the Durham Industrial Education Center in developing a program of study and the training which would provide the opportunity for qualifications for retail employment for both white and Negroes interested in this field of employment. These merchants currently hire more than 1,300 employees.

Durham's six commercial banks have individually indicated their employment policies do not include race as a consideration in hiring and that qualification for the job to be filled was the sole criterion.

Three insurance companies with home offices in this community have indicated that their employment will be based solely on the qualifications of the applicants to perform the desired task without regard to the race, color, creed, or national origin of such applicant.

Duke University has advised this Subcommittee that employment without regard to race has been its policy for sometime.

Several of the industries in Durham have been operating under the fair employment practices of the Federal Government for sometime as required of those industries who supply goods or services to the Federal Government.

The number of employees represented by the firms covered in this report exceeds 13,900.

In addition, the City and County of Durham have indicated that they will hire on the basis of qualifications under a fair employment practices policy. At the time of this survey the City of Durham had already made substantial changes in upgrading job opportunities for Negroes and expected that in the future

PICKETERS PETITION FOR OPEN ACCOMMODATIONS.

more changes of this nature would take place. The City of Durham currently employs more than 900 persons and the County employs 235.

The Mayor noted that the high point of the city's desegregation program was the agreement of local employers to give employment opportunities to the Negro and white workers alike.

When Woolworth's lunch counters desegregated in 1960, they witnessed a sharp decrease in white patronage for a time. The firm now reports that business is as good as, if not better than, before the sit-in demonstrations were conducted at the store. Other chain store and drugstore lunch counters have desegregated since 1960.

All 11 of Durham's motels and its leading hotel have desegregated.

After two weeks of work, the Durham Interim Committee reported on June 5, 1963, that 55 of 103 licensed food service establishments had announced that their doors would be opened to all persons, regardless of race. These businesses accounted for 75 per cent of the Durham area volume of food service.

As of June 19, 1963, establishments representing more than 90 per cent of the Durham area volume of food service had agreed

75

to serve the public without regard to race or color. This included all of the major restaurants, cafeterias, cafes, and grills of Durham. All motel restaurants and coffee shops had also desegregated. Liggett and Myers and American Tobacco Company cafeterias have been serving Negro employees since June of 1962, in conformity with the Fair Employment Practices Act of the Federal Government. All of Durham's theaters desegregated during the summer of 1963 and have remained desegregated.

The municipal recreational facilities, including swimming pools, and the municipal library are desegregated.

On June 4, 1963, it was announced that efforts were being made to drop all discriminatory practices in pupil assignments in both the county and city school systems.

There are about 300 Negro students in the predominantly white Durham city schools at all grade levels. The city school system has enrolled Negroes in white schools since 1957.

The County Board of Education acted upon requests by Negro students for reassignment to predominantly white county schools at its meeting June 24, 1963. This action of the county school board ushered in a new era for the system when it assigned three Negro students to predominantly white schools for the 1963-1964 school year.

In March of 1963 the Durham Jaycees held a meeting at which it approved the elimination of the word "White" from the requirements for membership. In June, the Jaycees rejected the nomination of the first Negro proposed for membership in its ranks. It later accepted Negro applicants.

The Chamber of Commerce is also open to Negro membership.

EDENTON

Population: 4,458; 38.1 per cent Negro

Mayor: John A. Mitchener, Jr.—Home: 203 North Granville Street; Telephone: Office: 482-3711; Home: 482-2363

Biracial Organization: Good Neighbor Committee

Chairman: Reverend Hugh S. Evans—Home: 302 West Queen Street; Telephone: Home: 482-4145.

Negro Action:
There has been a request that Negroes be hired as policemen.

Municipal Reaction:
A Good Neighbor Committee was named. The Mayor does not attend the Good Neighbor Committee meetings. The Committee exists to hear those who have complaints to make.

Adjustments:
Edenton has about eight Negro students in the high school and one in elementary school, all of whom are doing poorly. Most of those in the high school have failed two courses each.

The City has a separate recreation program for the Negro and the white. There are three tennis courts for the whites and one for the Negroes.

No Negro policeman has been hired because no Negro applicant has qualified, but the City is accepting applications from Negroes.

No adjustments have been made in the area of accommodations.

ELIZABETH CITY

Population: 14,062; 37.0 per cent Negro

Mayor: Levin B. Culpepper—Home: 502 Baxter Street; Telephone: Office: 335-7296; Home: 338-6147

Biracial Organization: Human Relations Committee

Chairman: Dr. W. N. Ridley, President, Elizabeth City State Teachers College; Home: 1825 Southern Avenue; Telephone: Office: 335-5923; Home: 338-6287

Negro Action:
The NAACP and the Southern Christian Leadership Conference co-operated with the students of Elizabeth City State College in organizing street marches, sit-ins, and entrance blockages against segregated restaurants during the summer of 1963. The street marches involved close to 250 persons at times.

The sit-ins resulted in arrests and convictions for trespass. The lower court sentences were appealed.

Later in the summer of 1963 the students boycotted segregated downtown stores.

Municipal Reaction:
The Mayor named a Human Relations Committee which began to deal with the Negro complaints. Negro student leaders have been permitted to attend most of the Human Relations Committee's meetings with wholesome effect. The City Council has

publicly endorsed the work of the Human Relations Committee and by resolution commended the Committee.

Adjustments:

A desegregated Industrial Education training program sponsored by the College of the Albemarle, the community college, is in progress.

Two Negro policemen have been hired and two Negro women have been added to the force on a part-time basis.

Supak, the largest employer of women in the City, now employs Negro women as well as white.

A subcommittee of the Human Relations Committee went to see the managers of the Supak Plant and discussed with them the desegregation of their employment practice. At this meeting it was announced by the management that the plant would henceforth hire qualified employees regardless of race.

Five downtown stores are hiring Negro salesclerks. The City is also accepting applications from Negroes for its non-menial jobs. Members of the merchants division of the Chamber of Commerce have advertised in the newspaper that they would accept employment applications on a merit basis without regard to race.

A variety store lunch counter is open to Negroes. The most difficult area in which to make adjustments has proven to be that of restaurants. Discussions between the committee and restaurant operators are continuing.

The theaters continue to be segregated.

The library and courthouse are desegregated.

There is one Negro in the nursing school and four Negro doctors practicing in the hospital.

The Chamber of Commerce is open to Negroes.

The Ministerial Associations merged and the white churches are open to any Negroes who wish to attend.

The City has adopted an ordinance to regulate picketing, requiring picketers to march ten feet apart, except when passing, prohibiting more than 15 demonstrators for a single cause within a city block area at one time, and prescribing the maximum size of placards. Picketers are required to walk within six feet of the curb and are required to be continuously in motion.

The atmosphere is conducive to more adjustments. The local white and Negro communities apparently have complete confidence in each other.

ENFIELD

Population: 2,978; 50.8 per cent Negro

Mayor: R. E. Shervette, Jr.—Office: 107 Halifax Street; Home: 310 West Burnette Avenue; Telephone: Office: 445-6761; Home: 445-3521

Biracial Organization: Biracial Committee

Chairman: Joseph Branch—Office: Whitfield Street; Home: Sherrod Heights; Telephone: Office: 445-2241; Home: 445-2021

Negro Action:
There is an active youth chapter of the NAACP in Enfield. The group organized demonstrations at the theater early in the spring of 1963. Shortly after demonstrations began, the theater was forced to close. The organization has focused its attention primarily at the desegregation of cafes, restaurants, and motels. They have also requested more job opportunities for Negroes.

August, 1963, was the month in which demonstrations were most intense. On August 29, 1963, more than 100 persons were arrested for their participation in demonstrations. By-standers threw bricks and bottles at the demonstrators on August 31. An ordinance to regulate picketing, which requires a five-hour advance notice before demonstrations, was violated.

Demonstrations continued through September, 1963, without success except in unifying the Negro community and in instructing the Negro community in its aspirations.

Municipal Reaction:
A delegation of Negroes led by T. H. Cofield, president of the adult chapter of the NAACP, met with the Mayor and persons selected by him in the spring of 1963 to establish a biracial committee. The Biracial Committee, composed of five whites and five Negroes, was appointed by Mayor Shervette in June, 1963, to receive community complaints. This Committee met at the call of its chairman, Joseph Branch, throughout the summer of 1963. The group became inactive in October or November, 1963, after conducting many discussions with merchants about their segregation policies, when street demonstrations continued.

The City passed an ordinance regulating picketing in response to the demonstrations.

Adjustments:

The Committee recommended that consideration be given to the hiring of a Negro policeman and applications have been taken for the position. The town board has considered the applications and has stated that when a vacancy occurs, or when the need arises, consideration will be given to the applicants. A Negro was employed by the City as a traffic officer four years ago.

Negro salesclerks were employed prior to the demonstrations and additional Negro salesclerks have been employed by downtown merchants since the demonstrations.

The theater remains closed and the Municipal Library is desegregated and is widely used by both whites and Negroes.

There are few public accommodation facilities in the town other than restaurants about which the Negro can be concerned.

The City passed new ordinances regulating demonstrations. These require that picketers march 15 feet apart, that they demonstrate before no more than one store in a block at any particular time, and that all demonstrators be eighteen years of age or older.

All court cases against demonstrators were discharged.

Courtrooms of the City have been desegregated.

FAYETTEVILLE

Population: 47,106; 35.9 per cent Negro

Mayor: Wilbur Clark—Office: Kyle House, 234 Green Street; Home: 1455 Pine Valley Loop; Telephone: Office: 432-6168; Home: 484-7211

Biracial Organizations:
1. Mayor's Biracial Committee
2. Good Neighbor Council

Chairmen:
1. J. W. Pate, Jr.—Office: P. O. Box 3665; Home: 614 Pearl Street; Telephone: Office: 485-1131; Home: 484-7345
2. R. O. McCoy, Jr.—Office: 427 Franklin Street; Home: 1517 Morganton Road; Telephone: Office: 433-2188; Home: 484-0087

Negro Action:

Student demonstrations under the direction of the NAACP were begun in May, 1963, with orderly marches into the downtown business district every afternoon. These demonstrations were halted for a few days while the Mayor sought adjustments in the policy of segregated public accommodations. Restaurants refused to desegregate and the demonstrations were resumed on a daily basis. The demonstrations concentrated on restaurants and theaters in the downtown area, with some attention being given hotels and department stores. The demonstrators usually numbered between 40 and 50 until the night marches started. City police did not make arrests during the early weeks.

Friday, June 14, 1963, police used tear gas to disperse mobs of Negroes and whites who crowded into the downtown area for the third straight day of protests against racial segregation. More than 200 Negroes were arrested on charges ranging from trespassing to blocking traffic on the city's main street.

Better disciplined demonstrations continued against the restaurants and theaters. The Mayor's Biracial Committee was appointed. Demonstrations by 40 to 50 marchers continued and there were scattered arrests for trespass. Negro and white servicemen from Fort Bragg joined the demonstrations. Night marches were resumed with between 300 and 400 persons participating, 50 per cent civilians and 50 per cent servicemen. The demonstrations were halted, unannounced, about one week prior to the public announcement of the five-point agreement on July 19, 1963.

The Fayetteville Freedom Council of the NAACP presented to the Mayor a statement of objectives as follows:

1. Upgrading of employment for Negroes in stores and banks.

2. Upgrading of employment for Negroes in all city establishments supported by public funds.

3. Desegregation of all facilities involving sale of goods or services in business establishments operated under license, including theaters and department stores.

4. Publication of pledge that desegregation and fair employment for Negroes are in effect, and establishment of a biracial committee to assure that the reform policies will be executed.

Municipal Reaction:

The Mayor appointed the Biracial Committee June 20, 1963. This was not the first biracial committee set up in Fayetteville.

Some progress towards equal civil rights for Negroes had been made in the community during the past several years.

The assignment of the Biracial Committee was to study the objectives of the Negroes and, by means of persuasion and voluntary agreement, to get the community's businessmen to make changes in policies consistent with as many of them as possible.

The second purpose of the Committee was of a long-range nature, concerned with private employment on a basis of ability and qualification without discrimination because of race. Expansion of the "Open Door" policy, the opening of tax-supported facilities and employment by governmental units to all citizens, and an organized effort by the local Negro community to train and qualify more Negroes for these opportunities were deliberated.

The Committee made a survey of conditions existing in community life partly to determine to what extent desegregation of facilities and increase of job opportunities had occurred. This was followed by negotiations to extend the reforms in policies.

A copy of the Committee's report appears in this book.

The Committee outlined its proposed plan of action to the Negotiating Committee of the NAACP Freedom Council at a meeting held June 26, 1963, and has since met with that committee numerous times.

On June 28 the Committee held a meeting to which both the NAACP Negotiating Committee, the Mayor and City Council members, and representatives of the press and radio were invited. At this meeting it gave a preliminary report of its survey.

The Committee has also held numerous conferences with businessmen and business groups, city and county officials, officers of organizations, and individual citizens, and received and investigated a number of complaints. Weekly reports by the Committee were published.

The NAACP Committee has co-operated with the Biracial Committee throughout. A five-point agreement between the two groups was contracted on July 19, 1963, as follows:

1. That the Mayor's Biracial Committee become a continuing steering committee to work for better race relations and equal opportunities for all citizens.
2. That the Biracial Committee make weekly progress reports to the local council of the NAACP and to the Mayor, City Council, and community at large.

MUNICIPAL RESPONSE TO THE CHALLENGE

3. That an immediate and concentrated effort be made for employment of Negroes in department and variety stores before September 2, 1963, and that Negroes be allowed to participate in training programs for all new employees.

4. That demonstrations will cease provided none of the businesses will revert to segregated policies or discriminatory practices; and that in the event of a grievance in any area, the Mayor's Biracial Committee and the Negotiating Committee will be given a reasonable opportunity to effect a satisfactory solution to such grievances prior to the renewal of said demonstrations.

5. That in the City of Fayetteville and in Cumberland County, city and county agencies will not take reprisals against employees who participate in this movement for human rights.

The Committee has held 23 meetings at the latest report.

The Mayor made a public commendation of both the white and Negro communities for the achievements made toward responsible leadership in the field of human relations. A copy of that public statement appears herein.

Adjustments:

The Veterans Administration Hospital and the United States Post Office have desegregated services, facilities, and employment policies.

Private utilities instituted a program designed to increase employment opportunities for Negroes and to upgrade present Negro employees in the immediate future.

The telephone company instituted a policy of hiring without regard to race.

Eleven variety and department stores desegregated their employment practices and their job training programs. All have Negro clerks on their sales forces and some employed Negro college students as extra help at Christmas.

City employment was opened to all on a merit basis. The Public Works Commission employs Negro foremen and has its first Negro clerical worker.

Nine hotels and motels, five lunch counters, and 22 restaurants and cafeterias desegregated and permitted their names to be publicized. All drive-in and indoor theaters desegregated.

Both bowling lanes, the miniature golf course, and one golf range desegregated.

The public library is open to whites and Negroes.

Thirty-one of 34 Negro applicants for transfer to former all-white schools were accepted in the fall of 1963. Both city and county school systems are now desegregated with more than 50 Negro students enrolled in formerly all-white schools.

The Cape Fear Valley Hospital desegregated its dining rooms, the only service that had remained segregated. There are three Negro doctors on the hospital staff.

The public swimming pool was desegregated.

GASTONIA

Population: 37,276; 17.9 per cent Negro

Mayor: G. Vic Phillips—Office: City Hall, 240 West Franklin Avenue; Home: 208 North King Street; Telephone: Office: 864-3211; Home: 864-0263

Biracial Organization: Human Relations Committee

Chairman: Marshall A. Rauch—Home: 1121 Scotch Drive; Telephone: Office: 629-2211; Home: 864-7797

Negro Action:

The only Negro demonstrations consisted of the picketing of the movie theaters for about one week in November, 1963. The picketing was discontinued by voluntary action of the Negroes. There has been no disorder.

Municipal Reaction:

A Human Relations Committee was formed. The Committee set up meetings between restaurant owners and two representatives from the Committee to discuss the feasibility of desegregating the restaurants. Gastonia had a committee as long ago as six years. A golf course was opened to both races 12 years ago and variety store lunch counters have been open about six years.

Adjustments:

The cotton mill and several department stores now have Negro personnel in sales positions.

As stated above, the lunch counters downtown have desegregated, as have almost all of the restaurants.

One of three outdoor theaters has desegregated. The two downtown theaters remain segregated.

Motel accommodations have been secured for Negroes by the Human Relations Committee.

A private bowling lane downtown admits Negroes.

Municipal golf course privileges were extended to Negroes in the late 1940's. The municipal library was recently desegregated.

There are presently two Negro students in each of two white high schools.

The hospital is completely desegregated and the Merchants' Association is open to Negro membership.

The city government passed a resolution supporting desegregated accommodation facilities and urging better job opportunities for Negroes in the community.

GOLDSBORO

Population: 28,873; 41.2 per cent Negro

Mayor: Tom R. Robinson, Jr.—Office: 147 South Center Street; Home: 308 East Chestnut Street; Telephone: Office: 734-0911; Home: 734-5017.

Biracial Organization: Biracial Committee

Chairman: James N. Smith—Office: 233 East Walnut Street; Home: 804 East Beech Street; Telephone: Office: 734-3271; Home: 734-2415

Negro Action:
Street marches were conducted and petitions for reforms to insure full "civil rights" to Negroes were presented to the city government.

Municipal Reaction:
A Biracial Committee was organized soon after demonstrations commenced with Ray Armstrong, former Superintendent of City Schools, and the Reverend B. R. Richardson as co-chairmen. A system of rotation of the chairmanship was adopted. White members of the Committee have visited the merchants in an effort to persuade them to lower their racial barriers, largely without success. The problem has been discussed at public meetings attended by both races.

THE GOLDSBORO BIRACIAL COMMITTEE REVIEWS ITS WORK. SEATED FROM *LEFT TO RIGHT*: JAMES N. SMITH, REVEREND M. W. MORGAN, RAY ARMSTRONG, MRS. GENEVA B. HAMILTON, MRS. SCOTT B. BERKELEY, JR. STANDING FROM *LEFT TO RIGHT*: HENRY WEIL, EARL WHITTED, JR., WALTER FOSTER, WILLIAM P. KEMP, JR., DR. KENNETH W. WILKINS, A. B. REID AND LEMUEL CRAFT. ABSENT MEMBERS ARE HUGH H. ALEXANDER, DR. H. F. COFIELD, MRS. VIRGINIA C. HENDERSON, DR. OSCEOLA JACKSON, JOE G. CAMPBELL, REVEREND J. ERTLE ARNETTE, GEORGE VANN, AND MRS. JEWEL W. WEATHERS.

Adjustments:

During recent months, several Negro clerks have been hired by downtown merchants. Drugstores have opened their fountains to all, including the mayor pro tem's drugstore. The municipal library does not discriminate. There are five Negroes in the predominantly white Junior High School, three in the High School, and one in a white elementary school. Meadowlane Elementary School, which serves Seymour-Johnson Air Force Base, is fully desegregated. Some Negro applications for transfer to predominantly white schools have been rejected.

"White" and "Colored" signs are still in evidence. The swimming pool in which the municipality had an interest has been closed to avoid demands to desegregate it. A municipally run teen-age center is not open to Negroes. A dairy bar which was opened to Negroes was subsequently re-segregated, because it stood alone among competitors.

An ordinance directed toward regulating demonstrations was proposed, but has not been adopted.

Under the auspices of the NAACP Juniors, the Negro community has established a "Study In" program for the purpose of training its members in fields and subjects which would qualify them for better work opportunities. There are currently some 30 young people studying speed reading, basic math, history, current events, music, and cultural topics two hours a night on Mondays and Thursdays under the direction of volunteer, retired public schoolteachers. This program is soliciting interest through sponsorship of two high school essay contests.

Women Volunteers:

Another Goldsboro development consists of the action of women who are forming an organization modeled on that of the Women's Good Will Committee of High Point.

GREENSBORO

Population: 123,334; 25.6 per cent Negro

Mayor: David Schenck—Office: 1025 Homeland Avenue; Home: 1916 Granville Road; Telephone: Office: 272-2175; City Hall: 273-0511; Home: 274-2048

Biracial Organization: Commission on Human Relations

Chairman: W. O. Conrad—Office: Western Electric Corporation; Home: 4212 Henderson Road; Telephone: Office: 299-2311; Home: 299-1486

Negro Action:

The first months of 1963 were marked by picketing at City Hall on three occasions in protest against discrimination in the hiring and promotion of policemen and other city employees. Then the attention of desegregation forces focused upon downtown public accommodation facilities and private employment. In April three students and one adult were arrested on charges of trespass during a demonstration at a drive-in restaurant. Three days later after mass demonstrations, the drive-in was desegregated.

Demonstrations were resumed on May 11, 1963, with activity concentrated on three chain drive-in restaurants. During a four-day period demonstrations continued, beginning with less than 30 persons and climaxing the last night with about 350 demonstrators concentrated at one drive-in. The drive-in closed early and the singing crowd proceeded to march to the central business area where a kneeling demonstration was held in front of a theater. After the march ended with the arrest of one white spectator on a charge of disorderly conduct, an official of the drive-in chain announced the desegregation of all its Greensboro units.

Beginning with the night of the march downtown from the drive-in, large-scale demonstrations were conducted in downtown Greensboro for 11 consecutive nights. The number of participants, predominantly college students, varied from about 500 to 2,000 persons each night. The principal targets were two cafeterias and three theaters. During the first full week, about 900 demonstrators were arrested on charges of trespass and the blocking of fire exits. In the second week of demonstrating another 600 persons were arrested on the same charges, except that nine persons arrested at sit-ins in the Mayor's office were charged with creating a nuisance in a public building and disorderly conduct. All charges of trespass were brought on warrants signed by the owner or manager of the business affected.

A march by about 760 persons on Friday of the second week marked the last demonstration of this phase of desegregation protests.

After an eight-day lull, during which progress was made around the conference tables, downtown demonstrations resumed under the continued direction of a college student leader. These demonstrations continued four straight days and involved from 200 to 850 persons, mostly non-student adults and children. On the last day 284 persons (including 94 juveniles) were arrested after a mass sit-down demonstration in the main downtown street intersection. The only other arrest during the week was of a white spectator who was charged with assault with a deadly weapon upon being found pressing a knife blade against the side of a college professor. No demonstrations have occurred since June 6, 1963.

The desegregation movement in the City has been directed primarily by four local organizations (membership predominantly Negro): the local chapters of the NAACP and CORE, the Greensboro Ministers' Forum, and the Greensboro Citizens' Association. In addition, a group called the Co-ordinating Council of Pro-Integration Groups was formed to co-ordinate the efforts and act as spokesman for all desegregation forces in the City.

The Co-ordinating Council of Pro-Integration Groups presented a program of demands entitled "The Action Ideal" to the City Council. This document was made available to the news media before the Councilmen had seen it.

Municipal Reaction:

After the second night of large-scale marches into downtown Greensboro, the directors of the Merchants' Association and the Chamber of Commerce met separately and passed resolutions urging all businesses to end discrimination based on race or color. These resolutions had only a limited effect, however, when support was not received from restaurant and theater operators.

A cessation of demonstrations was not achieved until a number of the target businesses had desegregated their facilities and a permanent Biracial Commission of Human Relations was established by ordinance.

On the same day that the list of demands was published, the Mayor appointed a Special Committee for the purpose of halting demonstrations and beginning consultations. The Mayor's Special Committee on Human Relations included representatives of the Chamber of Commerce, the Merchants' Association, the superceded Mayor's Committee on Human Relations, the Greensboro Ministerial Association and the four Negro desegregation

PETITIONERS SEEK TO DISCOURAGE PATRONAGE OF A SEGREGATED THEATER.

groups. This committee elected as their chairman a prominent Negro physician.

At a City Council meeting on June 3, 1963, the Co-ordinating Council of Pro-Integration Groups presented a proposal which included a ten-point program for meeting the demands of the desegregation forces. This was a revised version of the program proposed earlier called "The Action Ideal." The proposed resolution was referred to a committee of three councilmen with a request by the Mayor to report their recommendations by July 1.

Since demonstrations were continuing and tension was heightening as a result, the Mayor called a meeting of 23 community business leaders on June 6. The Mayor issued a strong statement on June 7 calling on all places of public accommodations to stop selecting their customers on the basis of race, color, or creed. In making this statement the Mayor pointed out the high costs to other businesses downtown and to the City of Greensboro which were being incurred to enforce the private business decisions of those insisting on a policy of segregation. The Mayor also announced the time and place for a meeting a week later for all affected businessmen to present their decisions in response to his request for complete desegregation. This marked the last day of mass demonstrations for the remainder of the summer.

The City Council passed an ordinance establishing a permanent biracial commission by amending the Greensboro Code of Ordinances with respect to administration on July 1, 1963, in accordance with recommendations of the Mayor's committee of three councilmen. The Commission on Human Relations was set up to have ten members, five Negroes and five whites. The five Negroes appointed included persons prominent in the desegregation groups. By the end of July the Commission on Human Relations had named these six subcommittees to concern themselves with different human relations problem areas: recreation, hotels and motels, public eating places, employment, education, and progress and information.

In recognition of the problem of economic reprisals against desegregated facilities, the Commission adopted the policy of not releasing information for publication regarding individual businesses which desegregate.

Adjustments:

At a series of meetings between the theater businessmen and the Mayor's Special Committee on Human Relations, a plan for gradual desegregation was worked out. On June 13, following the meeting between the Mayor and 35 owners and managers of public accommodation facilities, the Mayor was able to announce the desegregation of all four indoor theaters, an additional eight eating places (a total of 38 at that time) and three additional motels (making a total of five). Not included in those changing their policies were the two downtown cafeterias which had been major targets of the demonstrations. Five days later, on June 18, one of the cafeterias began serving Negroes without incident.

Desegregation of the theaters began on June 25. A two-week period was used during which 25 special invitation cards were passed out each week. These cards served to identify the holders who were to use them at any theater day or night from Monday through Thursday. The Police Department's special squad covered the theaters for the first days. No major incidents occurred during the two-week trial period. Two of the theater managers reported no major problems, although in one theater there were several occasions when people asked for ticket refunds and other indications of patronage loss. One theater has a balcony with a lower admission price and this section is still used most frequently by Negroes. Major credit for the successful desegregation of the theaters is attributed to the co-operation of the news media in avoiding publicity.

The desegregation of one cafeteria was carried out without any special arrangements.

By July 16, the city's four bowling establishments had agreed to a gradual desegregation program. There is presently an integrated bowling league in the City.

The City has promoted two Negro patrolmen to detective positions and assigned a Negro to a cashier's position in the tax office.

In the area of public schools significant adjustments have been made. For the past five years Greensboro has had only one desegregated school, which had 37 Negro pupils last year. This year about 220 Negro students have been assigned to ten schools previously segregated.

In July the Greensboro Housing Authority announced its official policy to be that "there shall be no discrimination either for or against any applicant for housing on account of race, creed, or color" in its low-rent housing units. One Negro family has moved into a previously all-white housing unit with no incidents.

Both the public golf and tennis courts are now open to Negroes.

Both hotels have desegregated their eating accommodations. One of the motels which desegregated in June reversed its position until such a time as other motels desegregate.

The Chamber of Commerce recently accepted representatives of three Negro firms and the Ministerial Association desegregated, although the only persons attending the Ministerial Association meetings are those who do not object to the desegregation practice.

Greensboro has acquired federal aid for a full-time employee to help analyze what qualifications employers expect of their employees and to design programs to train prospective employees for vacant jobs. A job analysis for this full-time employee is carried elsewhere in this book.

An ordinance was passed to require a permit before picketing.

GREENVILLE

Population: 23,860; 33.4 per cent Negro

Mayor: S. Eugene West—Home: 1101 East Tenth Street; Telephone: Home: 752-5575

Biracial Organizations:
1. Pitt County Interracial Committee
2. Good Neighbor Council
3. North Carolina Joint Council on Health and Citizenship
4. Progressive Citizens' Council

Chairmen:
1. Reverend Richard N. Ottaway—Office: P. O. Box 564; Home: 806 East Fourteenth Street; Telephone: Office: 752-2482; Home: 752-4521
2. Reverend W. J. Hadden—Home: 1042 West Rockspring Road; Telephone: Home: 752-7246
3. Dr. Andrew A. Best—Office: P. O. Box 417, 412 Cadillac Street; Telephone: Office: 752-2129; Home: 752-5587
4. Roscoe C. Norfleet—Home: 1401 Sixth Street; Telephone: Home: 752-2581

Negro Action:

There are two groups of Negroes working to present the Negro viewpoint. The oldest of these is the United Pitt County Citizens' League which is the chartered unit of the National Association for the Advancement of Colored People in the County. This is a loosely knit group of Negroes which primarily sponsors the annual Emancipation Proclamation Day on January 1.

The second group is the Progressive Citizens' Council. This group was organized several years ago to act as a political instrument for the Negro. Its first aim was to elect a Negro to the City Council. Having failed to help elect a Negro to the City Council, the group turned its full attention to civil rights, utilizing its well-established organization with representatives from nearly every Negro group in the community. This Council has made all the petitions to white groups dealing with civil rights.

On a Sunday in October, 1963, a group from Williamston demonstrated in Greenville in protest over the housing of some of their demonstrators in the Pitt County jail. This was without incident.

The only demonstration organized and enacted by local Negroes was "The Christmas Sacrifice" in December, 1963. This was first designed by the Progressive Citizens' Council to be a boycott of the downtown businesses; but after much debate in the Interracial Committee and the Progressive Citizens' Council, the boycott idea was amended to be a blackout of Christmas tree lights because it was strongly felt that a street boycott would prove to be confusing both to whites and Negroes. The blackout was very successful. By actual count, there were only six Negro houses in Greenville which burned Christmas tree lights during the holidays. This experience gave the Negro a sense of unity that he has generally lacked.

Many Negroes feel that the absence of street demonstrations has prevented the Negro from participating in one of the symbols of identity of his time. These persons feel that there is a certain lack of fulfillment in the whole civil rights movement for the Negro in this community.

The Progressive Citizens' Council has petitioned three groups. The first of these was the board of directors of the Greenville Merchants' Association. The board asked that the Interracial Committee have some one present in order to answer questions. The Negro board of directors moved to have a resolution published immediately.

The second petition was addressed to the City Council. The Council met in a special session to hear the group and went over the petition point by point. Immediately following this meeting, the Council published a resolution in the newspaper urging the people of Greenville to treat all persons without respect to color. The Council also established the Good Neighbor Council.

The third petition was addressed to the Greenville City School Board. The Progressive Citizens' Council met with this group to discuss its proposal. All the points outlined in the petition have not been met, but the Negroes feel that someone is working toward these ends.

The Progressive Citizens' Council's petition to the Chamber of Commerce and Merchants' Association of Greenville was dated May 7, 1963, and read as follows: We, the members of the Progressive Citizens' Council of the City of Greenville, hereby petition the Merchants' Association and Chamber of Commerce of Greenville, North Carolina, the following recommendations:

94

(1) To recommend to the merchants of the City of Greenville to abolish all racial discrimination in policies on the basis of race and color in respect to all the facilities that are available to all other citizens.

(2) To encourage the hiring of qualified Negroes as employees in all facets of public businesses in order to properly serve the public.

(3) That promotion be made on the basis of knowledge, education, efficiency, and ability to produce.

(4) That a committee from this Council be given a conference for a detailed discussion of these matters of interest to the progressive society for the benefit of all citizens.

Municipal Reaction:
Pitt County Interracial Committee:
In December, 1960, the Greenville Ministerial Association saw the need for the establishment of an organization to promote communications between the Negro and the white races. A Social Action Committee was appointed to establish such an organization. During early 1961 attempts were made by this Social Action Committee to create a new association from the existing white and Negro ones. However, the Negro leadership felt that the existing dual organization arrangement better served the needs of the community. The Negro association was primarily interested in educating the Negro clergy through weekly discussions.

Late in 1961 the Social Action Committee decided to attempt to establish an autonomous biracial organization. First, the group met with and exchanged ideas with the Lenoir Biracial Committee in Kinston. Next, each member of the Social Action Committee invited a layman to meet with the group to further discuss the creation of a biracial organization. After several meetings, a list of white people was drawn up to comprise a larger discussion group. In February, 1962, a group of 22 white citizens accepted an invitation for more discussions of the idea. After two meetings in February and March, 1962, it seemed obvious that the white community was willing to move prudently in the area of race relations. Someone was appointed to contact the Negroes and ask them to compose a group which would later merge into a biracial organization. This person who volunteered to contact the Negroes failed in this undertaking for almost a year; but in February, 1963, the chairman of the Social Action Committee called a meeting to hear a progress report. The report was that the Negro community was ready to participate in a biracial organization. Within two days, the Pitt County Interracial Committee was organized with ten Negroes and ten white persons. This group has been meeting regularly since.

The Pitt County Interracial Committee is entirely voluntary and is not sponsored nor sanctioned by any agency. *Ad hoc* committees or subcommittees are appointed as situations or projects warrant. Such committees are composed of an equal number of whites and Negroes.

Three subcommittees have had long and active lives. One is a subcommittee which has discussed desegregation with interested businesses. The second subcommittee is one working to establish an annual human relations institute in the community. The third subcommittee, which has only recently been appointed, is one appointed to propose a constitution for the Pitt County Interracial Committee.

The major objective of the Pitt County Interracial Committee is to establish an instrument of communication in the communities between the races through the sponsorship of regular public meetings where whites and Negroes can meet to discuss their mutual problems or their individual feelings and ideas.

Most of the desegregation of public accommodations and businesses has resulted from the personal efforts of the four-man subcommittee appointed to deal with the subject; however, many things have been accomplished informally through the individual members of the Interracial Committee, such as the promotion of the hiring of Negroes for extra Christmas help by one member, who first hired Negroes himself and then encouraged other businessmen to do likewise.

When demonstrations appeared forthcoming in May, 1963, the *ad hoc* subcommittee discussing desegregation with businesses investigated the existing laws of the City pertaining to demonstrations. The subcommittee was happy to find that there were no segregation laws in the city code. The subcommittee contacted city officials and informed them of the presence of an Interracial Committee and offered its services. The Mayor, City Manager, and Chief of Police were most cordial and receptive to this offer and immediately engaged the subcommittee as the effective interracial negotiating arm of the City. Mayor West decided that all businesses which might be a target for demonstrations be given an opportunity to discuss with the Negroes the actual segregation situation. During May, June, and July, this subcommittee met with the lunch counter operators, restaurant owners, theater owners, motel owners, and city officials many times. As a result of these discussions, the lunch counter operators desegregated their businesses early in the summer; the restaurant owners were of a divided opinion as to what adjustments they might make. Two restaurants immediately desegregated; others promised to desegregate when the whole group moved; and some pledged never to desegregate.

The theater owners reported that they would desegregate when the majority of the businesses in the City desegregated.

The motel owners met without reaching a consensus of purpose. Two motel restaurant operators were absolutely opposed to any change of policy in regard to their segregated practices. As of February, 1964, the motels were still undecided as to what to do. At one point three motels were ready to desegregate according to a plan, but one withheld and at a later date that motel voluntarily permitted a desegregated dinner in its restaurant. This situation remains confusing. It is felt by the Committee that a very serious error may have been made by using an all-white subcommittee in working with the motels.

Two restaurants have desegregated, and there have been isolated incidents of Negroes eating in normally segregated facilities. On October 10, 1963, the United States Air Force Band rendered a concert and stayed in motels all over the City with its Negro members.

The same subcommittee met with the board of directors of the Greenville Merchants' Association in July, 1963, to discuss a petition by the Progressive Citizens' Council. As a result of this meeting the board of directors immediately published a resolution stating that they encouraged all merchants to adopt nondiscriminatory employment and service practices.

This subcommittee met with the City Council in regard to the petition by the Progressive Citizens' Council. As a result of this meeting, the City Council immediately issued a resolution through the local newspaper stating that it endorsed nondiscriminatory employment and service policies and empowered the Mayor to establish a Good Neighbor Committee.

In September, 1963, the Greenville Ministerial Association desegregated its membership.

The subcommittee met with the city officials and county officials and accomplished the hiring of Negroes and the desegregation of city facilities such as the city hall and the courtroom of the Pitt County Courthouse.

Prior to the birth of the Interracial Committee, there were desegregated facilities in the County. Most prominent of these were East Carolina College, the Municipal Library, and the County Health Department.

The Pitt County Interracial Committee as a whole is actively engaged in a public relations and educational venture. It is actively seeking opportunities to speak to civic clubs, church groups, and others. The Committee seeks to commit responsible people of the community to responsible action. The co-operation with this program has been most encouraging.

East Carolina College desegregated quietly over the past years and now has some 60 Negroes enrolled, including a number living in the dormitories. The college has served as a great public example of how desegregation can be accomplished and how fruitful and beneficial the results can be.

The North Carolina Joint Council on Health and Citizenship:

The North Carolina Joint Council on Health and Citizenship was organized in August, 1960, as a successor to the Pitt County Group—an informal group of volunteer citizens which had been active in the development of a program against *ignorance* and *poverty* since February, 1957. The Council was founded by Dr. Andrew A. Best of Greenville as a nonpartisan, nonsectarian, nonprofit, volunteer organization. This Council is primarily concerned with the promotion of *total* health and *total* citizenship through education.

The Council's constitution includes the following purposes:

A. To provide a forum where ideas, information, and opinions may be co-ordinated, crystallized, and translated into action.

B. To be a center for organizing, harmonizing, and directing action in the attainment of our common aim—the elimination of ignorance and poverty, along with their by-products of illegitimacy, juvenile delinquency, and general maladjustment.

Now in its fourth year of organized activity, the council has geared its primary program to operate in co-operation with the schools. This program is aimed at increasing the over-all academic attainment of students. It also makes a major contribution through the resulting improvement of the health and hygiene habits of the most underprivileged segment of the population.

A present plan for expanding the council's educational program includes the circulation of four or five council-trained and supervised teachers through a number of schools and communities, teaching health and hygiene, with the provision that participating schools assign one local teacher to the touring teacher to learn from the touring teacher in order to release her the following year to a different circuit of schools and communities, while perpetuating the program in the particular school or community.

Another significant council activity is the sponsorship of a ten-week class designed to increase the competence and achievement levels of students. The weekly class is taught by Dr. Best and his staff. At present, the volunteer enrollment consists of 361 students from 22 high schools in ten counties. Some participants in the class travel more than 100 miles round-trip each week.

Local students from this project dominate the group which qualified to take advantage of new job opportunities which became available as a result of adjustments in the employment policies by local businessmen.

There have been four public mass meetings held in connection with the council's anniversary celebration. Large numbers of white and Negro people gathered to hear such prominent citizens as Dr. Samuel D. Proctor, Governor Terry Sanford, Congressman Herbert C. Bonner, and Secretary of the Department of Health, Education, and Welfare, Anthony J. Celebrezze. More than 5,000 people attended the rally in Ficklen Stadium in Greenville on November 10, 1963, to hear Secretary Celebrezze. These meetings have contributed a new dimension to understanding and cooperation in race relations in eastern North Carolina.

Adjustments:

During the past three years, each of four of the large department stores have hired Negroes in sales positions. The Interracial Committee has sought and is reported to be on the verge of obtaining a package-commitment by hotels, motels, restaurants, and theaters to desegregate simultaneously. Two motels have, in fact, desegregated their facilities and restaurant facilities are desegregated on a special arrangement basis.

The lunch counters and drugstores have been desegregated, and there are two downtown restaurants which serve Negroes. Another restaurant will serve Negro organizations.

The City has no public swimming pools. The old swimming pool became unserviceable and was filled in. The municipal library is desegregated and is frequently used by Negroes.

The County Hospital is segregated.

There is no token desegregation in the schools, although East Carolina College has some 60 Negroes enrolled. These students take an active part in college extracurricular activities.

The Good Neighbor Council was recently appointed by the Mayor. It is attempting to create employment opportunities for all qualified Negroes.

HENDERSON

Population: 12,740; 41.7 per cent Negro

Mayor: Horace E. Falkner, Save-Way Food Market, 603 Andrews Avenue; Home: 804 East Montgomery Street; Telephone: Office: 438-7114; Home: 438-5095

Biracial Organization: Biracial Committee

Chairman: Nathan P. Strause, Jr.—Office: Vance Trucking Company; Home: Country Club Drive; Telephone: Office: 438-6151; Home: 438-3294

Negro Action:

There have been no demonstrations by Negroes nor have any petitions been presented to the City Council or Mayor.

Municipal Reaction:

The Biracial Committee is composed of five whites and four Negroes. Since the Committee has been appointed, it has been working to obtain job opportunities for Negroes as sales personnel in stores.

Adjustments:

The variety stores which are primarily chain stores, desegregated their lunch counters before the Committee was appointed.

At the present time there are approximately ten Negroes hired as salesmen by several dry goods and other downtown stores.

All Negroes who applied for admission into white schools were accepted. These youngsters are in different grades and apparently are doing satisfactory work.

The motels and restaurants at the present time are hesitant to serve Negroes because they fear loss of revenue.

All city parks were contributed to the City by donors who placed reversionary clauses in their gift indentures should the parks be used by Negroes. Recognizing this, the Negroes have made no request that these public facilities be made available.

The local theater has not been requested to admit Negroes.

HENDERSONVILLE

Population: 5,911; 20.5 per cent Negro

Mayor: A. V. Edwards—Office: City Hall; Home: 417 Ninth Avenue; Telephone: Office: 693-4161; Home: 693-3328

Biracial Organization: Human Relations Committee

Chairman: Reverend A. J. Cox—Office: First Methodist Church; Home: 804 Fifth Avenue; Telephone: Office: 693-7011; Home: 693-7037

Negro Action:
No public demonstrations have occurred in Hendersonville; however, there have been numerous Negro rallies.

Municipal Reaction:
The Human Relations Committee was formed and has been at work.

Adjustments:
One Committee member, who happened to be a druggist, volunteered to meet with the organized association of druggists in Hendersonville and, after discussing adjustments with him, the Druggists' Association agreed that they would desegregate their lunch counters.

Although several meetings with hotel, motel, and restaurant owners have been held, there have been no adjustments made in their service practices.

General Electric Corporation and some of the dry goods stores have hired Negro salesclerks. A department store and others have committed themselves to hire Negro sales personnel.

103

JESSE L. JACKSON LEADS A STREET MARCH PETITIONING FOR ENTRANCE INTO SEGREGATED THEATER.

There are no Negroes in the white schools.

The Negroes have requested admission to the theater, but thus far the theater owner has said that he would only be willing to admit Negroes when the rest of the community's businesses are ready to adopt equally liberal practices.

The municipal library is open to Negroes, although it is not frequented by them.

Most of the recreational facilities are owned and are attended primarily by northern tourists.

HICKORY

Population: 19,328; 14.2 per cent Negro

Mayor: Julian G. Whitener—Office: Rhodes-Whitener Mills, 216½ Union Square; Home: 842 North Center Street; Telephone: Office: 327-4105; Home: 324-7278

Biracial Organization: Hickory Community Relations Council

Chairman: Reverend Cecil W. Noble—Office: Advent Christian Church, 1941 North Center Street; Home: 1925 North Center Street; Telephone: Home: 323-5718

Negro Action:

There have been no massive demonstrations in this community. In August, 1962, a small group of 45 high school and college-age Negroes picketed in front of a downtown grocery store with signs protesting the store's hiring practices. This lasted for approximately two hours.

Also in August, 1962, a local Negro dentist applied for membership in the Hickory Chamber of Commerce and was accepted. Shortly afterwards, another application was received from a Negro civic organization and this, too, was accepted. These were the first applications from Negroes ever received by the local Chamber. No applications have been received since, but these two members are in good standing. They, and their guests, have attended the Chamber's annual meetings in 1962 and 1963. No special provisions were made for seating and no problems developed.

Municipal Reaction:

Taking note of the demonstrations across the State in the spring of 1963, the Chamber of Commerce officials called in their

Negro members to discuss the situation as it related to Hickory. At this meeting, it was decided to form some type of organization to maintain communications between the white and Negro communities. A steering committee was formed, representative of the city government, the Chamber of Commerce and the Hickory Merchants' Association, and from this group developed the Hickory Community Relations Council. The Council was given official sanction by the City of Hickory by appointment at a regular meeting of the Hickory Board of Aldermen. The Council is composed of eight members, four white and four Negro, with one ex officio member, an appointee of the desegregated Hickory Ministerial Association, who serves as Chairman of the Hickory Community Relations Council. The chairman refrains from voting, but may exercise a vote in case of a tie. The terms of office of Council members are at the pleasure of the Hickory Board of Aldermen. The Council meets twice each month. The Hickory Community Relations Council adopted a statement of purpose and procedures, June 25, 1963.

After adopting a simple statement of purpose and procedures, the Hickory Community Relations Council set regular meeting dates twice each month, and adheres strictly to its schedule.

Press media do not cover meetings of the Council unless invited to do so. All releases to news media are made over the name of the chairman with the approval of the council members. The Council divides itself into subcommittees when occasions warrant special attention or study. These subcommittees are authorized to enlarge themselves with persons outside the council membership. Generally, however, the subcommittees consist of two members, one white and one Negro. The present active subcommittees are the subcommittees on merchants, downtown theaters, innkeepers, bowling alleys, recreation and government.

The City passed and published a resolution stating that all city owned and operated facilities would be immediately desegregated and that there would be no discriminatory employment practices in hiring and promoting of city employees.

The Chamber adopted a resolution endorsing the statement of purpose and procedures of the Council and offering meeting facilities for the Council.

Adjustments:
The Council has been working at some length on placing Negroes in industry. Several industries have already employed qualified Negroes. With the exception of hosiery mills, where employment is predominantly female, local industry has been employing Negroes in production jobs for several years.

All major retail outlets, both local and chain, have adopted nondiscriminatory employment practices and some Negroes may be observed in sales and service positions.

All "White" and "Colored" signs have been removed from city owned and/or operated facilities.

All tax listing facilities have been desegregated, as well as voter registration.

The annual "First Baby" promotion by the local newspaper and radio stations no longer specifies "White Baby."

All lunch counters in downtown department and variety stores have been desegregated.

Major restaurants have all been desegregated. No adjustments have been made, nor have any been requested, by taverns or beer parlors.

The major downtown hotel has been desegregated as to its eating and lodging facilities. A Negro church convention of 150 was recently accommodated at this hotel.

The four motels on the outskirts of town have indicated a willingness to desegregate, but have made no announcement at the time of this report. The downtown motel has desegregated.

Discussions are still going on with the management of downtown theaters and the bowling alley. Drive-in theaters are desegregated.

Activities of the City of Hickory recreation system are desegregated. Swimming pools and the Hickory Community Center are operated by the Hickory Community Foundation, a private contribution organization, and have not been desegregated; although discussions are being held with its board of trustees and officers. The City maintains a Community Center, library, and swimming pool in the Negro community.

The local library is a quasi-governmental operation. The land and building, books, and equipment are provided by a private estate as a gift to the community. Salaries and maintenance are provided by a special city tax supplement. No policy of discrimination has been announced and the Council, so far, has received no complaints from Negroes concerning discriminatory admittance practices. Negroes are admitted to Lenoir Rhyne College and the Catawba County Industrial Education Center.

No Negro students have been enrolled in the schools in the white areas, nor are there any white students attending the schools in the Negro areas. No rejected applications for transfer by Negro students have been brought to the attention of the Council.

There are three private hospitals and a county hospital which is under construction. When the bond election for the new county hospital was before the public, the question of whether the hospital would be desegregated was raised and the Mayor assured the community that the hospital would be desegregated in all respects.

HIGH POINT

Population: 66,543; 17.2 per cent Negro

Mayor: Floyd D. Mehan—Office: 501 Mangum Avenue; Home: 1227 Westwood Avenue; Telephone: Office: 882-8724, 882-9217; Home: 888-5883

Biracial Organization: Human Relations Commission

Chairman: Mayor Floyd D. Mehan

Negro Action:
Both CORE and the NAACP have active chapters in High Point. Demonstrations were organized May 23, 1963, to protest discrimination in accommodations. For five nights, Negroes marched through downtown High Point. Each night they attracted a larger crowd of whites, most of them young boys. On the fifth night of demonstrations trouble flared briefly. A smoke bomb and rocks were hurled at Negroes as they demonstrated before two theaters. On the sixth day, as a crowd of 3,000 whites waited downtown for the marchers and 50 highway patrol officers were moved into the City to aid local police, CORE leaders called a two-week truce in the demonstrations.

Demonstrations were resumed at intervals throughout the summer because the Negroes desired faster progress, until a cessation agreement was reached September 13, 1963.

Demonstrations included street marches, picketing, and blockading of theaters, restaurants, and stores. The Negroes issued the following petition:

In order to make clear the objectives sought by the local CORE and NAACP Chapters in continuing the demonstrations in High Point, we have outlined the following goals:

1. To help High Point become an "Open City" for all people regardless of race, creed, color, or religion.

2. More specifically, the desegregation of the theaters.

3. Desegregation of the bowling alleys.

4. Immediate acceleration of the program to employ and promote Negroes by our city government.

5. Immediate employment of Negro sales personnel by all major downtown and College Village Shopping Center stores.

6. Complete desegregation of all restaurants, motels, and hotels.

7. Establishment of a permanent Human Relations Commission.

Until these grievances are satisfactorily met, CORE and the NAACP will continue their efforts to achieve these goals through peaceful protest.

Municipal Reaction:

A temporary biracial committee of 12 members, eight white and four Negro, was named by the Mayor, with Capus M. Waynick as chairman of the Committee, on May 27, 1963. The Committee adopted a policy which has been continued by the permanent Human Relations Commission of holding meetings open to the public, press, and television.

The Biracial Committee approached hotel, motel, and restaurant owners to discuss their desegregating. All but one hotel and one motel desegregated, as did several of the better restaurant and drugstore counters.

Subcommittees talked with the theaters and bowling alley operators. The hospital and High Point College modified their policies and some other progress towards desegregation ensued.

A meeting of about 50 industrial leaders was held at the invitation of the Biracial Committee. On their own initiative, these

A PRAY-IN BEFORE THE CITY-COUNTY BUILDING IN HIGH POINT.

industrial leaders supported the purposes and program of the Biracial Committee. This program also had the full support of the Mayor and City Council.

Discontent with continued demonstrations was sufficient to convince the Mayor and City Council that an ordinance to require a permit to demonstrate was needed and one was prepared for passage on September 13, 1963.

In a final conference with Negro leaders before the Council met, the Negroes agreed to suspend demonstrations on these conditions:

> In order to further promote better relations among the citizens of High Point by recognizing and resolving critical problems:

> The Mayor will at once appoint a permanent Human Relations Commission that will continue the work that has in the past been assigned to the temporary Biracial Committee. This Commission will be charged with all phases of human relations problems. From time to time it will work upon juvenile delinquency, crime rate, employment, school drop-outs, public accommodations, etc.

> During the period of suspension of all demonstrations, it was agreed that reports would be made to the City Council and interested citizen groups.

At its meeting on Friday, September 20, the City Council passed an ordinance establishing the Human Relations Commission. Eleven members were selected, six white and five Negro, and the first meeting of the new Commission was held on October 3, 1963. Arnold J. Koonce was made Chairman, but resigned November 11, 1963.

The following committees were established within the Human Relations Commission: Job Opportunity and Training; Hotels and Motels; Restaurants and Public Eating Places; Community Needs; Public Institutions, Recreation, Theaters and Amusement; Community Progress and Information; Agenda Committee; and the Good Will Committee (Women, Men, and Youth). In the following days committees were staffed, areas of discontent determined, and discussions begun to resolve the determined problems. Not all committee members were members of the Human Relations Commission. The Human Relations Commission meets biweekly on a regular basis. An agenda and minutes of each meeting are mailed to all members.

An early action of the Human Relations Commission was the sponsoring of a biracial luncheon on September 30, 1963, at the YWCA. One hundred and sixty people representing 80 civic and church clubs were present for this occasion.

Another early action was the sponsoring of a biracial "Dutch" dinner meeting on Friday evening, October 11, 1963, in the Sky Room of the Furniture Exposition Building. This meeting was held for all members of the Commission, their subcommittees, the Mayor, City Council, and other interested persons. There were 120 interested citizens present for the occasion. The principal speaker was W. O. Conrad, Chairman of the Greensboro Human Relations Commission. He devoted most of his speech to discussion of how to increase work opportunities for Negroes.

On October 25, 1963, some 600 local white citizens sponsored an advertisement in the local daily newspaper urging the proprietors of public accommodations to proceed to remove from their operations all segregation and discrimination. These citizens pledged their continued patronage of those businesses which abolished the practice of segregation.

In the area of government considerable progress had been made prior to the Commission's activity. The City Council had expressed its determination that race should not be a factor in the employment policies or any other activity of city government. Negroes had already served as members of the Board of Education, Public Housing Authority, and Civil Service Commission. Approximately 10 per cent of the police force were Negro with High Point being the first city in the South to employ Negroes as full-time police officers. The public libraries had been open to all for some time.

Several areas of discontent with government were brought before the Commission. There was a feeling, for instance, that poor housing conditions in parts of the Negro community were the result of either discriminatory application of zoning regulations and/or lax enforcement of building codes by the building inspector's office. Investigation disclosed that zoning regulations were not being violated and that under the existing regulations such conditions could and did exist in both white and Negro neighborhoods.

A critical problem in the Negro community is lack of adequate housing. Members of the Commission have met with the president of the High Point Board of Realtors to find a solution to this problem. He and other realtors have since expressed a desire to build homes on a tract in the Urban Redevelopment area which would sell in the $6,000 to $10,000 price range. A survey of local financial institutions shows that home mortgage financing is available to any qualified applicant regardless of race.

Job opportunities is a major area of the Commission's concern. In response to specific complaints the Commission worked with officials of the Employment Security Commission to clarify its procedures. Members of the Commission have held and will continue to hold open forums with experts in the field of job training to accumulate helpful information for dealing with this important aspect of increasing job opportunities.

The committees of the Human Relations Commission have been reorganized into the following structure: Agenda Committee, Committee on Information and Grievances, Committee on Accommodations with subcommittees on Housing, Public Facilities, Recreation, and on Hotels, Motels, and Restaurants, and a Committee on Employment with subcommittees on Job Opportunity, Job Education, and Employer-employee Relations.

Adjustments:

Public recreational facilities and programs are generally open to all citizens without regard to color. Most recreational facilities supported by the United. Appeal are open to all citizens. All facilities of the Recreation Department of the City are desegregated. The municipal golf course and tennis courts are used regularly on a desegregated basis, and Negro citizens have participated in the city sponsored golf and tennis tournaments. Both municipal swimming pools are open to all citizens, and fishing at the municipal lake from banks and boats is desegregated. The annual Soap Box Derby, doll show, rifle marksmanship contest, and electric train race are open to contestants from all races. The municipal stadium has no segregated seating at its games and other functions. A Negro has served on the Parks and Recreation Commission.

Membership and full participation are open to all citizens in the High Point Symphony Orchestra, the local chapter of the North Carolina Symphony Society, the local Arts Council (Children's Concert and Cultural Program), the Community Concert Association, and the community theater.

Most privately owned recreational facilities continue to operate on a segregated basis.

Owners and managers of bowling lanes and theaters have been willing to discuss their policies with the Commission.

The High Point Memorial Hospital has had a desegregated staff for many years. The lunch counter was desegregated during 1963 and "White" and "Colored" signs were removed. During 1963 some change in the employment situation of Negroes took place both in government and private industry.

In the area of job opportunities, several industries and other businesses have indicated their willingness to employ qualified Negroes in jobs not formerly open to them. Most major downtown stores have hired Negroes as salesclerks. Ten Negroes are employed by the City in non-menial positions.

The Industrial Education Center is now open to all, although the relative number of Negroes at the school is still small. A determined program in job training will get underway in 1964. This program will include forums, workshops, and various training sessions. The YMCA has already initiated a high school night training session which is proving to be highly effective.

The hotels and motels present one of the better examples of good race relations by a single trade group. There are nine hotels and motels in the metropolitan area. Six are desegregated and have been for some time. Two of the segregated hotels classify themselves as primarily residential hotels. Efforts are continuing to desegregate the remaining three hostelries.

A majority of the public eating facilities in the City are serving all customers regardless of race. This includes most of the larger restaurants of the City. Most drive-in restaurants are now desegregated. Some of the drive-in restaurants which have indoor seating have not desegregated this aspect of their business.

Lunch counters in drug, department, and variety stores are desegregated.

The daily newspaper has discontinued the labeling of offenders of the law as Negro and white.

The Ministerial Alliance has been desegregated for many years.

JACKSONVILLE

Population: 13,491; 6.4 per cent Negro

Mayor: A. D. Guy—Office: A. D. Guy Insurance and Realty Company, 511 New Bridge Street; Home: 1001 Henderson Drive; Telephone: Office: 346-4171; Home: 346-3851

Biracial Organization: Mayor's Biracial Committee

Chairman: Mayor A. D. Guy

Negro Action:

There have been no demonstrations in Jacksonville. On June 2, 1963, three Negro men sought admission at a theater in a Jacksonville shopping center. On June 5 approximately 28 Negroes sought admission at the same theater. These attempts hastened the appointment of additional members to the Mayor's Biracial Committee, even though the Mayor had not completed the gathering of background information from all local business-men.

Municipal Reaction:

Several courses in health and hygiene have been taught by Civil Defense Instructors at the request of the Negro community. These were well attended both in Georgetown and in Jacksonville. Additional classes have been requested and are being planned to further assist the Negro populace in their effort to become aware of their community responsibilities.

During 1961 a representative of the Onslow County Ministerial Association suggested to the City Manager that a Biracial Committee be appointed by the Mayor. Due to the excellent relations existing between the Negro and white citizens at that time, no further discussion or plans were made concerning this subject by the Mayor and City Council.

On May 10, 1963, Major General J. P. Berkeley, Commanding General, Marine Corps Base, Camp Lejeune, and Colonel Ernest Fusan, Commanding Officer, Marine Corps Air Facility, visited the Mayor at his office to discuss the contents of a Department of the Navy Directive, SECNAV INSTRUCTION 53:50.2A. Following this conference plans were formulated to proceed in an orderly manner toward obtaining the desegregation of all public and private facilities within the City of Jacksonville. It was the Mayor's plan that prior to appointing a committee, that he and the city manager would personally contact the proprietors of all restaurants, motels, taverns, retail business establishments, and theaters within the city in an effort to obtain a consensus of these individuals toward desegregating their facilities.

These personal contacts determined that there was no adamant feeling against the desegregation of any of the services within the City, with the exception of the theaters. It was further determined that full desegregation was in progress at the lunch counters in a variety store, in two drugstores, and at chain restaurants and motels.

Adjustments:

Following the theater desegregation attempts, the Biracial Committee held a conference with Negro leaders and advised them that a committee from the Biracial Committee had gained an appointment, June 8, with the president of the theater chain in an effort to formulate a plan which would lead to complete desegregation of the local theaters. Following the meeting with the theater company president, a plan for desegregation of the local theaters was put into effect on June 24, 1963. In accordance with the plan, full desegregation of the theaters was realized during the week of July 22, 1963.

On June 13, 1963, the Mayor held a conference at City Hall with the proprietors of all restaurants, cafeterias, and taverns located within the City for the purpose of formulating plans for the desegregation of these facilities. The plan which was formulated permitted the desegregation of all restaurants, cafeterias, and taverns.

There has been total desegregation of hotels and motels.

The recreation facilities of the City have been desegregated without incident. The City employs a Negro recreation center supervisor. All private bowling alleys and amusements have desegregated.

The Onslow County Ministerial Association has advised the Biracial Committee that its members, by resolution, welcome all persons to join with them in worship services at their respective churches. This invitation is issued without reservation as to race.

A committee of the local NAACP visited the managers of retail establishments in quest of additional job opportunities for Negro citizens. The managers of three large department stores and one variety store assured the committee that all employees selected by their respective stores would be given equal opportunity regardless of race. Several department stores have hired

Negro salesclerks. Grocery stores have hired Negro check-out clerks.

The superintendent of county schools has reported that the white schools in the County and within the City have been desegregated at the elementary, junior high, and senior high levels.

The municipal library is desegregated.

KINSTON

Population: 24,819; 39.7 per cent Negro

Mayor: Simon C. Sitterson—Office: 220 East Gordon Street; Home: 905 West Road; Telephone: Office: 523-2106; Home: 523-5346

Biracial Organizations:
1. Mayor's Biracial Committee
2. Good Neighbor Council
3. Lenoir County Interracial Committee

Chairmen:
1. Dan E. Perry and E. K. Best, Jr.; Dan E. Perry— Office: 106 West Gordon Street; Home: 908 West Road; Telephone: Office: 523-5107; Home: 523-3987; E. K. Best, Jr.—Office: 300 South McLewean Street; Home: 1503 Tower Hill Road; Telephone: Office: 523-4768; Home: 523-5357
2. Henry C. Suddreth—Home: 1503 McAdoo Street; Telephone: Home: 523-4407
3. Reverend Douglas A. Bell—Home: 1407 West Road; Telephone: Home: 523-9708

Negro Action:
An adult and a youth chapter of the NAACP and a chapter of CORE are active in Kinston. The adult chapter of the NAACP is headed by a Negro motel owner. The NAACP youth group is actively engaged in encouraging qualified persons to register to vote. It is conducting a qualification of voters program to teach persons the required amounts of knowledge in reading and writing.

Highly organized demonstrations were sponsored by Kinston's Committee on Racial Equality under the leadership of University of North Carolina student, Kellis Parker, beginning June 13,

1963, against a segregated theater. These ranged over a period of a week. One hundred and four demonstrators were arrested the first night of demonstrations and 274 were arrested the second.

Monday night, June 17, 1963, two Negro men and two Negro women attended a meeting of the City Council and presented to the Council a list of 15 objectives on behalf of the Kinston CORE. The Kinston CORE was organized "in an effort to seek ways of removing barriers that prevent freedom of choice and equal opportunity in the Kinston community." These 15 objectives were summed up by the last, as follows: "Our overall objective is the general and complete desegregation of all aspects of Kinstonian life; the replacement of injustices with justice."

These 15 objectives were considered an ultimatum by the white community and immediately strong resentment and indignation developed among the white community against a "drastic and sudden" reversal of the social structure.

Demonstrations were resumed by the youth on July 16 and 17, 1963, and resulted in 347 arrests on charges of obstructing traffic, trespassing, and parading without a permit. The Negro adults indicated their support of a boycott against businesses with segregated employment practices by a street demonstration.

Municipal Reaction:

Simon Sitterson served as Mayor from July 1 to August 27, 1963, when he was elected to a full term. Former Mayor Guy Elliott named the Good Neighbor Council, May 14, 1963, before any local demonstrations had taken place. E. S. Brinton was named the chairman by Mayor Elliott, but he was succeeded in June by Henry Suddreth. The Council made up of five whites and four Negroes, strives to hold monthly meetings. Its project is to review with industrialists job opportunities for minority groups.

Tuesday, June 18, 1963, Mayor Sitterson appointed a special committee, known as the Mayor's Biracial Committee, to give consideration to the list of demands by the Negroes and to work toward some solution of the racial problem. Eleven Negroes and 11 whites were appointed to the Committee.

The Committee held its first meeting Wednesday, June 19, 1963, in the Mayor's office. Attorney Dan Perry and E. K. Best, Jr., were appointed Co-chairmen.

It was decided to direct the attention of the Committee to three

TYPICAL SCENE OF DEMONSTRATORS SINGING FREEDOM SONGS IN PROTEST OF SEGREGATED PUBLIC ACCOMMODATIONS.

areas: one, job opportunities; two, restaurants; and, three, the public library. These areas were three of the ones listed in the demands presented by the Negroes. Each member of the Committee was appointed to serve on one of these three subcommittees. A statement of purpose was unanimously adopted June 29, 1963. The statement adopted reads as follows:

We, the members of the Mayor's Biracial Committee wish to make this statement for the public record:

Responsible citizens and all people of good will must face the fact that peace in human relations is essential. We believe that the time is already past due for all of our citizens to be given fair and equitable treatment in all areas and levels of community life in Kinston and Lenoir County.

We feel it is morally wrong and not in keeping with a free, democratic society to continue a way of life which denies to a large segment of our population equal access to all public facilities and accommodations, equal employment opportunities, and equitable and fair treatment in general. We are convinced that we should, without further delay, seek the removal of all policies in both government and business which deny rights and services because of race.

We urge the city and county governments to encourage a policy of nondiscrimination in all phases of our public facilities, to adopt a policy of nondiscrimination in employment at the city and county level, to seek the equal treatment of all persons without regard to race, color or religion, and to urge private businesses to do likewise. We ask this, fully understanding the right of every individual to have the privilege of selecting with whom he will do business.

We earnestly call upon all citizens of Lenoir County to actively support these recommendations, and to do those things which will further improve human relations in our community.

This statement was published in the local newspaper and was endorsed by both the City Council and the Board of County Commissioners.

The Committee is now working to desegregate hotels, restaurants, parks, and playgrounds and to obtain more job opportunities for Negroes.

A special school board committee is working on school desegregation.

The City Council passed five new ordinances designed to protect Kinston and its citizens from violence. The new ordinances regulate parades and picketing by requiring permits. No one under eighteen years of age is permitted to parade or demonstrate before any local business establishments. Those who qualify for permits after a 24-hour application, are to conduct themselves in an orderly manner. No more than 12 persons are allowed in front of any establishment at a given time. Other regulations prohibit excessive noises and prohibit the blocking of sidewalks and entrances by demonstrators.

A voluntary Lenoir County Interracial Committee has functioned for 12 years. It is headed by the Reverend Douglas A. Bell and it sponsored a desegregated institute on human relations, February 9-16, 1964.

Adjustments:

Kinston now has employed five Negro policemen and two Negro firemen.

In June, 1963, two or three stores employed Negroes as sales-clerks.

Lunch counters at local drugstores and variety stores, with one or two exceptions, have been desegregated for more than two years.

The Council obtained an agreement with restaurant owners to desegregate their establishments, but this package agreement fell through at the eleventh hour because of the publicity given a demonstration held the very day on which the agreement was to have gone into effect. Several restaurants are serving Negroes, but most of the owners continue their segregated practice.

The Kinston Hotel will accommodate Negroes who seek lodging and meals on an individual basis. No motels are desegregated.

No theaters or private amusement centers are opened to Negroes.

The city parks and playgrounds are segregated.

On July 22, 1963, the Board of Trustees of the Kinston-Lenoir County Public Library announced, through a resolution, that "The main library shall be open to all residents of Lenoir County, regardless of race, creed, or color." The main library facilities have been used only to a very minor degree by Negroes since the change of policy was announced.

No applications for transfer by Negroes to predominantly white schools have been made.

The Industrial Education Center is open to the public without discrimination.

The Medical Association is open to Negro membership.

The Ministerial Fellowship has been desegregated for two years and its members are served at the Kinston Hotel each month. There was a desegregated Easter worship service at the Grainger Stadium on March 29, for the second consecutive year.

Grainger Stadium has had desegregated seating for the past two seasons. The baseball team is also desegregated.

The local newspaper does not refer to race except when pertinent to the news item. It has expanded its coverage of community activities to the Negroes in recent months.

Several new ordinances have been passed to deal with picketing and demonstrations. These are included in this book.

LAURINBURG

Population: 8,242; 39.6 per cent Negro

Mayor: W. D. Lytch—Office: 303 West Church Street; Home: 201 West Vance Street; Telephone: Home: 276-2873

Biracial Organizations:
1. Community Betterment Committee
2. Mayor's Biracial Committee
3. Scotland County Good Neighbor Council

Chairmen:
1. Sandy Shaw—Home: Wagram, N. C.; Telephone: Home: 369-2546
2. R. F. McCoy—Office: 139 South Main Street; Home: 708 Prince Street; Telephone: Office: 276-2812; Home: 276-2875
3. Andrew G. Williamson—Office: 100 Cronly Street; Home: Morrison Lane; Telephone: Office: 276-2631; Home: 276-1595

Negro Action:

The NAACP has an active chapter in Scotland County.

Negro business and civic leaders approached the Chamber of Commerce of Laurinburg and requested that the Chamber sponsor the establishment of the Community Betterment Committee on June 25, 1959. There have been no petitions to the City or other persons for reform nor have there been demonstrations in Laurinburg.

Municipal Reaction:

The Laurinburg Chamber of Commerce established and continues to sponsor the Laurinburg Community Betterment Committee. This action was taken as a result of the request by Negro business and civic leaders in October, 1958. The first meeting was actually held on June 25, 1959. The Committee serves as an agency for the free exchange of information and ideas among the citizens of Scotland County. The Committee consists of ten Negro citizens and ten white citizens of Scotland County who serve for a period of two years, one-half of the members being appointed in alternate years. The members are nominated by the white and Negro County Ministerial Association to the Chamber of Commerce which approves the nominations and makes the appointments.

In July, 1963, Mayor Lytch appointed a biracial committee, known as the Mayor's Biracial Committee, composed of seven white members and six Negro members. It was decided by the group to study the following areas of possible conflict: (1) employment opportunity, (2) voting, (3) segregation, (4) administration of justice, (5) government, (6) education and the uneducated, (7) housing, and (8) medical care. Out of these studies has come the local Scotland County Good Neighbor Council which is organized in connection with the State Council. This group is actively engaged now in improving job opportunities for all races. These three organizations are making progress in promoting understanding between the two races.

Adjustments:

Two Negroes are now employed as officers by the Police Department.

Two of the larger retail establishments in the City have begun a policy of accepting job applications without any restrictions as to race. These establishments have begun to employ Negro personnel in sales and clerical capacities.

There are no public accommodations which are desegregated.

Scotland Memorial Hospital is segregated to the extent that there is one floor to which Negro patients are assigned and all the staff doctors are white. Both white and Negro nurses are employed.

Both the public and private recreational facilities are segregated.

The schools remain segregated; the municipal library has desegregated.

The Ministerial Associations, the Merchants' Association, and the Chamber of Commerce are segregated.

LENOIR

Population: 10,257; 19.3 per cent Negro

Mayor: J. Harper Beall, Jr.—Office: P. O. Box 486; Beall Oil Company, 201 North By-Pass; Home: 114 Mimosa Lane; Telephone: Office: 754-6551; Home: 754-6155

Biracial Organization: Biracial Committee

Chairman: John C. Bernhardt—Office: Bernhardt Furniture Company, 135 Bernhardt Street; Home: 325 Woodside Place; Telephone: Office: 754-5381; Home: 754-3226

Negro Action: There have been no demonstrations by Negroes nor have any petitions been presented to the City Council or Mayor.

Municipal Reaction:

The Mayor has appointed a six-member Biracial Committee with three white and three Negro members. There are no subcommittees. This Committee is backed up by a 21-member personal advisory committee, composed of leading citizens of the community, which serves as a liaison with the public.

Adjustments:

One member of the Biracial Committee has hired a Negro secretary in his plant which employs between 50 and 75 persons in its business office. Word of this spread through the community, although there has been no publicity in the newspaper. Another Negro has been employed by a downtown department store as a shoe salesman.

There are two Negro policemen on the 24-member force. The City Council has now provided a patrol car and radio for these two policemen. The Committee is seeking more job opportunities for Negroes.

One hotel and all of the motels are desegregated.

A large variety store has desegregated its lunch counter and between 25 to 30 of the restaurants, cafeterias, and drive-ins are open to Negroes, which is 60 to 70 per cent of these businesses.

The two downtown theaters are open to Negroes in a segregated manner.

The mayor recently appointed a Negro to the Lenoir Recreation Commission which operates two centers.

There are several private amusement centers, such as bowling alleys; but there has been no request by Negroes for admission.

The municipal library is desegregated and there is one Negro attending the white high school, who is a member of its National Honor Society.

There are two private hospitals and a county hospital. The county hospital has desegregated its Negro floor and its services.

The City is building two new units in its recreation system.

The new swimming pool in the Negro residential section is desegregated. The swimming pool in the white residential section has not been opened yet, but the City Council has ordered that Negroes who present themselves are to be admitted.

There have been two mass religious meetings of white and Negro people, one in a white church and the other in a Negro church. In both, community singing was featured. So far as can be determined, all churches agree to admit Negroes to worship services and the Episcopal and Catholic churches have Negro members.

LEXINGTON

Population: 16,093; 16.9 per cent Negro

Mayor: C. V. Sink—Office: 30 East First Avenue; Home: 2 Vance Street; Telephone: Office: 246-2581; Home: 246-2738

Biracial Organization: Human Relations Committee

Chairman: Reverend Marlin T. Schaeffer—Home: 141 West First Avenue; Telephone: Church: 246-1617; Home: 246-4136

Negro Action:
During early June of 1963, there were three evenings of demonstrations in the form of street marches and sit-ins at several downtown businesses, including a cafe and a bowling alley. On the second night, Thursday, June 5, a mob of white youths gathered near the Negro section of town about 7:00 P.M. Two hours later the crowd had grown to more than 2,000. Both sides threw rocks, sticks, and bottles at each other. Windows in a Negro church nearby were broken. On June 6 another riot resulted in the shooting of two white men, a 25-year old photographer who was seriously wounded and a 24-year old man who was killed.

Following the riot, demonstrations ceased until early November, 1963, when there was a demonstration in association with the case resulting from the shooting on June 6. There have been no demonstrations since November.

A petition for school reassignment was presented by a number of Negro parents to the school board. This was presented too late for action in the 1963-1964 school year.

Municipal Reaction:

There was a Human Relations Committee in Lexington in 1951 and 1952 which was dissolved as a result of inaction.

The Human Relations Committee, which had been reorganized by the Mayor with ten members, five whites and five Negroes, before the June demonstrations, met for its first meeting approximately a week following the June 6 riot. Since its appointment, the Committee has grown to its present membership of 16, including seven Negroes and nine whites. It is anticipated that the Committee will further be expanded by an additional five members in the near future. At the present time the Human Relations Committee operates with four subcommittes. These subcommittees are the Subcommittee on Education, Restaurants and Theaters, Business and Industry, and Program and Publicity.

The Human Relations Committee proposed to the school board that it adopt the "Burlington Plan" which calls for the desegregation of the first three grades in the school system with the subsequent desegregation of two additional classes each subsequent year. The plan also calls for the parents of every child being given two alternate schools from which to choose the school in which to enroll their child, one a predominantly white and one a predominantly Negro school. This recommendation to the school board was not acted upon.

The Committee has worked extensively in the area of job opportunity and job training.

The present work of the Committee is focused upon the desegregation of two restaurants on U.S. Highway 85. This has not resulted in adjustments.

A recent radio editorial by WBEY suggested that the members of the Human Relations Committee join the NAACP, CORE, or some other organization and then all embark for Africa. This editorial was critical of the Committee chairman's northern background.

Adjustments:

There has been no breakthrough in the area of public accommodations, although the Human Relations Committee is presently seeking the desegregation of restaurants.

Most municipally sponsored activities are desegregated. The public library, golf course, and swimming pools have been de-

NEGROES PROMOTE ECONOMIC BOYCOTT DUE TO DISCRIMINATORY EMPLOY-MENT.

segregated. The swimming pools were closed last summer as a result of public dissatisfaction with this change of policy. It is anticipated that these swimming pools will be opened during the summer of 1964. The public parks are, for the most part, segregated.

The municipal hospital segregates Negro and white patients according to floors within the hospital. The hospital staff, on the other hand, is desegregated.

There are no Negroes presently enrolled in the white schools of Lexington; although there is a case pending in the Federal Court seeking the reassignment of seven Negroes to Lexington's white schools. The school board anticipates many applications for reassignment for the 1964-1965 school year and expects to desegregate most of the City's schools.

The Ministerial Association has been desegregated for a number of years. The YMCA, the Merchants' Association, the Chamber of Commerce, and the civic clubs of Lexington remain segregated.

Twenty-two per cent of the city employees are Negro. Recently three of these were upgraded by the City of Lexington from menial to non-menial jobs.

There are a number of Negroes taking courses at the Industrial Educational Center. A department store has upgraded two Negro women employees to sales positions and a variety and an apparel store have each upgraded one Negro woman employee to sales positions.

LUMBERTON

Population: 15,305; 26.4 per cent Negro; 2.8 per cent Indian

Mayor: R. A. Hedgpeth—Office: Fayetteville Road; Home: 205 East Nineteenth Street; Telephone: Office: 739-4285; Home: 739-6614

Triracial Organization: Good Neighbor Committee

Chairman: Horace Stacy, Jr.—Office: McLean and Stacy, Drawer 1087; Home: 604 West 31st Street; Telephone: Office: 739-7516; Home: 739-4086

Negro and Indian Action:

The NAACP is organized in the City under local leadership. There have been no racial demonstrations in Lumberton.

On March 16, 1964, the Robeson County Indians submitted a petition to the Robeson County Board of Commissioners requesting the provision of more job opportunities for Indians within the County.

Municipal Reaction:

On June 4, 1963, the Mayor appointed a Triracial Committee of 13 citizens, four Negroes, two Indians, and seven whites, at the request of the Ministerial Association, the Chamber of Commerce and Agriculture, and the Merchants' Association. The Committee has averaged a meeting every two weeks in addition to the work of the subcommittees on Merchants, Restaurants, Motels, and Theaters which have been working in pairs and groups of three. Each subcommittee was composed of one Negro, one white person, and where possible, one Indian.

A permanent Good Neighbor Committee was established in accord with the recommendations of the Triracial Committee. Mr. Horace Stacy, Jr., was named the chairman of the Good Neighbor Committee, which is composed of eight white persons, five Negroes, and two Indians. Of the 15 members, seven were

127

members of the original Triracial Committee. The first meeting of the Good Neighbor Committee was held March 31, 1964.

Adjustments:

The City employs some 46 Negroes and Indians, including two Negro policemen and a Negro school traffic safety director. Some merchants have indicated to the Committee that both Indians and Negroes will probably be employed by them in non-menial capacities in the near future. A department store employed two young Negro students as gift wrappers during the Christmas holidays of 1963.

There are no hotels or motels in downtown Lumberton; however, all of the motel operators on U. S. 301 and Interstate 95 have privately agreed to accept all paying customers for lodging and board regardless of race. Other restaurants on these highways also follow a nondiscriminatory policy towards Negroes and Indians.

Although the restaurants downtown have not desegregated, one lunch counter and one drugstore lunch counter serve both Negroes and Indians.

There are three theaters in the City, one owned by a chain and two which are locally owned. At this time there has been no disposition on the part of these businesses to desegregate; although both of the indoor theaters as well as the outdoor theater have separate facilities for each race.

There has been no request and nothing has been said about the desegregation of the private bowling alley. The golf course and swimming pools are owned by a private corporation to which the white public is able to subscribe.

The city library has been serving Indians and Negroes for six or seven years.

There are 30 Indians in the junior and senior high schools, although there are no Negroes in the white schools. There was a recent bond election which approved bonds for a new Negro and a new white high school. Although there was some discussion of building a single high school for both the Negroes and whites, both races indicated in the election their preference to have separate and equal facilities.

The Robeson County Hospital has a floor for Negroes. The Indians are served as whites throughout the hospital. Recently the hospital committed itself to locating private rooms for desirous Negroes whenever and wherever such private rooms are available.

Neither the Chamber of Commerce nor the Merchants' Association is open to Negroes. The Ministerial Association is open to Negroes and Indians.

The Triracial Committee has recommended that all community concerts and other community programs be conducted for the benefit and enjoyment of all citizens. The Committee has also recommended that the present Committee be dissolved and that a permanent Good Neighbor Council be established.

MONROE

Population: 10,882; 29.3 per cent Negro

Mayor: Dr. Fred M. Wilson—Office: 101 South Hayne Street; Home: 1112 Griffith Road; Telephone: Office: 283-3312; Home: 283-2771

Biracial Organization: Mayor's Better Citizenship Committee

Chairman: Reverend Harley Williams—Office: Central Methodist Church; Home: 1003 Lakewood Drive; Telephone: Office: 283-3186; Home: 283-2661

Negro Action:

There were three or four days of street marches to schools during August, 1963. These were quiet demonstrations led by white boys.

Recently the Monroe Youth Action Committee has made verbal requests to the Mayor's Better Citizenship Committee.

Municipal Reaction:

The Mayor's Better Citizenship Committee was appointed by the Mayor at the request of the City Council. The Committee meets twice a month. The City Council and the Chamber of Commerce adopted resolutions endorsing the opening of accommodation establishments to Negroes. In addition, the Methodist church adopted and published a resolution in support of the work and activities of the Mayor's Better Citizenship Committee. This resolution was well received.

This Committee is concerning itself with an industrial education program and the development of job opportunities for Negroes.

Adjustments:

One manufacturing firm has hired Negroes following the receipt of instructions from its national office. A department store and the ABC store also have hired Negroes.

Other than one drugstore which has been serving Negroes for over two years, there are no lunch counters or restaurants serving Negroes. One drugstore removed its counter stools in order to circumvent pressure to desegregate its seating.

The hotels, motels, restaurants, and theaters were considering a package desegregation agreement when the public demonstrations interrupted the discussions. Efforts to desegregate downtown eating establishments made during February, 1964, again failed to succeed.

All public outdoor parks, including playgrounds and a golf course, have been desegregated. The swimming pool was closed to avoid desegregation. There are two private swimming pools to which the white public subscribes. Some desegregation of indoor facilities is taking place at the Main Street Recreation Center.

The library remains segregated and there are no Negroes attending the white schools.

Neither the Ministerial Association nor the Chamber of Commerce is desegregated.

MOORESVILLE

Population: 6,918; 18.5 per cent Negro

Mayor: John C. Miller—Home: 244 Cedar Street; Telephone: Home: 664-1276

Biracial Organization: Good Neighbor Council

Chairman: Dr. Boyce A. Brawley—Office: 411 East Statesville Avenue; Home: 336 Cedar Street; Telephone: Office: 663-6301; Home: 662-3354

Negro Action:

During August, seven spokesmen for the South Iredell Citizens League presented an itemized list of eight requests to the City Manager and Town Attorney. The creation of a biracial committee led the list. Of next concern was the securement of better job opportunities.

Municipal Reaction:
The City Council endorsed the creation of a ten-member Good Neighbor Council by the Mayor, suggesting that it be composed of seven whites and three Negroes.

Adjustments:
Both Burlington Industries mills are employing Negroes on an equal employment practice basis. Although there has been discussion of downtown stores employing Negroes, no store has adopted this practice.

The City is in the process of constructing federal housing for Negroes and including in this development a Negro recreation center.

MOUNT AIRY

Population: 7,055; 4.9 per cent Negro

Mayor: Edward T. Clark —Office: Clark and Parker Lumber Company, 754 North South Street; Home: 1118 North Main Street; Telephone: Office: 786-5194; Home: 786-4855

Biracial Organizations:
1. Employment Activities Committee, a subcommittee of the Chamber of Commerce
2. Human Relations Council

Chairmen:
1. William K. Woltz—Office: Perry Manufacturing Company; Home: 232 South Park Avenue; Telephone: Office: 786-6171; Home: 786-2041
2. Reverend Kenneth B. Wilson—Office: First Baptist Church; Home: 213 Wrenn Avenue; Telephone: Office: 786-5185; Home: 786-6667

Negro Action:
On May 16, 1963, Mrs. Nannie N. Penn, Co-ordinator of the Surry County NAACP, and Mrs. John S. Lovill, Jr., President, met with the Town Board of Commissioners at its regular meeting and discussed representation on the Board of Education, equal opportunity in employment, representation on the town council, and the town's employment policy. The discussion developed that consideration would be given to the appointment of

a Negro when a vacancy occurred on the school board and that the City was striving to provide equal job opportunities to Negroes in its employment.

Demonstrations occurred on August 3 and 4, 1963, when groups protested segregation at several eating establishments. Upon the demonstrators' refusal to leave these establishments, they were arrested and charged with trespassing.

Municipal Reaction:

A meeting between the NAACP and the Town Board of Commissioners on May 16, 1963, resulted in a decision authorizing the Mayor to appoint a biracial committee. The Human Relations Council was appointed a few weeks later and the first meeting was held in late June or early July, 1963. The Committee has a membership of 13, including the Mayor and City Manager who are ex officio members. Reverend Kenneth Wilson was named the first chairman of the Human Relations Council.

The Mount Airy Employment Activities Committee, a subcommittee of the Industrial Expansion Committee of the Chamber of Commerce, made its first report in February, 1964. The report of this Committee which seeks job equality and opportunity for Negroes stated that progress had been made through its efforts. At the time of the report, two-thirds of Mount Airy's total employment management had agreed to employ Negroes solely on a qualification basis. Prospective employees who qualify on aptitude tests are to be given intensive-training job positions. It was reported that one industry had been employing Negroes for several years and that this experiment had proved very encouraging.

Since most of the industries are privately owned, the Employment Activities Committee has worked directly with the owners.

Adjustments:

All "White Only" signs have been removed from Mount Airy businesses.

Plans were formulated by the Employment Activities Committee and the industrial employers to announce on January 1, 1964, that they would henceforth follow an equal employment opportunity practice; however, the highly publicized demonstration held during August, 1963, upset these plans. At the present time about 65 per cent of the industrial employers have agreed that as of January, 1964, they maintain an equal employment opportunity practice. Several Negroes have already been employed and promoted by industry, including one Negro who has become the foreman over 15 white workers.

Twenty-five per cent of the town's 80 employees are Negroes and two of these employees are foremen.

Most restaurants and lunch counters have been opened to Negroes.

Mount Airy has no downtown motels and the only major hotel has closed due to competition from the modern motels on the U. S. 52 by-pass.

The library is open to Negroes and there is one Negro boy in the high school. Surry County schools have been desegregated without incident.

The greater Mount Airy Ministerial Association has six active Negro members.

NEW BERN

Population: 15,717; 41.3 per cent Negro

Mayor: Mack L. Lupton—Office: Lupton's Frozen Foods, 107 Craven Street; Home: 1510 Tryon Road; Telephone: Office: 637-3522; Home: 637-3973

Biracial Organization: Biracial Committee

Chairman: W. C. Chadwick—Office: Chadwick General Insurance, 214 Clark Building; Home: 621 Middle Street; Telephone: Office: 637-3146; Home: 637-3432

Negro Action:

Negroes have from time to time petitioned the Biracial Committee to work toward specified adjustments.

Municipal Reaction:

The Mayor appointed a Biracial Committee in August of 1963 with a white and Negro representative from the United States Marine Corps Air Station as observers.

Adjustments:

The lunch counters located in the chain stores have been desegregated for several years and are patronized by both races. Restaurants, hotels, motels, and theaters remain segregated, but the Biracial Committee is now engaged in a campaign to desegregate as many of these facilities as possible.

Negro sales personnel have been employed by many retail outlets in the downtown area. Business establishments other than restaurants, hotels, motels, and theaters actively solicit the patronage of both races. Some businesses, such as launderettes, which have traditionally catered to the white race only, have for several years been used by both races.

There are no municipal parks of any consequence. There is no municipal golf course. The municipal tennis courts are available for use and are used extensively by both races.

Nongovernmental recreational facilities remain segregated.

There are two libraries in the City in addition to those connected with school facilities. These are public libraries operated by nonprofit associations; one of which is patronized principally by whites, the other by Negroes. The former is located near a business district adjoining white residential areas. The latter is located near Negro residential areas. The former is the larger of the two and is not segregated. There are many Negroes who make use of it, and all are welcome to do so.

All of the schools in the Craven County and New Bern city administrative units are used by military personnel. A large portion of these schools are completely desegregated. Some particular schools are segregated, but this is due in large measure to the geographical location of these schools. Neither administrative unit has received any properly filed requests for transfers from a geographically segregated school to any other school. Either board will receive and process applications for transfer properly filed. Both boards have adopted and are in the process of adopting additional so-called "desegregation" plans.

City bus service is desegregated and has been since the early years of World War II. Buses are loaded from front to back on a "first come, first served" basis. Seating arrangements in bus and airline terminals in the area are also desegregated.

A motel was constructed several years ago by Negro investors on U. S. Highway 70, west of New Bern, which accepts Negro patrons only. Adjacent to this is a Country Club for Negroes only. There are many restaurants and several clubs in the City which cater to Negroes only.

NEWPORT

Population: 861; 5.9 per cent Negro

Mayor: Leon A. Mann, Jr.—Home: Town of Newport; Telephone: Home: 223-5541

Biracial Organization: Biracial Committee

Chairman: Mrs. Floyd Garner—Telephone: Home: 223-5911

Negro Action:

There have been no demonstrations by Negroes nor have any petitions been presented to the City Council or Mayor.

Municipal Reaction:

The Mayor appointed a four-member Biracial Committee which meets monthly.

Adjustments:

Of the three soda fountains in Newport, two have desegregated their service and seating and the third has not been requested to do so.

There is no hotel, motel, municipal park, theater, or restaurant. The municipal library is desegregated.

The park facilities are owned and operated by the Cherry Point Mutual Veterans Housing Association and are segregated.

The Council made a survey of how many eligible adult Negroes were registered to vote and determined that 70 per cent were registered.

OXFORD

Population: 6,978; 43.9 per cent Negro

Mayor: T. C. Jordan, Jr.—Home: 410 Raleigh Street; Telephone: City Hall: 4119; Home: 5618

Biracial Organizations:

1. Good Neighbor Council
2. Biracial Commission

Chairmen:

1. Hugh M. Currin—Office: Williamsboro; Home: Tranquil Circle; Telephone: Office: 5543; Home: 5796
2. Has not been selected

RALEIGH

Negro Action:

In June, 1963, four or five demonstrations were conducted by the Negroes, one of which turned into a near riot.

Subsequent to the June demonstrations the Negroes picketed and thereafter boycotted stores against which they had complaints. Among the unusual approaches adopted by the Negroes was repeated requests to city officials that new committees be created to handle racial problems. First, they requested and organized a Good Neighbor Council; second, a Biracial Committee; and third, the Granville County Co-ordinating Committee, an all-Negro organization.

Municipal Reaction:

The Good Neighbor Council, composed of eight members, four white and four Negro, worked primarily in the area of job opportunities and job training and was able to secure approximately a dozen different jobs for Negroes in ten department and grocery stores, primarily as salesmen, cashiers, and meat department personnel. The industries in the area have been hiring Negroes for many years. This practice is heaviest in the electronics industry.

The Biracial Committee, composed of ten members, five white and five Negro, approached the hotel and the three motels and received a commitment from the hotel and one motel to serve Negroes upon request; however, after continued demonstrations, the commitment was dissolved and there have been no requests by Negroes to either the hotel or motel to be served by them. John K. Nelms was selected chairman of the Biracial Committee.

The Biracial Committee met with all of the restaurant and drive-in owners simultaneously. Subsequent to that meeting, delegations were sent around to talk to individual proprietors about lowering racial barriers.

In May of 1964 the white citizens of Oxford organized the Biracial Commission to supersede the Biracial Committee.

Adjustments:

A lunch counter in a variety store and one in a drugstore began and have continued to serve Negroes since prior to the June demonstrations.

One drive-in restaurant embarked upon a 30-day trial period of serving Negroes and three others committed themselves to such a trial period, but never undertook it. The drive-in which

137

did embark upon the 30-day trial period has discontinued its practice of serving Negroes.

The three local restaurants flatly refused to consider a trial period.

The theater also refused to engage in a trial period.

The city parks, a ballpark and a swimming pool, have been closed since the water reservoir burst two years ago. The recreation system is being reorganized, but there has been no thought concerning whether the new program will serve Negroes.

A new public library has been constructed through private contributions. Although this library is desegregated, there remains a public library which serves the Negro community.

There have been no requests by Negroes to be admitted to the white school.

There is a Negro and a white hospital in the City, both completely segregated.

The Ministerial Association is desegregated and a Negro is serving as its chairman.

Neither the Chamber of Commerce nor the Merchants' Association has Negro members.

RALEIGH

Population: 93,931; 23.6 per cent Negro

Mayor: James W. Reid—Office: Professional Building; Home: 108 North Lord Ashley Road; Telephone: Office: 828-0551; Home: 833-4310

Biracial Organization: Community Relations Committee

Chairman: W. C. "Buck" Harris, Jr.—Office: Insurance Building; Home: 2815 Lakeview Drive; Telephone: Office: 833-9711; Home: 787-1754

Negro Action:

The Raleigh Citizens Association is a dominant Negro group which has been active in the community for some time. It was organized to encourage Negroes to register and vote, and to seek job opportunities for Negroes.

Both the NAACP and CORE have active chapters in Raleigh. There are two major Negro colleges, Shaw University, and St.

Augustine's College, located within the city limits of Raleigh and close to the downtown area.

Street marches were held during the spring and summer of 1963. They were primarily directed at public accommodations, such as hotels, restaurants, and theaters, and were implemented to a great extent by students from Shaw and St. Augustine's, as well as sympathetic students from North Carolina State and other white colleges of the community.

Municipal Reaction:

Early in May, 1963, a group of leading businessmen of the community, at the request of Mayor W. G. Enloe, established a "Committee of One Hundred" to determine the course the City should take in dealing with the problems brought about by the demonstrations. Victor E. Bell, a local banker, was chosen as Chairman of the group, and over a six-week period a considerable amount of progress was made toward ending the deteriorating municipal situation, which was concentrated in the downtown area.

The Committee met with Negro leaders and with representatives of target businesses and on a voluntary basis, many downtown restaurants, one major hotel, and several motels opened their facilities to Negroes. It was agreed that the demonstrations would end, and that no publicity was to be given that any particular business had desegregated. A Mechanics Committee, headed by Dr. James Boyd of St. Augustine's College and Dr. Charles Lyons, Jr., Executive Secretary of the North Carolina Teachers Association, was to carry out the gradual desegregation.

The Biracial Committee submitted its resignation, but recommended to the new city administration and Mayor Reid that a permanent committee be appointed to assure continued communication at a high level between leaders of the races of the community, in an effort to work positively toward solution of problems.

On July 26, 1963, the Mayor's Community Relations Committee was appointed by the Mayor. It was composed of 15 members representing almost every phase of the business and community life, including members from the hotel and motel associations, the restaurants association, major industry, the colleges, retail business, the banks, State government, and the legal profession. The Committee was not directed to proceed with the immediate desegregation of every facility in the City; but rather, by a careful study of the many sides of the problem to determine what was best for the City of Raleigh and to recommend this action to the community.

It was noted that almost 24 per cent of Raleigh's population was Negro, and that the community could not realize its greatest potential if this segment of the population were in any sense held down and not allowed its full opportunity for development and contribution to the community.

In October, W. C. Harris, Jr., Raleigh attorney and former member of the General Assembly, accepted the chairmanship of the Committee. Dr. Charles Lyons, Jr., was named Vice-Chairman.

The Committee issued a "Statement of Purpose" which was widely acclaimed. The statement read:

Raleigh is a good community by many measures. A basic good will among individuals, among groups and races does exist here. The Mayor's Community Relations Committee expects to keep its attention focused on the good things of Raleigh, to build on them and, hopefully, to expand them.

The Committee sees its purpose to be that of assisting the people of Raleigh to create progressively a sense of community oneness. In this desirable community each person will be recognized as a full member.

This Committee does not have the authority to set specific objectives for the community. We would, however, be misleading to ourselves not to have in mind an awareness of the form in which full community membership must ultimately be manifested. In our opinion the measure of full membership will be recognizable when each person in Raleigh is equally privileged on the same terms as any other privileged person:

1. To participate in the political decisions by which the community is governed;
2. To enjoy the services provided by public authority;
3. To receive accommodations and services offered by the business community to the public;
4. To participate as qualified in the economic opportunity afforded by the community and to become prepared for such opportunity; and
5. To contribute to and participate in all activities of a non-private nature aimed at community development, improvement, and happiness.

This Committee thinks of itself as a vehicle of the people of Raleigh to use as they themselves progressively become aware of steps which ought to be taken, and express by work and deed the desire to take them.

In furtherance of that purpose the Committee will try:

1. To facilitate the good will of the people in Raleigh.
2. To serve as a focal point for the identification of problems in the area of human relations, and more specifically race problems, and for possible solutions to those problems.
3. To facilitate community progress by encouraging the creation of new opportunities for private employment and public service solely on the basis of merit and qualification.
4. To aid in the creation of a climate and atmosphere in our community which will generate solutions to problems before they reach crisis proportions.
5. To encourage the members of the community to adopt an attitude of tolerance and open-mindedness toward freer communication between white and Negro members which in turn will promote understanding and co-operation toward a free community.
6. To work toward the creation of a fresh hope which will aid Raleigh in becoming a more ideal American community for all of its people.

Subcommittees were formed to work with various aspects of community relations, and meetings have been held with individual merchants and with groups of merchants to discuss the progress of desegregation of all public facilities.

A survey was publicized which showed that none of the local businesses which had desegregated facilities had suffered financial loss to any great extent. This report was widely circulated to all businesses, to make them aware of the success of efforts so far.

The Committee met with student leaders from the various local colleges and universities upon their return to Raleigh in the fall, and advised them of the progress that had been made in the City and the continuing long-range plans that were being carried out.

A survey of job opportunities was made in the community through the co-operation of the Employment Security Commission, and a list of these distributed to the schools and colleges. A survey was made among the major builders in the area, and it was found there was equal opportunity in the building trade for Negroes, and that many of the most skilled tradesmen were Negroes. It was pointed out that there is a shortage of truly skilled people in the building trade.

In January of 1964, at the request of the community, the City Council of Raleigh authorized the hiring of a full-time community relations executive secretary to maintain daily contact with

PETITIONERS DEMONSTRATE ON STEPS OF THE STATE CAPITOL.

businesses and industries that are concerned with desegregation problems. This person would work out of the Municipal Building as a city employee. Several candidates have been interviewed by the Committee, but at the moment a suitable person has not been found. The Council has agreed that the salary of the executive secretary would be paid by city funds.

A "Community Relations Week" was planned by the Committee with the co-operation of the Raleigh Civic Council and the Raleigh Ministerial Association for the second week in June, 1964.

Adjustments:

All variety store and downtown drugstore lunch counters are desegregated. Six major and 20 minor restaurants, constituting one-third of Raleigh's licensed restaurants, are desegregated.

The two major downtown hotels with over 600 rooms, several motels with over 100 rooms, and all indoor theaters have desegregated.

One bowling alley desegregated, but re-segregated when another refused to adopt the same policy.

The public library facilities have been desegregated for several years, and Negroes have enrolled in Needham Broughton High School and Enloe High School, as well as in other classes throughout the school system.

All city recreational facilities, including the swimming pools, have been opened to the Negroes.

In municipal government, Negroes serve on several advisory boards and commissions. A Negro serves on the City Council and was named by the Mayor as chairman of the major public works and planning committee.

All public workers are employed and promoted upon a merit basis.

Two variety stores hired four Negroes in sales, three behind lunch counters and the other as a window-trimmer.

Seven department stores and four grocery chains employ Negroes as salesclerks. Three industries employ Negroes for production and office work. A utility actively seeks Negroes for jobs which have gone exclusively to whites in the past.

The Chamber of Commerce and the Merchants' Association are desegregated and welcome participation by Negroes in all community projects.

REIDSVILLE

Population: 14,267; 33.2 per cent Negro

Mayor: Julius J. Gwyn—Office: Gwyn and Gwyn, 108 South Main Street; Home: 414 Maple Avenue; Telephone: Office: 349-4364; Home: 349-9358

Biracial Organization: An informal biracial conference

Chairman: Mayor Julius J. Gwyn

Negro Action:
Negro leadership in the Negro movement has come from the churches, the Negro labor union at the American Tobacco Company, and the NAACP. The Negro labor union has been integrated with the white union under an order of the Federal government. The NAACP has worked closely with the church leadership.

When the Negro youth lost confidence in the older leadership, they formed a youth chapter of the NAACP and included mem-

143

bers from outside the City. This youth chapter brought strong pressure for making the biracial conference an official adjunct of the municipal government.

On June 11, 1963, NAACP Adults, Young Adults, and Youth organizations petitioned the Mayor and his biracial conference for reforms as follows:

I. Equal employment and upgrading of Negroes in all city establishments supported by public funds including the following:
   (A) Hiring of Negro doctors, nurses, and other personnel in public health establishments.
   (B) Hiring of Negro clerks and typists in city government.
   (C) Hiring of Negro personnel in public establishments receiving city contracts.

II. Desegregation of all public facilities, such as:
   (A) Swimming pools, playgrounds, parks, recreational parks, etc.
   (B) Schools: Assignment of students without regard to race, creed, or color.

III. Complete desegregation of all hospital and medical facilities; complete integration of patients, doctors, and nurses.

IV. Upgrading of employment for Negroes in all stores and banks in the City of Reidsville.
   (A) Hiring of Negro clerks
   (B) Hiring of Negro cashiers
   (C) Hiring of Negro typists
   (D) Hiring of Negro managers, assistant managers and department heads, etc.

V. Desegregation of all facilities involving monetary exchange in business establishments operating by virtue of granted license(s). Also desegregation of all facilities and accommodations provided therein for use by customers. Among such are: Theaters:
   (A) Seating
   (B) Rest rooms
   (C) Lounges
   (D) Concession stands

VI. General announcement indicating that desegregation and fair employment practice for Negroes are in effect.
   Provision for expediting the aforementioned policy:
   (A) Newspaper statements (local).
   (B) Radio announcements (local).

On July 25, 1963, the Rockingham County youth and young adult branches of the NAACP sent the Mayor and his informal biracial conference the following recommendation: "We, . . . recommend that Negroes be hired in the clothing and variety stores. We also recommend that the theater be integrated by August 10, 1963. If these recommendations have not been complied with, we will begin our selective buying campaign in the City of Reidsville on August 12, 1963, and demonstrations if needed." Although a boycott program was threatened in August, no program of coercion was instituted by the Negro community. As of May 1, 1964, there have been no public demonstrations in Reidsville.

Municipal Reaction:

The Mayor serves as moderator of an informal biracial conference with a floating membership which meets weekly to deal with racial matters. All meetings of the biracial conference have been suspended indefinitely by agreement. Leading citizens played an important role in the conference. White participants were selected because of their positions of responsibility and influence in the community. People who were widely known for their "liberal" views were avoided. This included the white ministers.

There was an agreement with the press not to publicize the names of participants, meeting dates, or accomplishments of the conference.

The City Council published a general policy declaration supporting nondiscrimination in employment and in the use of public facilities. In addition, the board of directors of the Merchants' Association adopted a resolution recommending that employers hire upon qualifications alone. The Chamber of Commerce adopted a resolution patterned after the one adopted in Charlotte.

The entire conference group has met with small segments of the business community. The Mayor has carried on much of the outside discussions himself.

The biracial conference enlisted the support of the civic clubs in its work. In August, 1963, the board of directors of the Chamber of Commerce passed a resolution pledging their support to all places of public accommodations which desegregated.

Adjustments:

Substantial steps have been taken to expand employment opportunities for the Negro.

145

Department store managers met with the biracial conference and agreed to employ on a nondiscriminatory basis.

The American Tobacco Company desegregated its cafeteria and toilet facilities and adopted a fair employment practice in August, 1963.

All variety stores, major financial institutions, and super markets have expressed a willingness to employ and promote employees on the basis of merit.

The voluntary hiring of clerks in retail stores has been the most outstanding accomplishment of the biracial conference. The promotion of Negroes in super markets has been obvious. The Negro leadership has assisted in the location of qualified applicants for job openings. Super markets have placed Negro personnel at cash registers and at check-out counters.

The City is without a hotel and there has been no question raised concerning the desegregation of the motel.

A program of controlled desegregation of the theater was worked out between a subcommittee of the biracial conference and the theater management. Prior to the new arrangement, there was a balcony reserved exclusively for Negroes. Civic clubs and church groups were unanimous in requesting restaurants and the theater to serve the public without restriction, expressly upon the understanding and covenant that these groups would support and make special effort to patronize these establishments, particularly during the specific hours of controlled desegregation. The psychological balance of responsibility and pledge of support was crucial in prevailing upon the restaurant and the theater owners to make the requested adjustments. Negroes are now admitted to the main floor of the theater without restriction. There is a slight price differential between the admission on the main floor and the balcony. Since the control program of desegregation was discontinued, relatively few Negroes have continued to use the main floor.

Desegregation of restaurants was arranged through a program to have a specified number of Negroes appear for service at each of the restaurants on the same day, at the same designated hour, in order that no restaurant appear to be taking independent steps. Different days and different hours were selected in order to introduce desegregation to a wide range of the community. Desegregation days were limited to twice a week over the three-week trial period. Substantially all restaurants have de-

segregated after this three-week controlled attendance program.
There are two newly organized private swimming pools restricted to whites; however, the public parks and the public swimming pools have been opened during the past year. The Municipal Recreation Commission, with Negro participants, voted to open the swimming pools and parks without publicity. This policy went into effect approximately one month before the community at large became aware of it through Negro swimmers actually using the pools.

The city branch of the Rockingham County Library renders service to Negroes and has done so for three years. All Negro branches of the public library have been closed and consolidated with the formerly white units. Employed personnel was integrated into the staff of the formerly white units.

The hospital has been desegregated with the exception of wards. The staff began desegregating a year ago, and since then there has been desegregation of rooms and the cafeteria.

Approximately 24 Negroes were assigned to predominantly white schools for the 1963-1964 school year.

ROANOKE RAPIDS

Population: 13,320; 11.4 per cent Negro

Mayor: Leroy W. Morris—Office: Leroy's Fairway Foods; Home: 234 Vance Street; Telephone: Office: 537-4127; Home: 537-3361

Biracial Organization: None

Negro Action:
There have been no demonstrations by Negroes nor have any petitions been presented to the city council or Mayor.

Municipal Reaction:
Five or six years ago there was a request by a Weldon physician for admission to the staff of the county hospital. No action has ever been taken on this request.

Adjustments:
Negroes are served and seated at downtown lunch counters; but other than that, the community is thoroughly segregated.

ROCKINGHAM

Population: 5,512; 27.3 per cent Negro

Mayor: John W. Gore—Office: Rockingham Dairy Products, 617 West Washington Street; Home: 513 Stanley Avenue; Telephone: Office: 895-5273; Home: 895-4939

Biracial Organization: Good Neighbor Committee

Chairman: W. H. Entwistle, Sr.—Office: Hamlet Road; Home: 916 Fayetteville Road; Telephone: Office: 895-6381; Home: 895-3047

Negro Action:

Although there has been a request that public accommodations be desegregated, action toward this end has been tabled until the United States Congress acts upon its pending civil rights legislation.

Municipal Reaction:

The Mayor appointed a seven-member Good Neighbor Committee composed of four whites and three Negroes. This Committee has been most concerned with securing better job opportunities for the Negro. There are some 1,800 trainable persons under forty-eight years of age residing in Richmond County.

Adjustments:

An Industrial Education Center has been secured for the City and County. The County jointly with two neighboring counties petitioned for participation in the work of the North Carolina Fund and was selected.

A textile mill and several retail stores hire Negro employees.

One variety store has desegregated its eating facility, the largest in the County.

There has been no petition by Negroes for transfer to white schools.

ROCKY MOUNT

Population: 32,147; 35.2 per cent Negro

Mayor: John T. Minges—Home: 1608 Waverly Drive; Telephone: Home 442-7430

Biracial Organization: Good Neighbor Committee

Chairman: J. B. Brewer, Sr.—Office: Brewer Paint and Wallpaper Company; Home: 1016 Eastern Avenue; Telephone: Office: 446-7171; Home: 446-5712

Negro Action:

In April of 1963, the Rocky Mount Voters and Improvement League, a Negro organization about five years old which coordinates the activities of the local chapter of the NAACP and the Southern Christian Leadership Conference, appeared before the Mayor's Good Neighbor Committee and requested that plans be formulated which would lead to the desegregation of public-owned facilities and those facilities open to the general public. The League further requested that additional employment opportunities be made available to the Negro citizens and that qualified Negroes be given positions of responsibility wherever practicable.

Other action on the part of the Negro citizens was two consecutive days of orderly picketing at one restaurant during July, 1963.

Municipal Reaction:

A former mayor, approximately ten years ago, appointed a ten-member biracial committee which was enlarged subsequent to the 1963 demonstrations, named the Good Neighbor Committee, and given specific tasks to perform by former Mayor William B. Harrison. The Good Neighbor Committee is composed of 24 members, equally divided by race and further divided into three yearly classes with three-year staggered terms.

In defining the powers of the new Good Neighbor Committee, Mayor Harrison presented the following:
The Committee is:

1. A private body and its meetings are not open to anyone other than members unless invited by the Mayor or Chairman of the Committee.

2. Not to publicize its deliberations or work except in special situations where both full Committee and Mayor approve.

3. Not to take action on any matter that can and should be taken up before a legally constituted board or community committee already set up for that purpose until that board or committee has finally acted on the matter and an impasse has developed. In this case it should only act as a mediator and not as a fact-finding or a judicial body.

A SIT-DOWN IN DOORWAY OF SEGREGATED RESTAURANT.

4. Not to be an action committee for any program or special interest group other than within the scope of purposes defined for the Committee.

5. To elect for a one-year term at a time, its own chairman, vice-chairman, and secretary, at a meeting to be called by the chairman in the month of June of each year, at which meeting newly appointed members of the Committee will assume their duties.

6. Authorized through its chairman to set up any committees it deems necessary to better carry out the purposes of the Committee.

7. Free to solicit aid from any individual, group, or organization on any matter within the scope of the purposes of the Committee.

8. To meet at least quarterly.

Upon receiving the request from the Rocky Mount Voters and Improvement League, the Good Neighbor Committee appointed a six-member *ad hoc* subcommittee composed of one member of the Good Neighbor Committee as Chairman, and five Negro and white non-Good Neighbor Committee members to attempt to develop a long-range plan to provide all persons equal citizenship. This committee drafted Rocky Mount's "Blueprint for Progress," a copy of which appears elsewhere in this book. This "Blueprint for Progress" was subsequently adopted by the Good Neighbor Committee and endorsed by leading business, civic, fraternal, and religious organizations. This "Blueprint" calls for priority attention to be given to job training and job opportunity. The Good Neighbor Committee feels that before the average Negro can assume full citizenship, he must be given greater economic challenge and opportunity, that it is not enough to make jobs available, that the Negro must be trained to compete for jobs with whites and must be trained to perform satisfactorily when employed.

The Job Opportunity Subcommittee assumed the responsibility of personally contacting the majority of the businesses in Rocky Mount, primarily the industrial, retail, and institutional establishments, and determining the employment policies of these businesses.

The Subcommittee found that many businesses were ready and willing to adopt equal employment practices. It also found a tremendous shortage of qualified Negro workers with skills in demand. Local Negro leaders recognized this and are assisting the Job Training Subcommittee to provide Negroes with necessary job training.

The Job Training Subcommittee undertook to assist the progress of both races in training the unemployed for obtaining job positions and in training the employed for job promotions. The initial approach of the Job Training Subcommittee was to identify the existing facilities and agencies available for such training.

With respect to individuals of school age, the Job Training Subcommittee determined that the responsibility must be borne by the public school system. There was an examination and recommendation that the local Negro senior high school make the necessary preliminary surveys and assemble the staff necessary to institute a Distributive Education Program.

Adjustments:

Much progress has been made in providing better employment

NORTH CAROLINA AND THE NEGRO

for Negroes. Retail stores, industries, government, and financial institutions are now employing Negroes on an equal basis.

The Mayor and City Council have appointed additional Negroes to many of the important city boards and commissions, which is a continuation of a practive begun ten years ago. All public-owned facilities are open to all citizens. Since September, 1963, there are 21 Negro students enrolled in previously all-white schools. These students requested admission to the white schools and were assigned by the Board of Education in almost every case to the school requested.

Some progress has been made in the field of public accommodations. Several restaurants and motels are serving Negroes on a limited basis. Organizations, composed of restaurant and motel owners, are at work on further desegregation of these facilities. The responsibility for public accommodations desegregating rests with the Good Neighbor Committee, but action in this regard has been delegated to the representative motel and restaurant associations.

The Chamber of Commerce and Merchants' Association are actively engaged in making more jobs available for all citizens. Each of these organizations accepts applications for membership from any individual or business.

There are excellent lines of communication between the Negro and white leadership.

SALISBURY

Population: 21,297; 28.1 per cent Negro

Mayor: Louis J. Harrison—Office: City Hall; Home: Dogwood Road; Telephone: Office: 633-2311, 633-3775; Home: 636-5596

Biracial Organization: Community Service Committee

Chairman: W. C. Stanback—Home: 1722 Park Road; Telephone: Home: 633-9249

Negro Action:

The last demonstration occurred over 15 months ago when the Negroes demonstrated in front of a theater. Prior to that, there was some picketing of lunch counters three years ago which resulted in the desegregation of lunch counters. The conservative Negro elements in the community have orally requested some relief in the area of public accommodations.

Municipal Reaction:

Action was taken by the City. The Chamber of Commerce and the Merchants' Association each passed a resolution endorsing the fair employment of Negroes and the opening of public accommodations to Negroes. The Mayor appointed the Community Service Committee over three years ago and this Committee continues as a standing committee composed of seven members, four white and three Negro.

Adjustments:

There have been approximately 14 new job opportunities made available by department stores through opening sales positions to Negroes.

Three of the better motels and all of the lunch counters have desegregated without incident.

Two of the finer restaurants have desegregated, as have two of the theaters. There are few park facilities and no swimming pools. Other than occasional use of the outdoor facilities by Negroes, the park and recreational facilities continue to be segregated.

There are libraries for both the white and Negro communities; however, Negroes are permitted to use and do use the white library.

There are three Negroes attending the white high school for the first time this year.

The Rowan Memorial Hospital is a private hospital. Nevertheless, the eating facilities have recently been desegregated. Other hospital services have been desegregated for several years. There are Negro nurses on the staff.

When and if planned public housing is constructed, it will be open to both Negroes and whites.

The Ministerial Association, the Chamber of Commerce, and the Merchants' Association have Negro members. Both the Merchants' Association and the Chamber of Commerce appointed follow-up committees to encourage implementation of their resolutions endorsing desegregated public accommodations and the offering of better job opportunities.

SANFORD

Population: 12,253; 37.3 per cent Negro

Mayor: Tommy C. Mann—Office: Mann Implement Company, 312 South Endor Street; Home: 502 North Steele Street; Telephone: 776-2912; Home: 775-3892

Biracial Organizations:
1. Good Neighbor Council
2. Human Relations Committee

Chairmen:
1. Gordon Fogle—Office: 115 South Steele Street; Home: 406 Brinn Drive; Telephone: Office: 776-4532; Home: 775-2772
2. John R. Dossenbach—Office: 211 Wicker Street; Home: 713 Fitts Street; Telephone: Office: 775-4237; Home: 776-1951

Negro Action:
There were demonstrations by high school students during the Christmas holidays of 1963.

Municipal Reaction:
Upon the request of a number of prominent private citizens, in June, 1963, the Mayor appointed a 12-member committee composed of six Negroes and six whites. This Committee served until October.

The Mayor appointed a 45-member Human Relations Committee with eight Negroes included, which began meeting December 30, 1963.

Adjustments:
One grocery store has employed a Negro cashier, and a number of industries have committed themselves to employ qualified Negroes when they present themselves.

The motels on the highway on the outskirts of town were approached by members of the Council without success. The downtown hotel was not approached.

Before Christmas, 1963, 36 of 40 restaurants and all lunch counters agreed to serve Negroes when they came in to be served, but not when they came in mass to test the practice of the establishment. The exceptions to the agreement were the motel restaurants on the highway. However, since the Christmas demonstrations, the 36 restaurants and all the lunch counters which participated in the agreement have determinedly re-segregated.

The theater is owned by a chain and there has been no communication between the owner and the Council.

The City operates both a Negro and a white swimming pool and park system.

The public library is segregated and operates a Negro branch in the Negro community. The industrial schools have had many Negro applicants and participants. No Negro applicant has been admitted into the white public schools.

The hospital employs Negro nurses' aides and there are two Negro doctors on the staff. Segregation exists to the extent that Negroes are usually placed at opposite ends of the hall from the whites.

The Ministerial Association made a public announcement that Negroes are invited to attend all the churches. The Ministerial Association, the Chamber of Commerce, and the Merchants' Association all are without Negro membership.

SHELBY

Population: 17,698; 22.7 per cent Negro

Mayor: Dr. Hubert S. Plaster—Office: Royster Building; Home: 525 South Washington Street; Telephone: Office: 487-6307; City Hall: 487-4021; Home: 487-4077

Biracial Organization: Human Relations Committee

Chairman: Reverend John E. Lawrence—Office: First Baptist Church; Home: 405 West Marion Street; Telephone: Office: 482-3467; Home: 487-6132

Negro Action:

There have been no demonstrations or picketing of any consequence.

Municipal Reaction:

Upon the request of the Ministerial Association, the Mayor appointed a Human Relations Committee, effective July 1, 1963. This Committee met monthly for the first three months and now meets bi-weekly. There are nine white and five Negro members for a total of 14. The Committee has four subcommittees.

Adjustments:

One subcommittee has been working for better job opportunities for the Negro. One industry presently is employing Negroes extensively in its operation. It was stated that one grocery store has a Negro woman bagging groceries. There are no Negro salesclerks downtown in either department stores or other stores.

All lunch counters with the exception of two drugstore lunch counters serve Negroes and have since before the Committee was appointed in the spring. The restaurants do not serve Negroes.

Neither the motels nor hotels serve Negroes, nor do the two indoor theaters.

The City operates two park systems, one for the whites and one for the Negroes. The system is segregated. The major difference is that the white park includes a golf course which is not open to the Negroes.

The City operates a library with a branch in the Negro community. The main library has been desegregated. There are four Negro students attending the white high school.

Cleveland Memorial Hospital is segregated with a floor for the Negroes, although there is a Negro doctor who has staff privileges.

One subcommittee is working with the public housing authority which is at present working to acquire federal housing, primarily to replace Negro rental slums.

The Ministerial Association is desegregated. The Merchants' Association and the Chamber of Commerce do not have Negro membership.

SMITHFIELD

Population: 6,117; 35.2 per cent Negro

Mayor: Hugh C. Talton—Office: Turnage and Talton Super Market; Home: 103 East Rose Street; Telephone: Office: 934-8106; Home: 934-2666

Biracial Organization: Human Relations Committee

Chairman: Reverend Charles H. Mercer—Office: Centenary Methodist Church; Home: 904 Crescent Drive; Telephone: Office: 934-2333, Home: 934-8597

Negro Action:
There have been no demonstrations or picketing.

Municipal Reaction:
Upon the request of private white and Negro citizens, the City Council approved the recommendations of the Mayor for a 12-member Human Relations Committee composed of seven white and five Negro members. Since the Committee's appointment in July, it has met monthly.

Adjustments:
The Committee has worked to secure better job opportunities for the Negro. It established a class for Negroes who wanted to obtain better jobs. This class met weekly for 12 to 15 weeks. The Committee secured two sales positions for Negroes in department stores; however, one of the Negroes hired resigned and the other has been informed that he is temporary.

All of the governmental offices have declared publicly that they will consider all job applications without regard to race.

Three drugstores serve Negroes as a result of having been requested to by the Human Relations Committee. There is some question whether either motel on the highway will serve Negroes either in its restaurant or sleeping accommodations.

Other restaurants have been contacted concerning their serving Negroes.

A subcommittee has concerned itself with public housing and has primarily worked for the removal of discriminatory signs throughout the City.

The theater is segregated with a balcony being provided for Negroes.

There are no public parks. The library is desegregated and is frequented by both whites and Negroes. There have been no requests by Negroes for transfer to white schools.

The county hospital is desegregated, although some Negroes are grouped at one end of the hospital floor. The hospital employs Negro nurses and Negro doctors have staff privileges.

The Ministerial Association has invited the only Negro minister in the community to join it.

The Chamber of Commerce does not have any Negro members.

STATESVILLE

Population: 19,844; 21.1 per cent Negro

Mayor: J. G. Bagnal, Jr.—Office: Forest Products, 110 South Jackson Street; Home: 428 Summit Avenue; Telephone: Mayor: 872-1144; Office: 872-2746, 872-5274; Home: 873-4472

Biracial Organization: Biracial Council

Chairman: Frank Goforth—Office: 501 South Center Street; Home: 634 Oakdale Drive; Telephone: Office: 872-2451; Home: 873-9634

Negro Action:
The hospital has been the subject of considerable discussion. The hospital obtained money under the Hill-Burton Act and built a Negro wing with it. The Negroes have requested that the entire hospital be desegregated. Negroes requested desegregation of the municipal pool.

Municipal Reaction:
The Mayor appointed a Biracial Council which is now being expanded. The Negro members of the Council were the ones who made contacts with the merchants to discuss the desegregation of facilities.

Adjustments:
Negroes are employed in some of the factories and as salesclerks in downtown retail stores.

Lunch counters have desegregated. Almost all restaurants and the hotel have desegregated. The single theater has been desegregated for a long time.

Park areas have been desegregated. The swimming pools have been the biggest problem. There are white and Negro swimming pools which were built with money derived from a bond issue and equally allocated to each. The Negro desire to use the white pool has met with resentment in the white community.

The library has been desegregated and it is frequented by the Negroes. Eight Negroes are enrolled in formerly white schools, four in the first grade and four in the high school.

The Merchants' Association is desegregated. The Chamber of Commerce has no Negro members and has never been presented with a request for Negro membership.

CIVIL RIGHTS ADVOCATES MARCH FOR REFORM.

TARBORO

Population: 8,411; 31.1 per cent Negro

Mayor: Dr. E. L. Roberson—Office: 3901 Main Street; Home: 807 Main Street; Telephone: Office: 823-2105; Home: 823-3035

Biracial Organization: Community Relations Committee

Chairman: Dr. Howard S. Hussey, Jr.—Office: 3901 Main Street; Home: 908 St. Andrews Street; Telephone: Office: 823-2105; Home: 822-2375

Negro Action:

There is an active chapter of the NAACP in Tarboro.

Eight Negro citizens among whom was the president of the NAACP requested the organization of the Community Relations Committee. These eight Negroes enlarged their group into an organization named the East Tarboro Citizens Council. Dr. Moses Ray, the chairman of the East Tarboro Citizens Council, also serves as vice-chairman of the Community Relations Committee. The East Tarboro Citizens Council serves as a back-up organization for the Community Relations Committee. Their prime concern has been job opportunities and adult education.

In the summer of 1963 a group of high school students requested service at a segregated restaurant on one occasion and left peacefully when requested to do so by the local chief of police. As of May 1, 1964, there have been no demonstrations in Tarboro.

Municipal Reaction:

The Mayor appointed a 13-member Community Relations Committee in July, 1963. This Committee is composed of eight whites and five Negroes. As a result of the Negroes' concern with adult education, a subcommittee was appointed to confer with the Tarboro School Superintendent and a representative of the Industrial Educational Center of Wilson. The subcommittee worked out an adult education program with these institutions. The East Tarboro Citizens Council screened the applicants and assumed a major role in the development of the program. All 55 applicants are participating in classes which are designed to lead to a high school equivalency certificate.

The Community Relations Committee is working closely with the Industrial Development Board and every effort is being made to give the first employment opportunities to the Negroes who have completed their high school equivalency program.

The Committee sent questionnaires to all food and chain stores, existing manufacturers, as well as a new industry that is to locate in Tarboro, requesting information on the employment practices of these businesses. In every instance, the replies were favorable in that all concerns stated that if they had openings for additional jobs in the future, that they would consider applications from qualified Negroes on the basis of merit and in free competition with other applicants. The new industry is actively recruiting Negro labor on a completely nondiscriminatory basis and another new industry has announced that it will employ Negroes and whites on a 50-50 basis.

Adjustments:

Three lunch counters in drugstores and variety stores are desegregated. This was done voluntarily by the individual business establishments and not as a direct result of the efforts of this Committee. No one had suggested that restaurants serve Negroes until recently and that is now under discussion.

One store has employed a Negro saleslady; food stores have begun to employ Negroes; and another business has employed a Negro in its gift wrapping department.

Theaters remain segregated.

The main library has been desegregated for some time. Recently a Negro was named to the library board.

The schools are run by Edgecombe County School District Number 1. There are no Negroes attending the white schools since there have been no applications for transfer as of May 1, 1964.

A separate summer recreation program and swimming pool is operated for the Negroes and whites. There has been no effort to desegregate these.

The hospital staff is desegregated, although patients are segregated.

The City has two ordinances dealing with demonstrations, one passed in 1956 on parading and the other passed in 1961 on picketing. The 1956 ordinance has a companion face-mask ordinance and was aimed primarily at the Ku Klux Klan.

The city tax listings have been desegregated.

The Merchants' Association will accept membership applications from Negroes.

THOMASVILLE

Population: 15,190; 21.2 per cent Negro

Mayor: Thomas F. Johnson—Office: Ragan Knitting Company; Home: 709 Welborn Street; Telephone: Office: 476-7741; Home: 476-7186

Biracial Organization: Biracial Committee

Chairman: Harry B. Finch—Office: 16 Salem Street; Home: 2 Clark Street; Telephone: Office: 476-7992; Home: 476-7991

Negro Action:

Negroes conducted street demonstrations and a reactionary fired a shot into a Negro church.

Municipal Reaction:

The City Council appointed a six-member Biracial Committee composed of four whites and two Negroes. This Committee deals with only one problem at a time and continues work on that problem until there has been some accomplishment. The Committee meets at least monthly. One of the projects of the Committee was to meet with the Negro PTAs to discuss the high rate of drop-outs and to encourage parents to make an all-out effort to keep their children in school.

Adjustments:

Six retail stores have hired Negroes as salesmen.

The industrial school, located between Lexington and Thomasville, has been publicized. At the present time only 16 of the 200 participants are Negroes.

The Committee worked with the two motels and the restaurants without bringing about any adjustments. The theater remains segregated.

The two swimming pools and the city parks have been desegregated.

There are two county libraries, one in the white community and the other in the Negro community. Although both are open to Negroes, the one located in the white community is seldom used by Negroes due to its inconvenient location.

There are six Negroes in the white schools.

Both the Chamber of Commerce and the Ministerial Association are desegregated.

WARRENTON

Population: 1,124; 20.5 per cent Negro

Mayor: W. A. Miles, Jr.—Office: W. A. Miles Hardware Company; Home: Fairview Road; Telephone: Office: 257-3439; Home: 257-3645

Biracial Organization: Biracial Committee

Chairman: James M. Stoney, Jr.—Office: Emmanuel Episcopal Church, North Main Street; Telephone: Church: 257-3891; Home: 257-4395

Negro Action:

The NAACP has a Warren County chapter. There have been no demonstrations. The Negroes requested the Mayor to form a biracial committee on June 13, 1963.

Municipal Reaction:

After giving the County Commissioners an opportunity to organize a county-wide biracial committee, the Mayor appointed a seven-member committee composed of four whites and three Negroes. This Committee has been working primarily to secure better job opportunities for the Negro. It discusses Negro grievances, acts as a mediation board, and advises the Mayor.

It has been determined that the Warrenton Biracial Committee does not properly serve the community. The Mayor, the County Commissioners, and interested Negro and white citizens have decided that there should be a county-wide biracial committee.

Adjustments:

Five downtown retail stores have hired 12 Negroes as salesmen. Five grocery stores have hired Negroes and one has trained a Negro as a cashier.

There have been no efforts to desegregate accommodations. The theater continues a balcony for Negroes. This balcony brings in about 20 per cent of the annual revenue to the theater even though the County has a 65 per cent Negro population.

The municipal libraries continue segregated.

The NAACP recently secured an injunction against the school board to prevent it from dismissing Negro petitions for transfer to white schools.

There are no municipal recreational facilities.

The County Board of Commissioners had all "White" and "Colored" signs removed from the Courthouse.

WASHINGTON

Population: 9,939; 40.2 per cent Negro

Mayor: A. Thomas Stewart—Office: Stewart's Jewelry Store, North Market Street; Home: 1307 Summit Avenue; Telephone: Office: 946-2611; Home: 946-2193

Biracial Organization: Biracial Committee

Chairman: Ashley B. Futrell—Office: *Washington Daily News;* Home: 1206 Summit Avenue; Telephone: Office: 946-2145; Home: 946-5068

Negro Action:

Following negotiations between the white and Negro citizens it was agreed that so long as adjustments are observable, the Negroes will not organize demonstrations or picket stores.

Municipal Reaction:

The 25-member Committee is composed of sixteen whites and nine Negroes, according to the ratio of Negroes to the total community population. The nine Negroes were recommended by the Negro community and the Mayor accepted them. The Committee meets monthly. There are several subcommittees.

Adjustments:

The Committee has an industrial as well as a retail job hunting subcommittee. There are now some 60 Negroes among the 400 employees of a shirt factory and there are commitments on the part of the larger chain-department stores to hire Negroes as salesclerks.

Hotels remain segregated. There is some amount of desegregation anticipated among the restaurants. The theaters are segregated.

The municipal library is desegregated.

The parks are desegregated and the tennis courts which were formerly reserved for whites are now used by Negroes as well. There are teen-age clubs and craft shops for both whites and Negroes and these remain segregated.

The Beaufort County Courthouse and other public buildings are to be desegregated. All "Colored" signs will be taken down in public buildings. The hospital has agreed to hire two additional Negro registered nurses.

The two Ministerial Associations recently held a biracial dinner.

WELDON

Population: 2,165; 49.6 per cent Negro

Mayor: Sterling B. Pierce—Office: 310 Washington Avenue; Home: 700 Sycamore Street; Telephone: Mayor: 536-3911; Office: 536-3024, 536-4563; Home: 536-3827

Biracial Organization: None

Negro Action:
The Negroes have requested that a biracial committee be appointed and they have suggested those Negroes whom they would like to have serve on such a committee.

Municipal Reaction:
The Mayor thought that the appointment of a biracial committee was a good idea until after he and the City Council visited with the City Council of Danville, Virginia. At present there is a consensus among the white community that no biracial committee should be appointed. This belief has been reinforced by a reaction to the suggestions for Negro appointments to the committee.

Adjustments:
Negroes have requested service and have received it from the two restaurants, one downtown and the other on the by-pass.

There has been a request that a Negro be placed on the school board, but this has not been done. No Negro has applied for transfer to the white schools.

A Negro dentist serves both white and Negro patients since there is no white dentist available.

WHITEVILLE

Population: 4,683; 26.5 per cent Negro

Mayor: Junius K. Powell—Office: Powell, Lee and Lee, Pinkney Street; Home: 105 West Frink Street; Telephone: Office: 642-2849; Home: 642-2078

Biracial Organization: Biracial Committee

Chairman: Steve Wall—Office: *The News Reporter;* Home: 104 West Calhoun Street; Telephone: Office: 642-3162; Home: 642-4762

Negro Action:
The NAACP has a local chapter.

The Negro members of the Biracial Committee filed these objectives at the initial meeting: That each Negro child be assigned to the school nearest his home, that inns and lodges admit all persons without discrimination with regard to race, that employers not discriminate with regard to race in employing new help, and that Negroes be given equal consideration for membership on public and governmental boards.

Municipal Reaction:

The Mayor appointed a 13-member Biracial Committee consisting of seven white and six Negro members. This Committee met twice a month until April, 1964, when it began meeting monthly. The Committee was enlarged at the request of its Negro membership by the addition of seven white members and one Negro member in January, 1964.

Adjustments:

There has been some success in getting manufacturers and retail businesses to hire Negroes in non-menial jobs. Two manufacturing companies have organized training programs for Negro women with the intention of hiring the participants in their businesses. A garment manufacturing plant has expanded its all-Negro unit. Another plant has employed about 12 Negroes, merging them with white employees without incident.

One retail merchant has hired a Negro as a shoe salesman and two other retail stores have hired Negroes as salesclerks.

Drive-in restaurants without seating capacity serve Negroes. Hotels, restaurants, and lunch counters remain segregated.

A Negro has been added to the police force.

The municipal library has always been desegregated.

The hospital continues to be segregated.

There are no municipal parks other than those attached to the schools. There have been no applications by Negroes to be transferred to the white schools.

The Merchants' Association does not have any Negro members.

WILLIAMSTON

Population: 6,924; 50.3 per cent Negro

Mayor: N. C. Green—Office: 1008 East Main Street; Home: 108 Academy Street; Telephone: Office: 792-4142; Home: 792-2620

GOLDEN A. FRINKS AND MRS. SARAH SMALL, LEADERS OF THE WILLIAMSTON
SOUTHERN CHRISTIAN LEADERSHIP CONFERENCE MOVEMENT, STAND BEFORE
GREENE MEMORIAL CHRISTIAN CHURCH.

Biracial Organization: Community Relations Committee

Chairman: Rush W. Bondurant—Office: East Main Street; Home: 102 West Marshall Avenue; Telephone: Home: 792-2741

Negro Action:

On Sunday, June 30, 1963, peaceful demonstrations were begun in the town of Williamston by the Negro community under the leadership of the Southern Christian Leadership Conference to protest bad living conditions and racial discrimination in Williamston. Following this and on 29 consecutive nights through July 31, 1963, demonstrations took place by a number finally increasing to 231, with the consent and protection of the local police and municipal authorities.

These demonstrations consisted on practically all occasions of marching from the Negro meeting place at the Greene Memorial Christian Church on East Main Street to the City Hall where the demonstrators would sing songs for approximately fifteen minutes to an hour. They would then return to the church. On each occasion through July 31 the demonstrators marched under

167

the protection of members of the Williamston Police Department and Martin County Sheriff's Department. The police remained with the demonstrators at all times until they returned to the church.

Other acts consisted of demonstrations in front of the local movie theater and numerous instances of daytime picketing on Main Street and at local motels and restaurants. Monday evening, July 8, violence threatened. Crowds attending increased progressively until on the last few nights as many as approximately 1,500, other than the demonstrators, congregated at and congested the area in front of the City Hall and the adjacent intersection. On July 30, 1963, a group of persons interfered with the march of the demonstrators toward the City Hall and there developed a stalemate in Main Street for several hours until peace officers were finally able to disperse the crowds. Major violence was again averted. On the following night a demonstration was held in front of the City Hall under the protection of numerous highway patrolmen, assisting the local Police Department and the County Sheriff's Department.

During this period no person was arrested for demonstrating, but more than 100 arrests were made for trespass. Many were arrested several times. A period of discussion was agreed upon between the Negro and white communities on the 29th day of the demonstrations. The Negro community presented its demands to the City Council.

A quiet period lasted until the Board of Commissioners of the Town of Williamston adopted an ordinance requiring a permit to parade, which the Negroes interpreted as an act of bad faith.

On the night of August 9, the demonstrators attempted to march from their usual meeting place at the City Hall and 54 persons were arrested for violation of the parade ordinance, disturbing the peace, and interfering with the free flow of traffic. Another attempt was made without a permit on August 22, but the crowd was dispersed without arrest. On the night of August 29, 1963, the group again attempted to proceed up Main Street without a permit and was stopped in the vicinity of the courthouse. Violence erupted, sticks, bottles, bricks and other missiles being used. Eleven Negroes were arrested, some for inciting to riot. On the following day during noon approximately 300 children attempted, under the leadership of grown persons, to leave the Hayes School, Negro, and march up Washington Street. A permit had been applied for, but was not granted. The demonstrators were stopped within one block of the school where they engaged in throwing bottles and other missiles. These demonstrations produced mass arrests.

On August 10, 1963, some of the demonstrators instituted an action in the Martin County Superior Court seeking an injunction to prohibit the Town of Williamston from enforcing the parade ordinance, and instituted an accompanying action seeking a declaratory judgment invalidating the parade ordinance. Hearings were held on August 17, 1963, and the Court dismissed both actions on September 4, 1963.

During September there was a school boycott by Negroes which lasted several days.

After four months of demonstrations, the leaders of the movement invited ministers, students, and laymen from the Boston area to join them in their struggle in mid-November, 1963. On November 13, 15 New England ministers and students announced their intention to participate in a parade and demonstration with local persons on the following day.

The police and sheriff's departments informed these ministers and students of the requirement of a parade permit and provided them with an application form. The ministers and students informed the Town in writing that they would not comply with the ordinance.

On November 13 the Town of Williamston obtained an injunction from a Superior Court judge prohibiting any march, parade, or demonstration in the Town of Williamston without a lawful permit, and same was duly served previous to any attempted march.

On the following day, these white ministers and students, together with 60 Negroes, largely juveniles, marched from their usual meeting place to the Martin County Courthouse where all adults were arrested, not only for violating the parade ordinance, but also on other charges such as disturbing the peace and interfering with the free flow of traffic. On the same night another group attempted to march and demonstrate and 23 were arrested on this occasion on the same charges.

Upon the call for hearing of the injunction proceeding, the demonstrators had the case and all other criminal cases then pending removed to the United States District Court for the Eastern District of North Carolina. At the time of the removal,

FREEDOM
MARC

MUNICIPAL RESPONSE TO THE CHALLENGE

the Town had obtained another injunction, made necessary by the arrival of new leaders. During December the demonstrators instituted two more actions in the federal court seeking to prohibit the enforcement of the parade ordinance. The Town and State immediately filed petitions for remanding the cases (other than the two instituted in the federal court) to the Martin County Superior Court. All cases are now pending in the United States District Court, awaiting a decision of the United States Circuit Court of Appeals, Fifth Circuit, concerning the appealability of a decision of a United States District Court judge ordering the remanding of similar cases. Hearings were held in connection with these matters in the United States Court of Appeals January 10, 1964.

Mass meetings or "Freedom Rallies" were held nightly by the Negro community. These rallies and demonstrations ended abruptly when President John F. Kennedy was assassinated.

An economic boycott was organized against discriminating downtown merchants. This boycott continues to some degree.

Local Negroes sent a "Freedom Choir" to Boston for ten days during the Christmas holidays, 1963. There were eight or ten adults in the party of 43 that made the trip. The others of the group were young people between the ages of thirteen and sixteen. A "Freedom Rally" was held in the Ebenezer Baptist Church in Boston's south end. The Boston NAACP Chapter coordinated the Massachusetts end of the program.

The local Negroes have requested interested parties in Boston to adopt Williamston as a special desegregation project.

On Monday, February 10, 1964, a school boycott was organized at the E. J. Hayes School; 191 high school students and 183 grammar school students were present out of a combined enrollment of 1,440 students.

Three Boston clergymen arrived on February 29, 1964, with a 1,700-pound shipment of food and a promise of renewed anti-segregation demonstrations.

On March 19, 1964, an application was made for a permit which was granted for picketing on Main Street in the Town of Williamston, the same taking place in an orderly and peaceable manner.

Approximately 30 white New England ministers, students, and laymen arrived in Williamston on March 24, 1964, to participate in renewed demonstrations. The activities of these persons consisted of placing themselves in front of the churches in town where they remained for an extended period. Three visiting clergymen were arrested and jailed for violating the town's picketing ordinance the first day of their visit. Approximately 26 of these persons and local persons were arrested on trespass charges during the week prior to Easter and eight were arrested for an attempted demonstration without a permit. This group left town a few days after Easter.

During the fall months of 1963, a concerted effort, supported by numerous distributions of handbills, resulted in a boycott of Williamston business establishments.

During September, 1963, a boycott of the Negro schools took place, lasting a few days.

Without variation, the demonstrating groups have consisted of approximately 20 per cent adults, many of them being non-residents, the others being juveniles down to the age of ten or twelve years. All activities have been under the leadership of a representative sent to Williamston by the Southern Christian Leadership Conference, working with the local unit.

The local Negroes are now sponsoring a voter registration campaign.

CORE has supplied the local Negro community with both financial and human resources.

The Negroes seek a board of education plan for the desegregation of the public schools, the desegregation of the local library, and the desegregation of public accommodations. They have also requested the enactment of a public accommodations ordinance and the removal of "White" and "Colored" signs. A major request has been that the hospital desegregate its facilities.

Municipal Reaction:

The Mayor and town authorities agreed with local Negroes to a period of discussions on July 31, 1963. During the subsequent peace, the town police arrested parents of teen-agers who had participated in the street demonstrations on a charge of contributing to the delinquency of minors.

The Mayor appointed a biracial committee, designated as the Community Relations Committee, with R. W. Bondurant as Chairman. The Committee held its first meeting July 11, 1963, and this Committee has had numerous regular and special meet-

A NONVIOLENCE DEMONSTRATION CLASS PRACTICES ON SCHOOL GROUND.

ings since that time for the purpose of keeping lines of communication open and attempting to solve problems.

The City Council listened to the Negroes present their demands and accepted and adopted two of the Negroes' proposals. One called for the removal of segregation signs from municipal buildings and the other called for the integration of the tax listings.

At their regular monthly meeting, on August 5, 1963, the Board of Commissioners of the Town of Williamston adopted its "parade ordinance." This ordinance required a permit for any demonstration, march, or parade. Demonstration leaders were notified of this action. This ordinance also required a 24-hour notice before the holding of any street demonstrations. The petition for a license required a description of the nature of the planned demonstration, a listing of the names of all minors who would be participating, an estimation of the number of participants, an outline of the route that would be followed, and other pertinent information.

The Martin County Board of Commissioners voted to discontinue the county's participation in the federal surplus food program in November, 1963. This decision was reviewed on March 3, 1964, and it was decided to wait until October, 1964, before considering the restoration of the food program. Meantime, the County claims to have ample ready cash for needy families as a result of the establishment several years ago of a trust fund by the will of Mrs. Carrie Biggs Morrison, a Martin County native. During January and February, 1964, the County Welfare Department furnished food and clothing assistance to 83 persons as compared to a monthly average of assistance to 2,446 persons in 1963. Food in the amount of 543,215 pounds was distributed in Martin County under the federal food surplus program during an eleven-month period in 1962-1963.

The Community Relations Committee felt that the library would be a good beginning point for its work. However, when members of the biracial committee approached the library board about desegregating this facility, many local citizens criticized the members of the Committee for even suggesting such a step.

The library is considered to be a private institution because it was donated to the community by the woman's club and other groups. The Town paid over $1,000 a year to the library for the librarian's salary. The Town promised to discontinue payments to the librarian's salary unless the library desegregated. Since the library remains segregated, the Town discontinued payments of the librarian's salary as of January 1, 1964.

During demonstrations, the drugstore and cafe locked their doors whenever demonstrators or Negroes attempted to enter.

A county commissioner and a local minister, who is a member of the Community Relations Committee, went to Boston to counteract some of the publicity which the Negroes had received there.

Williamston and Martin County officials have called for a lowering of racial barriers in public facilities and for the adoption of equal employment practices.

The hospital board went on record as favoring desegregation but there have been some complications in effecting this policy. These are being worked out.

The Community Relations Committee is presently in the process of being enlarged with the result that there will be a more representative group of local Negro citizens along with a larger number of white members.

Adjustments:

All signs with reference to race have been removed from all town and county properties. The County court's seating has been desegregated.

The Town of Williamston and the County of Martin have announced that employment conditions will be on a desegregated basis. All Town of Williamston and County of Martin tax listings are on a non-segregated basis.

The County has no Negro students enrolled in its white schools. The Board of Education of Martin County is considering applications from students for reassignment to different schools. The Williamston unit of the Industrial Education Center is desegregated.

The directors of the Martin County Hospital have announced that their facilities are no longer segregated and that employment practices will be without regard to race. A variety store and two department stores have each employed or upgraded a Negro as a salesclerk. Many Williamston merchants have announced a new practice of employing clerks without regard to race. Several lunch counters desegregated and then re-segregated when demonstrations were resumed in August, 1963. In one case, the booths were removed in order to avoid further question about the seating of Negroes.

During the entire time, there have been a limited number of instances in which Negroes have attended the white churches. At the usual Easter Sunrise Service a large number of local Negroes were in attendance. Ministers of both races participated in the services. This was accomplished by the local Ministerial Association, which desegregated during March, 1964. Desegregation of the Association required the inviting of the two local Negro ministers to join the Association.

After efforts to accomplish the desegregation of the local white private library met with failure, the governing body of the Town withdrew its financial support. The local private Negro library still receives this support.

WILMINGTON

Population: 44,013; 36.4 per.cent Negro

Mayor: O. O. Allsbrook—Office: Sealtest Foods, Southern Division, 2040 Oleander Drive; Home: 179 Colonial Drive; Telephone: Office: 762-6681; Home: 762-3821

Biracial Organization: Wilmington-New Hanover County Biracial Committee

Chairman: Reverend Hunley A. Elebash—Office: St. John's Episcopal Church, 831 Forest Hills Drive; Home: 911 Hawthorne Road; Telephone: Office: 762-7719; Home: 763-6682

Negro Action:

The NAACP and CORE have chapters in Wilmington. These organizations sponsored well-organized and orderly marches in June, 1963, by as many as 200 Negroes and sponsored picketing of retail stores, restaurants and theaters as well as sit-ins against discriminating restaurateurs.

In mid-June, 1963, at least 174 demonstrators were arrested for trespassing after they had entered a hotel and three restaurants and refused to leave when requested.

Municipal Reaction:

The Board of Commissioners of New Hanover County, together with the city of Wilmington, appointed a Biracial Committee to formulate and implement plans for the orderly handling of problems dealing with race relations.

The Wilmington-New Hanover County Biracial Committee was formed May 28, 1963, by the Mayor and the chairman of the County Commissioners. The Committee is composed of 18 white and eight Negro members. It has the following subcommittees: (1) Public accommodations, with three white and two Negro members; (2) Employment, with four white and no Negro members; (3) Education, with five white and no Negro members; (4) Public relations, with three white and one Negro member; (5) Youth, with two white and two Negro members; and (6) Health, Welfare and Safety, with three white and two Negro members.

The Committee meets on the first and third Mondays at 4:00 P.M.

The Committee was organized to create a better understanding between the races in the community, to serve as a means of communication between the people affected by racial problems, to seek peaceful and lawful solutions to community problems, to encourage businesses serving the public to adopt voluntarily a policy of open public accommodations, to encourage employment of qualified people without regard to race, and to encourage all citizens to eliminate discrimination based on race, creed, or color.

The Committee made a public statement on June 10, 1963, calling on all citizens in New Hanover County to give their fellow citizens fair and equitable treatment in all areas and levels of community life; and urging the city and county governments to encourage a policy of desegregation in all phases of public accommodations and to adopt a policy of nondiscrimination in job opportunities on the city-county level; and urging the city and county governments to urge private businesses to also adopt nondiscriminatory practices.

In compliance with the requests of the Wilmington-New Hanover County Biracial Committee, the County Board of Commissioners passed a resolution on June 7, 1963, expressing confidence in the Biracial Committee and resolving that the Board encourage a policy of desegregation in all phases of public accommodations and stating the Board's policy of not discriminating in job opportunities on the county level and urging all citizens of New Hanover County to adopt similar policies.

On January 22, 1964, the Biracial Committee issued a statement in which it said that it believed it had failed in most areas of its endeavor except that of increasing job opportunities and employment for the Negro because of its failure to keep the public informed of its activities with the result that the "community's problems" became the "committee's problems."

Adjustments:

For several years the Wilmington Police Department has been hiring without regard to race.

Several recently appointed boards and commissions have included members of both races.

Thirteen local merchants upgraded or hired 22 Negro salesclerks.

In addition to the City and County, six of Wilmington's largest industries have stated their policy of hiring without regard to race.

A cafeteria, restaurant, and all lunch counters agreed to desegregate in co-operation with a plan proposed by the Biracial Committee. The plan was worked out by the New Hanover Restaurant and Drive-in Association.

No hotel or motel operators have agreed to desegregate; municipal parks have completely desegregated; the hospitals in the area are privately owned; and no theaters have desegregated.

There are Negro students attending the predominantly white schools.

No business schools are open, although the Industrial Education Center is desegregated.

The public library is desegregated and has a biracial board of directors.

The Ministerial Association and the Merchants' Association have desegregated.

WILSON

Population: 28,753; 39.3 per cent Negro

Mayor: John D. Wilson—Office: 206 Gold Professional Building; Home: 101 Warren Street; Telephone: Office: 243-2034; Home: 243-2842

Biracial Organizations:
1. Citizens Committee
2. Good Neighbor Council

Chairmen:
1. Monroe G. Fulghum, Welfare Officer, Courthouse; Home: 1400 Branch Street; Telephone: Office: 243-6166; Home: 237-3983
2. Reverend Charles Hubbard—Office: First Methodist Church; Home: 1206 Branch Street; Telephone: Office: 243-3728; Home: 243-2046

Negro Action:
Negro civic clubs joined the Chamber of Commerce in urging the Mayor to establish a good neighbor council.

Municipal Reaction:
The Citizens Committee, which has been in existence for several years, made a survey of the various industries and business establishments in order to determine the number of Negroes they employed and in what capacities. With this information, the

Committee then approached the heads of these industries and the business establishments to prevail upon them to employ qualified Negroes in nontraditional jobs. A conference was also held with the Superintendent of the Employment Security Commission to urge improvement in that agency's policy of job referrals.

In June, 1963, the Mayor formed the local Good Neighbor Council upon the suggestion of Negro civic clubs and the Chamber of Commerce. The Council was composed of ten persons, six whites and four Negroes. It has since been expanded to 19 members. There was an initial agreement among the members of the Council that they would seek to deal with the total problem of human relations in the community and not just single aspects of it. The Council and the Citizens Committee co-ordinated their efforts to resolve unemployment among qualified Negroes in the community. The City Council endorsed the Mayor's appointment of a Good Neighbor Council.

The committees appeared before both the City and County Boards of Commissioners at one of their regular meetings and recommended to them the following:

1. That signs pertaining to race be removed from all city and county property.
2. That all citizens be given equal job opportunities in all county and city departments of government.
3. That the present practice of separate tax listings be abolished.

Adjustments:

Signs pertaining to race that were on drinking fountains, rest rooms, and in the courtrooms have been eliminated. The City has employed a Negro as a calculating machine operator-clerk in the Municipal Building and is seeking Negro women applicants for secretarial work. Segregated tax listing has been abolished.

The variety stores, department stores, and banks are receiving employment applications from Negroes and will hire without regard to race.

A Negro man has been employed by a department store as a window dresser and a bottling company has employed a Negro on one of its regular truck routes.

An industry which did not employ Negro women now employs more than 40 Negro women. Another industry is employing more Negroes and has upgraded two, including a Negro girl as a skilled worker.

The Darden High School is screening promising juniors and seniors who are not planning a college career to interest them in secretarial and clerical training, and to prepare them for trades in the Industrial Education Center.

The lunch counters were desegregated before the Good Neighbor Council was organized. The Good Neighbor Council is presently working with food handlers in an attempt to get a package agreement with the entire group.

The library and all city recreational facilities have been desegregated.

WINSTON-SALEM

Population: 111,135; 37.1 per cent Negro

Mayor: M. C. Benton, Jr.—Office: 106 City Hall; Home: 2901 Country Club Road; Telephone: Office: 722-4141; Home: 722-5883

Biracial Organizations:
1. Mayor's Good Will Committee
2. Good Neighbor Council
3. Urban League

Chairmen:
1. Tully Blair—Home: 1917 West First Street; Telephone: Home: 722-2523
2. and 3. Joe S. Rice—Office: 337 Witt Street, S. W.; Home: 325 Arbor Road, N.W.; Telephone: Office: 724-5544; Home: 722-8018

Negro Action:

Widespread lunch counter protests were experienced in 1960. They began in Winston-Salem on February 8 of that year. During the following three months, until May 10, there were intermittent protests and demonstrations and openings and closings of lunch counters.

Municipal Reaction:

Prior to 1946, occasional biracial committees were established in Winston-Salem. Their accomplishments were not significant because, as one community leader states: "They always 'bogged down' for the lack of a program and because too often the white people did the planning *for* the Negroes rather than *with* them."

The beginning of a definite program designed to improve race relations and the racial problems in Winston-Salem began in 1946. That year, after careful study the community council requested that a race relations survey of the community be made. The survey was a part of a nationwide project financed by the General Education Board of the Rockefeller Foundation. A biracial advisory committee of 40 members, later increased to 60, was established to sponsor the project and work with the various visiting consultants. The survey was made, being directed and staffed by the National Urban League and its research staff that had made community studies for many years. The findings and recommendations of the local survey were published in a six-volume report.

Soon after the community survey report was made the chairman of the local advisory committee stated: "Some recommendations can be carried out immediately, but others may take five, ten, or twenty years. . . . the reports give us a definite long-range program such as we have never had before. It is our belief that the responsible, intelligent people of both races, working together with patience and perseverance, not only can carry out the recommendations in the survey, but can make our community an outstanding one in this area of human relations."

One of the immediate and most significant results of the survey was the establishment in the City in 1949 of a biracial council with an executive secretary. Soon thereafter the council became a chapter of the Urban League. From the beginning the membership of this agency has been representative of the most responsible professional, religious, and business leadership of the community with an equal number of Negro and white members. This council has performed a number of important functions. It furnished the first really effective and continuing channel for communication between Negroes and whites in the City. It provided an orderly program by which interracial problems could be presented and discussed. It also served as a quiet, but effective method by which many interracial problems could be handled. It has not attempted to deal with all racial problems. The more critical and controversial problems have been studied and handled by specially appointed community biracial committees. The Urban League has placed its basic emphasis on education, housing, and job opportunities for Negroes. It has not served in Winston-Salem as a propagandistic organization.

Soon after the 1960 sit-in protests began in the City, the secretary of the Retail Merchants' Association, the City Manager, a Wake Forest professor, and the managers of the principal stores involved arranged for a study of the problem. Numerous conferences were held with both Negro and white citizens and with the store managers. In order to find out what the white people who traded in the variety stores thought about the situation, 842 adult white customers, while shopping in four variety stores, were interviewed during two successive days. Two methods of interviewing were used. One was a brief interview designed to elicit a spontaneous, off-the-cuff response. The other was an interview designed to probe more deeply and obtain more reasoned thoughts about the problem. Actually, the second employed the same approach and the same questions used in the brief interview, but it involved considerably more time. The results of the interviews, including the initial statement and the questions, were as follows:

The variety stores want to find a workable solution to the lunch counter problem. If they decide to open the lunch counters and serve everybody without regard to race:

	790 Brief Interviews		52 Depth Interviews	
	Number	Per Cent	Number	Per Cent
1. Do you think most people would accept that plan?				
Yes	253	32	36	69
Undecided or do not know	113	14	14	27
No	424	54	2	4
2. Do you ever eat at these stores?				
Yes	628	79	41	79
No	162	21	11	21
3. Would you accept the plan?				
Yes	368	47	38	73
Undecided or do not know	39	5	1	2
No	383	48	13	25
4. Would you continue to trade at these stores?				
Yes	700	89	49	94
Undecided or do not know	16	2	1	2
No	74	9	2	4

The Mayor appointed a Good Will Committee on April 1, 1960, composed of ten Negro men and ten white men. Subcommittees were appointed and they met numerous times with the merchants individually and as a group and with Negro protesters. The members of the subcommittees decided that it would be unwise and unfair to make any recommendation which the merchants could interpret as being imposed upon them. The Committee concluded that its function should be to discuss every possible facet of the problem with the merchants and then mutually reach an agreement as to what seemed to be the most intelligent, fair, and workable solution. Significantly, at one of the meetings with the merchants, the manager of one of the variety stores proposed that the eventual solution would be desegregation of the sit-down counters. However, there were further openings and closings of the lunch counters and demonstrations. Eventually, on May 23, 1960, the stores mutually agreed with the Committee to open their lunch counters on a desegregated basis. The effect of the decision was immediate desegregation.

Two months after the lunch counters were desegregated, all the managers reported that their general business was back to about normal. All agreed that they saw only improvement in the future. One manager said the only regret he had was that the decision was not made four months earlier. A manager of one of the larger variety stores, describing desegregated eating at his counters, said: "You would think it had been going on for fifty years."

Recognizing the national Negro movement and its potential for Winston-Salem, the Mayor appointed a permanent biracial committee early in May of 1963. This committee, known as the Mayor's Good Will Committee, was originally composed of nine white and nine Negro members. It now has a membership of 30. The first meeting of the Committee was held on May 22, 1963. The first action of the Committee was to draft a statement of purpose. In part, the statement reads as follows:

The fact that Winston-Salem is not now experiencing specific incidents of open discord in race relations, as has been the case in other cities and States, is not the result of chance, but of sincere efforts and co-operation in finding solutions to problems.

It is the belief of this Committee that a continuation of this approach will be effective in avoiding any open discord and in making further progress in areas related to the achievement of equal rights and opportunities for all citizens.

The Committee accepts as its ongoing objective the achievement in Winston-Salem of access to all public facilities for all citizens, regardless of race, creed, or color.

The Committee is organized into five subcommittees, each working in one of the following areas: hotels and motels, restaurants, theaters, education, and employment. Meetings of the main Committee were held every two weeks for the first three months in order that immediate attention could be given to the major problems involved. At present meetings are held monthly.

In the summer of 1963 the Mayor also appointed a Good Neighbor Council with Joe S. Rice, the president of the local chapter of the Urban League, as its chairman. The Winston-Salem chapter of the Urban League is the only League chapter in North Carolina. The Good Neighbor Council has never met due to the effective work of the Mayor's Good Will Committee in the areas of concern in which it had been anticipated that the Good Neighbor Council might operate.

During the period from 1946 to 1960, numerous and significant changes were made in customs involving interracial relations in the City—due to a favorable climate of public opinion and a realistic facing of conditions on the part of many people, businesses, industries, and government.

There occurred the desegregation of the following: the public schools (if only token), public libraries, city buses, ministers' conferences, and the public golf course. There was the removal of signs indicating separate rest rooms and drinking fountains in public buildings and the abandonment of separate seating arrangements at the Reynolds Auditorium, the Coliseum, the baseball park and community center. Some Negroes were employed as mail carriers, police officers, and members of the fire department. Concerts and lectures at both Salem College and Wake Forest College were open to the public and all people were seated on a desegregated basis. Also, each school invited and entertained integrated learned societies and other educational groups. Wake Forest competed with and entertained on its campus, desegregated debating and athletic teams.

From 1960 to 1963 many changes took place. Some of the largest industries desegregated both work in their plants and eating in their cafeterias. Several businesses and industries employed Negro engineers, draftsmen, secretarial and clerical workers, and others in positions above unskilled labor. Both Salem College and Wake Forest College desegregated. A sizable number of Negroes were employed as clerks in retail stores. Racial barriers to public recreation facilities, including swimming pools, were removed. The city-county school system began operating on the policy of permitting children to attend the school nearest their homes. All lunch counters desegregated.

Adjustments:

To date the permanent biracial committee has reported the following changes effected in 1963.

1. All major hotels and motels have lowered racial bars.

2. All the major eating establishments (about 50), except three cafeterias, have removed racial barriers.

3. All theaters, downtown as well as drive-ins, accept patrons without regard to race.

4. The Committee sent questionnaires to 18 industries and businesses regarding policies on employment of Negroes. All 18 responded and each stated they now employ Negroes. Each stated they now have some Negroes in positions above unskilled jobs. Also all, except one that reported some minor exceptions, state their Negro employees have the same rights and privileges of all employees. All the companies replied that they would be willing to meet with the subcommittee on employment to discuss the question of how employment opportunities for Negroes in Winston-Salem and Forsyth County may be improved. Employment is strongly emphasized because the Committee is of the opinion that it and education or training are among the most basic factors involved in the advancement of the Negro's position in American society.

Both the Bar Association and the Junior Bar Assiciation are desegregated. The new City-County Memorial Hospital will be completely desegregated when it opens in 1964.

Winston-Salem has been selected as the site for the North Carolina Performing Arts School. This foundation-supported school will be operated on a nondiscriminatory basis. The Governor's School for gifted high school students is also a non-segregated institution.

GUIDELINES FOR ESTABLISHING
A BIRACIAL COUNCIL*

A biracial council is primarily a community relations organization. Its aims are to encourage the active participation of every citizen in the community's economic, educational, and political life. It seeks to guarantee such right of participation. Its work largely consists of the governmental function of education. Its means of fulfilling its function is through persuasion.

A biracial council should be endowed with the most authority possible since it must work through persuasion. It should be appointed by the municipality's mayor or the chairman of the county commissioners and might arise through the authority of an ordinance creating it as a permanent part of the governmental structure. Additional recognition should be elicited from civic, professional, and religious organizations.

The mayor's leadership in establishing the biracial council as well as his timely recognition of its work will contribute significantly, if not essentially, to the atmosphere in which the council operates. The mayor's own attitude and expressions help to mold the community's disposition toward the council's work.

It is important that a biracial council have members who understand and appreciate its purpose, who are capable of persuading, and who have the stature and respect, through the indicia of the organization, required to be recognized and heard. It is important to have members who have a co-operative spirit, whatever their personal views. Most of these persons will be progressive minded. Individual cases may require the placement of militant parties on the council, but this action is not often desirable and usually proves unprofitable.

Membership should be as broad as possible. It should, therefore, consist of around 18 persons in a 50-50 Negro and white ratio. The group should include most of the following: A Negro and white teen-ager, housewife, teacher, minister, merchant, realtor, industrialist, laborer, and restaurateur. Member's tenure should be agreed upon before any appointments are made. This tenure should be approximately three years. It is desirable to have three classes of six with yearly staggered terms. Nominating groups should include the Chamber of Commerce, the Minis-

---

* By John Brooks.

terial Association, the Merchants' Association, the Board of Education, and the Negroes' community development organizations such as the NAACP, CORE, and the Southern Christian Leadership Conference. Neither the mayor nor the members of the governing board should serve on the committee, but they should be readily available to advise and consult with the committee.

Municipalities of 10,000 or more should have a full-time biracial council worker such as an executive secretary or administrator. Communities of less than 10,000 should seek the establishment of county-wide biracial councils. These councils also would be well advised to have a full-time administrator.

The council should elect its own chairman, vice-chairman, and secretary. It should meet at least monthly and should publish quarterly reports.

One of the first actions of the council should be to make a survey of the community's discrimination and segregation practices. A program to bring about adjustments in these practices should then be designed. Work to carry out the program should proceed as much as possible through established community organizations such as the Merchants' Association, the Board of Education, the Industrial Education Center, and the realty association.

Committees should be established on essential areas of concern. These might be organized in somewhat the following order: Agenda Committee; Committee on Information and Grievances; Committee on Accommodations with subcommittees on Housing, Public Facilities, Recreation, and on Hotels, Motels and Restaurants; and a Committee on Employment with subcommittees on Job Opportunity, Job Education, and Employer-employee Relations. Committee members and subcommittee chairmen should be members of the biracial council. Subcommittee members might be additional interested persons with special qualifications helpful to the work of the particular subcommittee.

The biracial council should consider the establishment of educational programs aimed at diminishing prejudices, training the non-skilled, educating the illiterate and encouraging the full economic, educational, and political participation of every citizen. A council should reflect upon the words of Thomas Jefferson in 1816: "If a nation expects to be ignorant and free, in a state of civilization, it expects what never was and never will be."

III

Municipal Declarations

The purpose of this book is to furnish guidelines from the experiences of certain North Carolina communities which may help other communities dealing with the problem of Negro discontent and the Negro petitions for first-class citizenship. We present 55 municipal reports of Negro action and the reaction of cities and towns in various parts of the State.

From some of the cities have come important declarations of attitude and purpose. These declarations emanate from areas in which the Negro population is large as well as from other state areas where the percentage of the Negro people is much less. It is the opinion of the Mayors' Co-operating Committee that some of these declarations should be published in this book and several of them follow.

Mayor Brookshire, of Charlotte, who has taken a lead in promoting racial justice in the State's largest city, is quoted herein. The position of the Mayor of Greensboro is also stated. An ordinance by the City Council of Greensboro creating its Commission of Human Relations is reproduced with a job description for an executive director for the Commission.

One article in this section of the book comes from the Mayor of Fayetteville, Wilbur Clark, and because of the interesting experiences in that city, where the presence of soldiers at Fort Bragg distorts the problem to some extent, this report seems worthy of special attention.

Another exhibit is a statesmanlike "Blueprint for Progress" prepared by a committee of six citizens in Rocky Mount, which lies in Edgecombe and Nash counties. This declaration is of such thoughtful character that it is reproduced in the belief that it can be of value throughout the State.

MAYORS' CO-OPERATING COMMITTEE REVIEWS THE MANUSCRIPT OF THIS BOOK IN MAYOR STANFORD BROOKSHIRE'S OFFICE. FROM *LEFT* TO *RIGHT*: BROOKSHIRE, *CHAIRMAN*. O. O. ALLSBROOK, DAVID SCHENCK, HARPER BEALL, JR., EARL W. ELLER, AND FLOYD MEHAN. ABSENT MEMBERS ARE M. C. BENTON, JR., WILBUR CLARK, LEVIN B. CULPEPPER, R. WENSE GRABAREK, WILLIAM B. HARRISON, AND JAMES W. REID.

Published also is a report to the government of New Bern written by W. C. Chadwick, Chairman of the City's Biracial Committee.

Various estimates have been made at national and local levels of the cost of segregation in dollars and cents. One estimate is that discrimination on account of race and color costs the nation some 30 billion dollars annually. That figure is more than half the enormous cost of the total program of the nation for self-defense and for defense of freedom throughout the world. While this economic consideration is not paramount in the Committee's thinking, it is recognized as of increasing importance to a modern society.

GUIDELINES IN COMMUNITY RELATIONS*

1. Recognition and acceptance of inevitability of changes in our long existing social and economic patterns are necessary. Negroes have made it abundantly clear that they are no longer willing to accept indignities and disadvantages of second-class citizenship.

2. Responsibility of each community is to seek and to find its own solutions.

3. Choice is clearly between accepting changes and using them constructively for community betterment or resisting changes with disastrous results.

4. Of the three measures thus far employed, (1) legal, (2) protest actions, and (3) biracial co-operation, the last has produced the best and perhaps the most lasting results in the preservation of racial harmony, progress, and prosperity.

5. Biracial councils carefully constructed of top leadership of both races to population ratio, in regular meetings, can (it has been proved) develop mutual understanding, promote good will and develop co-operation.

6. It is important to involve total community leadership—business, civic, and church.

---

* By Stanford R. Brookshire.

7. Initiative should originate with local government, which should remove all unconstitutional ordinances and offer employment to all citizens on merit basis, without favor or discrimination.

8. Social conscience, civic pride, and economic considerations can make proper climate for change.

9. Progress can be made only when prejudice gives way to reason, animosities to good will, apathy to action.

10. We must emphasize the importance of equating responsibility as a two-way street.

11. Emphasis on full utilization of human resources is essential. People are either an asset or a liability to their community.

12. Discrimination based on color is morally and legally wrong and economically unsound.

13. Constructive effort through removal of inequities and providing educational and economic opportunities without bias is a basic attack on poverty and crime.

14. There must be conversion of problems to opportunities to build better communities, a better nation, a better world.

A PIEDMONT NORTH CAROLINA MAYOR SPEAKS OUT

Although Greensboro led early in the admission of a number of Negro students to white schools, a period of disorderly Negro demonstrations ensued. Mayor David Schenck issued a statement which incorporated an appeal to the businessmen and other citizens of Greensboro to confront the issue of the Negro petitioners in a spirit of good will and helpfulness. This vigorous appeal follows:

The City of Greensboro has a proud tradition of progress toward the idea of equal treatment of all without regard to race, creed, or color. Our municipal facilities, the Coliseum, the golf course, the library, tennis courts, and playgrounds have been open to all for quite some time. Our City buses were desegregated quietly years ago. Employment of the Negro by the City has increased rapidly and we now employ persons on the basis of qualification and merit without regard to race. There are no laws on our books that refer to segregation or integration. This City was the first in the South whose retailers announced equality of employment in sales forces. This decision was reached quietly two years ago. The Greensboro Chamber of Commerce and the Greensboro Merchants' Association were among the first such organizations in this area to publicly advocate an equal treatment policy in all business establishments. Greensboro was the first city in this area to announce that agreement was possible with theaters for change in their policy for service to all persons without regard to race. Many of the finest restaurants of the City as well as the downtown lunch counters are open to all. Our largest motels have served all races for quite some time. Unfortunately, and to the detriment of all citizens regardless of race, recent efforts to negotiate the matter of equal service in business establishments has been met by increased turmoil and demonstrations in our downtown area. Good faith has been shown by those who have sought to mediate these issues as evidenced by the accomplishments already named. Now, as an act of good faith on the part of the demonstrator, let mass demonstrations and deliberate attempts at arrest cease. We intend to uphold the law in this City and to preserve the peace of the community.

Now, to those establishments whose policy of segregated services are being protested, let me say this: We recognize the right under law of the property owner or business proprietor to use his property and conduct his business in any fashion he chooses so long as public safety and morals are not violated. But how far must your city government and your fellow businessmen go to protest that right? Must the business of downtown Greensboro be disrupted; must the City be brought to a point of serious explosion; must extra policemen, sheriffs, highway patrolmen, and even the National Guard, be kept on alert to enforce your private business decision?

I say to you who own and operate places of public accommodations in the City, the hotels, motels, and restaurants, that now is the time to throw aside the shackles of past custom. Selection of customers purely by race is outdated, morally unjust, and not in keeping with either democratic or Christian philosophy.

The rights of property will, I hope, remain inviolate; but the right of a business operator, by stubborn refusal to meet change, to cause his entire City to suffer the grave consequences of his own private decision, is questionable. As Mayor of Greensboro, therefore, I now call on all places of public accommodations in the City, specifically the restaurants, theaters and hotels and motels to immediately cease selection of customers purely on the basis of race, and to open their doors to desirable customers of any race, color or creed.

To accomplish this goal, I am requesting owners or managers of these establishments in Greensboro to attend the meeting on Thursday of next week to make their decision known. This meeting is set for Thursday, to give each business the opportunity to take this request to its top management. In many cases ownership is away from our City.

To give the community an opportunity to act on this matter, I request that demonstrations be halted, for only in an atmosphere free from threat and ultimatum can any progress be made.

The time to act, my fellow citizens, is now. This City cannot long endure the impasse of inaction, nor can it expect to progress half climbing to the future, and half shackled by outdated prejudices of the past. The citizens of this City both white and Negro are *all citizens* and must be accorded equal rights and opportunities. By the same token all must share the responsibility for maintaining the peace of the community. All of both races must share the responsibility of making our City one of opportunity, one of understanding, one in which we are proud to live. Our economy, our job opportunities, our work, and our recreation depend on the co-operation and sharing of responsibility for all the people. When our image in the nation is damaged, for whatever reason, our citizens of all races, suffer. Let us now move to restore to Greensboro the progressive spirit which is rightly ours.

This outspeaking of Mayor Schenck attracted wide attention and on June 8, 1963, the day after it was uttered, the President, John F. Kennedy, attending a conference of mayors in Honolulu, referred to it as follows:

The improvement of race relations and the fulfillment of human rights are a continuing problem and continuing challenge. I do not propose to limit our mutual concern to one brief address. I hope to meet with many of you in the White House in the near future. I must say I was impressed by the willingness of so many mayors to move ahead in this area. Yesterday I read where Mayor David Schenck of Greensboro, it appears—and this is a story in *The New York Times*— appealed to all of the businessmen of the community in North Carolina and said, "I say to you who own and operate places of public accommodation in the City, the hotels, motels, and restaurants, that now is the time to throw aside the shackles of past custom. Selection of customers purely by race is outdated, morally unjust, and not in keeping with either democratic or Christian philosophy." So spoke the Mayor in North Carolina, and I think it is good advice for all of us.

AN ORDINANCE AMENDING THE GREENSBORO CODE OF ORDINANCES WITH RESPECT TO ADMINISTRATION

BE IT ORDAINED BY THE CITY COUNCIL OF THE CITY OF GREENSBORO:

Section 1. That Chapter 2 of the Greensboro Code of Ordinances is amended by adding a new article at the end of said chapter as follows:

ARTICLE XV.   COMMISSION ON HUMAN RELATIONS

Section 2-252.   Creation and duties

There is hereby created a commission to be known as the Commission on Human Relations. The duties of the commission shall be as follows:

(a) To study problems of discrimination in any or all fields of human relationship and encourage fair treatment, and mutual understanding among all racial and ethnic groups in the city; and

(b) To anticipate and discover those practices and customs most likely to create animosity and unrest among racial and ethnic groups and by consultation seek a solution as these problems arise or are anticipated; and

(c) To hold such meetings as the commission may deem necessary or proper to assist in carrying out its functions; and

(d) To make recommendations to the City Council of the City of Greensboro for action it deems necessary to the furtherance of harmony among racial and ethnic groups in the city; and

(e) To appoint, at its discretion, subcommittees to concern themselves with specific human relation problems. These subcommittees may be composed of citizens who are not members of the commission; except that the chairman of each subcommittee must be a bona fide member of the commission; and

(f) To perform such other duties as may be assigned it from time to time by the City Council.

Section 2-253.   Membership and appointment

The commission shall be composed of ten (10) members, all bona fide adult residents of Greensboro, who shall be appointed by the City Council for terms to expire on the 15th day of August. The time herein fixed for appointment is directory and not mandatory.

Section 2-254.   Terms of office; vacancies

The terms of office of the members of the commission shall be one (1) year. Appointments shall expire simultaneously at the termination of a regular tenure. Members shall hold office until their successors are appointed and qualified. Any vacancy resulting from a cause other than expiration of term shall be filled only for the unexpired portion of the term. Members shall not succeed themselves after serving a third full term without an intervening period of one year, and appointment for the unexpired portion of a year shall be considered as appointment for a full year.

NEGRO POTENTIAL VOTERS REGISTERED, 1960.

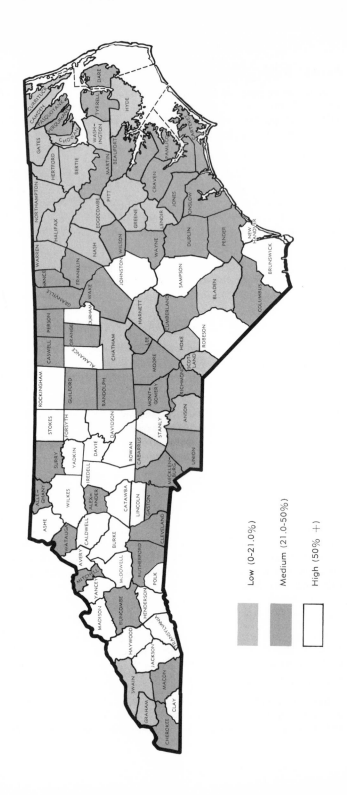

Low (0–21.0%)

Medium (21.0–50%)

High (50% +)

Section 2-255. Removal

A member may be removed by the council for cause. If a member shall miss all of the meetings held during any period of sixty (60) days without excuse granted by the commission, this may be considered as cause for removal.

Section 2-256. Officers

The commission shall elect a chairman from its members and shall elect a secretary, each of whom shall serve for such time as may be fixed by the commission. The secretary may be either a member of the commission or an employee of the city. Should the chairman or secretary be absent at any meeting, the commission shall elect a temporary chairman or secretary to serve at the meeting.

Section 2-257. Expenditures and compensation

The commission shall make no expenditure or contract any indebtedness for which the city shall be liable without the approval of the council. Members of the commission shall serve without compensation.

Section 2-258. Regular meetings

The commission shall hold meetings regularly at least once each month unless there is not sufficient business to warrant a meeting, but not more than sixty (60) days shall expire without a regular or special meeting of the commission. Regular meetings shall be held on such days and at such hours as may be fixed by the rule of the commission.

Section 2-259. Special meetings

Special meetings of the commission may be called by the chairman by notice given in writing and delivered personally to each member or left at his residence not less than twenty-four (24) hours prior to the time fixed for the meeting. If all members of the commission are present at the special meeting, however, then the requirement as to prior written notice shall be deemed to be waived. It shall not be necessary to state in the notice of a special meeting the nature of the business to be transacted at such meeting, and any business may be transacted at any special meeting that might be transacted at a regular meeting.

Section 2-260. Place of meetings; all meetings public

All regular and special meetings of the commission shall be held in the city hall or in the annex, except when adjourned to another place. All such meetings shall be open to the public.

Section 2-261. Quorum and vote required for recommendations

Six (6) members of the commission shall constitute a quorum, but the concurrence of at least six (6) members shall be required before any recommendation is made on any matter considered.

Section 2-262. Rules of procedure

The commission shall adopt such rules and regulations as may be necessary for the proper discharge of its duties, which shall be filed with the city clerk.

Section 2-263. Report to council

The commission shall submit from time to time, but not less than once annually, a report of its activities and recommendations to the council which shall be filed with the city clerk and made a part of the official minutes of the city council.

PERMANENT HUMAN RELATIONS MACHINERY

Several North Carolina cities have opened offices where the work of biracial organizations function. There is a growing sense of the need of full-time workers in this field of service. Greensboro has decided to employ an executive director to work under the direction of the city government and the Commission on Human Relations, and the following indicates the action at Greensboro, defining the job, indicating what is expected of the employee, and inviting applications for the job:

DEFINITION

This is a highly specialized position involving independent performance on a wide variety of human problems and relationships. Work of this kind is distinguished by responsibility which relieves the city manager, the mayor and the Commission on Human Relations from detailed handling of problems of a complex social nature. This is normally handled without significant guidance or review. This function also is a full-time activity in carrying through on programs initiated by the Commission on Human Relations. Because of the nature of intergroup and interracial problems and the need to solve these problems by counseling and guidance, no formalized set of rules or guidelines can be established. The distinct image of our city is reflected in every action taken by this office. Dynamic and effective communications must be maintained between the business community and the city government, between the churches and social organizations and the city government, among other government bodies and our city government, and among all of these in an unending co-mixture.

All actions of this office must be oriented toward minimizing conflict and tension among ethnic groups and directed toward securing equal rights for all citizens of the community.

TYPICAL DUTIES

1. Serve as permanent full-time city employee, working under the broad general direction of the city manager, and the Commission on Human Relations.

2. Daily contact with public establishments, church, and social groups on problems of human relations.

3. Prepare talks for delivery to civic and social groups for presentation by either the director or the chairman of the Commission.

4. Conduct research and maintain source files in the area of human relations, with emphasis on what other communities are doing, particularly looking at not only the successful approaches, but those that have been ineffective.

5. Organize and prepare workshop material for intergroup training programs.

6. Organize and plan workshops for business and social groups, leading toward harmony among the races.

7. Act as secretary of the grievance committee for the Commission on racial and other ethnic problems.

8. Investigate all complaints and prepare factual reports for the grievance committee.

9. Recommend action areas to the Commission.

10. Prepare agendas for commission meetings, including the preparation of background material for each item of the agenda.

11. Work with educational groups in preparing programs for improving adult education and minimizing school drop-outs.

12. Prepare all press releases for the City and the Commission on racial and ethnic problems.

13. Maintain working relationships with all voluntary groups in the city working on human relations problems.

14. Maintain close liaison with all government agencies, City, State and Federal, regarding human relations problems.

15. Prepare reports for the Commission and the council on human relations problems and on the commission's activities.

MINIMUM QUALIFICATIONS

1. Extensive knowledge of psychological and social forces involved in the integration of minority groups into the economy and culture of the community.

2. Thorough knowledge of the economic forces at work in the community that affect the welfare of minority groups.

3. Thorough knowledge of community resources that can be utilized to further the objective of the City Council and the Commission.

4. Thorough knowledge of all civil rights legislation affecting the community.

5. Ability to maintain objective standards in the evaluation and handling of cases requiring official action.

6. Ability to work with people.

7. Ability to collect and analyze social and economic data and to prepare reports.

8. Ability to speak and write effectively.

EXPERIENCE

1. A minimum of four years as a full-time community relations worker, either with a private or business organization.

2. Responsibility should have been diversified, including community education, community organization, working with policy makers as well as functional committees, program planning.

3. Specialization in such fields as housing, fair employment programs, etc., while helpful is not as important as generalized ability such as a community relations consultant.

EDUCATION

1. College degree, preferably in one of the social sciences, with graduate work in such fields as sociology, community organizing, group dynamics, adult education, psychology or political science.

PERSONAL CHARACTERISTICS

1. Should possess a high degree of personal integrity and character, with an outstanding record of honesty.

2. Should be a forceful and persuasive speaker and writer.

AN EASTERN CITY'S REPORT*

To The Honorable Mayor, Members of the Board of Aldermen, and City Manager of the City of New Bern:

The Biracial Committee which was appointed by the Mayor on behalf of the city government has been organized for five or six weeks and has studied the problem with which our City is faced to a very considerable degree, and your Committee desires to make this report to you at this time. I have been asked to present the report to you as chairman of the Committee.

We have found that a good many of our business establishments have for some time been undertaking to provide our Negro citizens with job opportunities when these jobs were available, and when qualified people could be found to fill them. We have also found that in a few hardship cases which had affected merchants to a large extent the Committee has been able to make proper contacts between the businessmen and the Negro population, and the problem involved has been solved to the extent that those individual establishments do not now face any trouble.

We have found in looking over the activities in other cities in the nation and State that in places where the people are willing to co-operate, a feeling of good will has been established and that in those places there has been no strife and there have been no incidents which caused friction or dissension in the community in which the proper attitudes were accepted by both races.

We have also found that in some places where violence was brought about because of the unwillingness of either group to be reasonable, there has been considerable dissension and a great deal of trouble, and in some cases deaths, as well as a good many court cases. We have some very good illustrations of which we could go into detail with this city administration if you should desire, but we are of the opinion that all of you are familiar with these; however, we will name two or three instances. In the State of Maryland there has been considerable confusion, violence, and mob action on the part of both races in the City of Cambridge; but in the City of Salisbury, Maryland, the people decided they would go about solving the problem in a reasonable and co-operative way, and they have in the City of Salisbury, Maryland, a peaceful, happy citizenship among all the races and no violence at all has taken place in the City. Another illustration is Little Rock, Arkansas, which gave this nation a very unfavorable picture in the minds of nations across the world, and in doing so, much violence, many heartaches, and much trouble was created there so that the national government became involved in that dispute. We have found that as a result of all this, the thing which was brought about by force is what could have been brought about by a co-operative spirit; now we understand that Little Rock,

* By W. C. Chadwick, Chairman of the Biracial Committee.

GOVERNOR TERRY SANFORD GREETS PARTICIPANTS AT THE JULY 3, 1963, CONFERENCE TO DISCUSS THE NEGRO PROTEST MOVEMENT.

Arkansas, is desegregated and the people are beginning after a long period of trouble to get back in their ordinary ways of life. This same thing happened in Birmingham, Alabama.

To bring the situation closer home, several of our cities in North Carolina, such as Charlotte, Asheville, High Point, Raleigh, and even closer, Jacksonville, have avoided a lot of dissension by the business people, the community, and the community leaders of both races acknowledging the fact that they could no longer go along with the policies which had been practiced for over one hundred years. These places which I have just mentioned, of their own accord, under proper leadership, did desegregate and they have had a comparatively quiet and peaceful development of their communities.

Your Biracial Committee has had many meetings with individuals, business concerns, and other interested people in which we have discussed with these business concerns and individuals the necessity for an attitude of co-operation in order to avoid in our community a reversal which could affect us for many years. In this connection your Committee has found that all of our people realize that the idea of desegregation of public accommodations facilities and recreational facilities must come about. We have also found that all of these people with whom we have had contact realize that it can be done, and an attitude of amity will continue to prevail in our community if it is done voluntarily rather than by violence and force.

We have had the Governor of North Carolina's special representative, the Honorable Capus Waynick, here on two different occasions to talk to the groups to which we have requested him to talk, and he has explained in detail what happens in a community which decides to be fair and just in the matter as opposed to one which takes the other position and has to be eventually forced—either by law or demonstrations or boycotts, or all three. One of General Waynick's statements is, "This is the greatest drama of the century." He has also said in another statement, which we quote, that the problem can be solved if the local community desires it solved, and he termed it in this way: "Do you want to be a part of the problem or a part of the cure?"

It is your Committee's candid opinion that all of us should become a part of the cure, which means the laying of plans for good will and community development. Your Committee is of the opinion that if our community acts now and promptly, in a positive way, to bring about desegregation of our public accommodations and other businesses, that we will establish in the minds of the people of our State a community which our State and nation can be proud of, and which will go down in history as a great forward step.

Over a period of years some of us who are older have become aware of the fact that many of our cities in the State have developed and attained progress because of far-sighted vision on the part of their community leaders. Many of these cities to which we refer a few years ago were smaller than our community, but today because of the vision and leadership of the community and the unselfish attitudes displayed in those communities, those cities have grown by leaps and bounds, and it is our opinion that our City can grow and develop into a most desirable place not only for our own people to live, but also become attractive to people from other places to come to our City and develop their businesses. The fact of the matter is actually: Is our City ready to assume its rightful position in our

GENERAL CAPUS M. WAYNICK, CONSULTANT TO THE GOVERNOR ON RACE RELATIONS, TALKS WITH A CONFERENCE PARTICIPANT ABOUT PLANS FOR RACIAL CO-OPERATION.

PETITION FOR DESEGREGATION

State by solving the immediate, urgent problem of desegregation and setting an example for others to follow, or are we going to take the other position and wait until we are forced to do so by unpleasant methods?

Your Committee unanimously recommends to the city administration and to the community that we step forward with one accord and solve the problem, and solve not only this problem but all problems facing us, and lay the groundwork for development, for happiness, for prosperity, which could be done if we assume the proper attitude. To the Biracial Committee, this seems the only fair and logical approach which can be made for our future happiness and welfare.

Your Committee fully realizes the importance and urgency of the situation. We realize it is a break from precedents. We realize it is not an easy thing to do. However, the temper of the nation now says, "Go ahead." We, the citizens of New Bern, are a part of a great State, a great nation, and we cannot long resist a movement which is brought about by a sympathetic nation to remedy a wrong which has existed so long.

Since the above circumstances have been developed by your Committee and presented to our various business groups—especially the public accommodations facilities, they have advised this Committee that it is their opinion that the city administration should go on record in a public statement, acknowledging the findings of this Committee as set forth above, and that the city administration should publish a statement requesting all of our people to co-operate and bring about a situation of harmony, good will, and a happy community.

FAYETTEVILLE'S CITY SURVEY—1963*

I. GOVERNMENTAL SECTORS OF COMMUNITY LIFE

A. FEDERAL OFFICES: The Veterans Administration Hospital and the United States Post Office are fully integrated in services, facilities, and employment policies. All jobs come under Civil Service.

B. CITY OF FAYETTEVILLE:

1. Voting: All registered citizens may vote.

2. Commissions and Boards: The City Board of Adjustment, and the Recreation and Parks Advisory Commission each have a Negro member.

The Public Works Commission employs a Negro "white-collar" worker, and trains and employs Negro foremen.

3. Many city facilities, including swimming pools and public libraries, are now integrated.

---

* By the Mayor's Biracial Committee.

4. Employment by the City Council and/or City Manager is open to all on the basis of merit. Actual employment, in a clerical position, has been offered to a Negro.

Positions in the Police Department and in the Fire Department are open on a basis of examination by the Civil Service Commission.

5. Schools: Some progress in desegregation of City Schools is being made—31 of 35 applications from Negroes for admission to white schools in the fall of 1963 have been accepted.

C. CUMBERLAND COUNTY:

1. Voting: All registered citizens may vote.

2. Commission and Boards: No Negro members.

3. Employment: There are two types of employment: elective and appointive. The sheriff is an elected official. In 1957 the County voted, by referendum, to permit the sheriff to employ and dismiss his subordinates. Following this, the county commissioners gave that same power to every county department head.

The Sheriff's office employs 42 people, of whom three are Negroes —two deputies and one employee in the county jail.

The Board of Health operates under the State Merit System in the selection of employment; it presently has four Negroes as employees—two nurses, one assistant, one janitor—out of a total of 30 employees.

The Welfare Department operates under the State Merit System. Of a total of 49 employees, four are Negroes—two caseworkers, one homemaker, one janitor.

The offices of the Clerk of Superior Court, Register of Deeds, Tax Collector, Tax Supervisor, Veteran's Service Office, Clerk of Recorders' Court, and County Accountant and Treasurer, have no formal barriers to employment of Negroes, but the pattern is one of total white employment.

4. Cape Fear Valley Hospital is integrated in services, facilities, employment, and membership of the trustees. Of a total of 365 employees, 75 are currently Negroes; there are three Negro physicians on the staff. The only facility not totally desegregated is the cafeteria, which serves from a single line, but has separate small dining rooms for white and for colored employees because it does not have a large enough one to seat all of them.

5. County Guidance Center offers its services to all. Its Advisory Council is integrated. Employment is on the basis of qualifications, under the Merit System.

6. ABC Board states it has no formal policy which bars employment to Negroes.

D. STATE OF NORTH CAROLINA:

1. Employment Security Commission offers service to all persons. It operates under the recently announced policy by Governor

Sanford which ended bias in State employment. Negroes serve on the staff in many positions.

2. The Fayetteville Technical Institute has had a policy of integration since it opened. Applications and records do not list race, but it is estimated there are between 25 and 30 Negro students now. Employment is open to all qualified persons.

II. PRIVATE ENTERPRISE

A. MANUFACTURING: Burlington Mills, Cape Fear Feed Products, Fasco, Inc., and Planters Chemical Corporation have integrated employees, who include a substantial number of Negroes, working side by side with white workers.

B. VARIETY AND DEPARTMENT STORES: Ten downtown variety and department stores were to start a policy of hiring persons on the basis of merit alone, without regard to race, creed, or color, on or before September 2, 1963. They are: The Capitol Department Store, Belk-Hensdale Company Department Store, Fleishman's Big Store, J. C. Penney Company, Sears, Roebuck and Company, Raylass Department Store, Eagle Stores Company, Inc., S. H. Kress and Company, McCroy's, and F. W. Woolworth and Company. In addition, Roses' 5-10-25¢ Store in Eutaw is now accepting applications on the basis of merit.

C. RESTAURANTS: In addition to the five downtown lunch counters that were desegregated before 1963, a total of 20 restaurants, including 11 large ones, are currently desegregated; they are as follows:

A. and W. Root Beer Drive-In, Bragg Boulevard	Howard Johnson's Restaurant
	Kleha's Charcoal Steakhouse
A. and W. Root Beer Drive-In, Raeford Road	LaFayette Lanes Restaurant
	Morris Cohen Delicatessen
Dunkin' Donuts Restaurant	Prince Charles Hotel Dining Room
Green Lantern Restaurant	Reaves Walgreen Drugs,
Hardee's Drive-In,	Eutaw Shopping Center
Bragg Boulevard	Reaves Rexall Drugs, Tallywood
Hardee's Drive-In, Raeford Road	Richman's Steakhouse
Hialeah Restaurant	Roses' 5-10-25¢ Store, Eutaw
Holiday Inn Restaurant	Strieb's
Horne's Restaurant	Tropical Restaurant

D. HOTELS AND MOTELS: Nine major hotels and motels are now open to travelers of all races; they are as follows:

Ambassador Motel	Horne's Motor Lodge
Bel Aire Motel	Howard Johnson's Motor Lodge
Coachman's Lodge	LaFayette Hotel
Driftwood Motor Lodge	Prince Charles Hotel
Holiday Inn	

E. AMUSEMENTS: The drive-in theaters in the community have been desegregated for some months. B. and B. Bowling Lanes, La-Fayette Lanes, Putt-Putt Golf—Bragg Boulevard, and Realistic Ranges are open to all people. Other indoor amusements have begun a program of desegregation.

F. NEGRO BUSINESSES: A check of 15 Negro business concerns, such as restaurants, beauty parlors, barbershops, filling stations, funeral homes, and sign companies, revealed that white people seldom apply to a Negro business for employment. All concerns checked stated that they would not refuse a person employment because of his race. Two, a filling station and a sign painter, have employed whites.

G. PRIVATE UTILITIES: Private utilities have instituted a program designed to bring about more employment opportunities for Negroes and to upgrade present Negro employees in the immediate future.

All of these businesses have opened their doors in a spirit of doing what is right for the community. As operators of private businesses they retain the right to refuse undesirable customers of any race.

III. BUSINESS, HEALTH AND WELFARE, CULTURAL, AND PROFESSIONAL ORGANIZATIONS AND AGENCIES

A. BUSINESS ASSOCIATIONS: The Chamber of Commerce, Downtown Fayetteville Association, and Cape Fear Industries are integrated both as to membership and as to attendance at meetings.

B. HEALTH AND WELFARE AGENCIES:

1. The United Services Fund and its member agencies are, with two exceptions, integrated: The American National Red Cross, Salvation Army, Air Force Aid Society, USO, USO Travelers Aid, Fuller School for Exceptional Children, Girl Scouts, Boy Scouts, Cumberland County Better Health Foundation, Cumberland County Mental Health Association. These agencies offer services and facilities to all; all hold open public meetings, and all but two have Negroes on their Boards—those two have no policies against it. Those that employ professional workers open employment on the basis of merit. The two non-integrated agencies are the YMCA and the Girls' Residence.

2. Chapters of volunteer state and national associations in the county surveyed are: Cumberland County Association for the Blind, Cumberland County Unit of the American Cancer Association, Cumberland County Chapter of the National Foundation, Cumberland County Heart Association, Cumberland County Society for Crippled Children, and Cumberland County Tuberculosis Association. All offer their services and facilities without regard to race. The four that have meetings open them to the public. Most of them have colored people on their boards.

3. Cultural Organizations: The Fayetteville Chapter of the North Carolina Symphony Society has no policy about attendance

at concerts. The Civic Music Society restricts membership to white people.

4. Professional Organizations: The Fayetteville United Ministerial Fellowship is integrated.

District Number 14 of the North Carolina State Nurses Association, which comprises three counties, is open to professional nurses regardless of color.

The Cumberland County Medical Society is segregated. The North Carolina State Medical Society's scientific meetings are open to Negro doctors.

The Cumberland County Dental Society is segregated. The North Carolina State Dental Society does not open any meetings to Negro dentists.

The Cumberland County Bar Association is segregated. The seminars of the State Bar Association are open to Negro attorneys.

The local units of the North Carolina Education Association are segregated.

FUTURE PLANS

The Biracial Committee and the entire community have reason to be grateful to all the business establishments, the NAACP Negotiating Committee, the individuals and organizations that have voluntarily assisted not only in the survey, but also in the establishment of a better atmosphere in the community, and in the advancement of fair treatment for all citizens.

On the basis of our findings to date and our future plans, we feel the demonstrations are no longer necessary or helpful. The Mayor's Biracial Committee has reported this feeling to the NAACP Negotiating Committee.

The Biracial Committee has already begun work on the second phase of its responsibilities, and plans to work or continue work on the objectives it has outlined for itself, such as:

1. Explain to and discuss with any interested citizens or group of citizens the survey and the work of the Biracial Committee.

2. Ask the City Council and the County Board of Commiss'oners to appoint "Good Neighbor Councils" in accordance with the request of the Governor.

3. Continue to work with restaurant owners who have not already opened their doors to all citizens, to persuade them to do so.

4. Continue to work with motels that have not yet desegregated.

5. Arrange a meeting with officers of banks and savings and loan associations to ask them to adopt fair employment policies for Negroes.

6. Approach small retail stores to ask them to make employment available to all on the basis of merit.

7. Approach grocery stores to ask them to make employment available to all on the basis of merit.

8. Approach additional industries and manufacturers to ask them to make employment opportunities available to all.

9. Approach labor unions about integrating their membership.

10. Request health and welfare associations and professional organizations to consider opening their membership to all.

11. Continue to hear complaints from any citizens about unfair treatment and to investigate them and make recommendations when possible and desirable.

12. Study with Negro leaders the opportunities to train and qualify more Negroes for job opportunities.

13. Study with Negro leaders ways to improve living conditions, family budgeting, etc., to study school drop-outs and other factors in their communities.

On the basis of this survey and program of future plans, the Mayor's Biracial Committee asks the co-operation of the entire community, both white and Negro citizens. We believe that only by working together to further better race relations, can we make this a better community for all its citizens.

MAYOR'S RESPONSE

Speaking for myself * and for the City Council, I am honored and pleased to receive this report.

The real credit for what has been achieved here belongs to all the people of Fayetteville, and I commend and thank the vast majority of the citizens of our City, who, by their tolerant understanding, deep concern, and steady support, have made this progress possible.

There are those, however, who merit special commendation. I would like, especially, to express appreciation to J. W. Pate, Jr., as Chairman, and all members of the Mayor's Biracial Committee for the constructive work they have done in behalf of the City. They have given unselfishly, even courageously, of their time and effort to resolve this difficult problem. I intend to ask this Committee to continue its labor in furtherance of efforts to bring about more opportunity, prosperity, and good will to all our people. The contribution that these citizens have made, and will continue to make to this community, is deserving of the highest praise.

* Statement by Mayor Wilbur Clark on July 19, 1963.

Equally, I want to express my appreciation for the responsible and patient work accomplished by the negotiating committee, representing our Negro citizens.

Together these Committees have served all of us well and honorably. They have acted in good faith and their contribution to progress has been significant.

Also, I wish to thank the news media of our City and their representatives who, as they wrestled with the responsibility of fair reporting, have shown up our community only in the light of actual conditions in the discharge of their trust and obligation to the public. All of these people must continue to assume their share in all honesty of purpose and duty in a manner which will reflect honor and credit unto themselves.

I feel very strongly that this now is a time in which the people of Fayetteville can find a real cause for pride in themselves and in their community.

The events of recent months have placed a great responsibility on all of us. White and Negro citizens alike have been challenged as never before to place the welfare of their community ahead of personal considerations. We have been compelled to place reason above emotion, common interests and co-operation above conflict. It has been a difficult time, but the wonderful spirit of this community has prevailed. The people of Fayetteville have shown that they know the meaning of responsible citizenship.

I do not say that we have totally solved this problem, as matters of concern that have been hundreds of years developing cannot be completely wiped away in a few months, or even a few years. To a large degree, these are intangible things which only time and patient understanding can erase.

The important thing, and justification for our pride today, is the fact that we have, as a community, recognized certain injustices incompatible in a free society. Furthermore, we have taken positive steps to insure privileges of American citizenship for all of our people, and to gain for this community the advantages that accrue from a united and purposeful citizenry.

It will be extremely difficult for future generations to fully appreciate what this generation has achieved in the field of human relations. They should, nevertheless, derive untold benefits from these achievements. They will be indebted to this generation and I am hopeful that they will pay that debt by assuming proper responsibility and attitudes as they assume advantages in the new opportunities that we have unleashed through resolute and realistic action.

This report, with the actions already taken which it relates and the actions to be taken which it foretells, marks a milestone in the improvement of relations among all of our people. We cannot move forward in any area unless we are united and willing to resolve our differences and work together to exploit our great potential; and, by working together, in the spirit of this report, we can, with real meaning, make Fayetteville the City of History and Progress.

*"A BLUEPRINT FOR PROGRESS"**

Throughout the history of the City of Rocky Mount the Negro and white races have lived and worked together in peace and harmony. In such an atmosphere of good will we have all grown and prospered. This relationship is not by accident, but is born out of a deliberate effort to develop mutual respect for the rights and needs of others. To foster and promote this development there was organized in our City about ten years ago a Biracial Committee composed of a small group of its citizens. This Committee served a useful purpose as a means of communication on racial problems when they arose and thereby made a great contribution to our City. With the development of racial tensions throughout our State and nation in recent months the Mayor of our City, in conformity with a policy recommended by the Governor of our State, appointed an advisory committee known as the Mayor's Good Neighbor Committee. This Committee is composed of 24 citizens of our City representing both races equally, and every segment of our economic, social, religious, and cultural life. The members of the Biracial Committee were included in the membership of the new Committee. The purposes of the new Committee, as stated by the Mayor, are as follows:

1. To promote peaceful relations between the races.

2. To work to correct overt injustices whenever and wherever it seems prudently possible.

3. To exert its full power to prevent racial trouble in Rocky Mount, especially the use of force, violence, and coercion by any group, at anytime for any purpose.

4. To act as the medium of communications between the two races in the event of trouble and attempt to resolve the problem at hand.

5. To help create an atmosphere of fairness and understanding in the fields of employment and job development and urge employers to give equal job opportunities and pay to Negroes where it will not seriously jeopardize their businesses.

6. To give guidance and help to Negroes so they may share equally the responsibilities and rewards of full citizenship.

7. To encourage and try to motivate all of our people, especially our youth, in utilizing the educational opportunities available to them today and to seek out sound career guidance and job opportunities.

---

* By the Mayor's Good Neighbor Committee, City of Rocky Mount.

A BIRACIAL FRIENDSHIP CIRCLE SINGS FREEDOM SONGS.

8. To work to develop a public opinion intelligently informed on interracial conditions and their serious implications for the community at large.

The Good Neighbor Committee immediately set out to perform the task assigned to it by the Mayor and very quickly accomplished some very concrete results. Working through special or subcommittees, and in some cases as individuals, the Committee very quickly got several uptown stores, financial institutions, and business firms who had previously employed only white personnel, to employ Negroes to fill positions of responsibility and dignity. By the same procedure, the Committee negotiated with public accommodation establishments to open their services to all without regard for race. During the same period, the Committee and other responsible citizens in our City collaborated with manufacturing establishments and plants in the employment of additional Negroes and assisted in the placement of qualified Negroes on the payroll of these plants.

Paralleling this effort, the Rocky Mount City Government placed additional qualified Negroes on its payrolls. Several Negro representatives have been appointed to official City Committees and Boards, including our City School Board, Library Board, Public Housing Authority, City Board of Health, Zoning Adjustment Board, and Boxing Commission.

During the same period the Rocky Mount School Board, without controversy, assigned 21 Negro children to schools previously attended only by white children, for the first time in the history of our City. This transition has been accepted without trouble or disruption of our school program.

The Good Neighbor Committee presented its proposed program to the Board of Directors of the Rocky Mount Chamber of Commerce and the Board of Directors of the Rocky Mount Merchants' Association, and it was approved by both Boards with a pledge of full support.

While the Committee felt it was making satisfactory and noteworthy progress in dealing with isolated racial cases and problems as they arose, it felt that a more basic, formal and long-range plan for dealing with the race situation in our City should be developed. The Chairman of the Mayor's Good Neighbor Committee suggested to his Committee and to the Rocky Mount Voters and Improvement League that "A Blueprint for Progress" for Rocky Mount be drawn up and this idea was approved by both groups. The Chairman then appointed a committee of six citizens to draw up such a blueprint, one being appointed from the Mayor's Good Neighbor Committee, three recommended by the Rocky Mount Voters and Improvement League, and two representing the public at large. This committee developed and presented to the Mayor's Good Neighbor Committee such a plan and that plan is hereby adopted as follows:

"A Blueprint for Progress"

A plan to solve the problems growing out of the race situation in Rocky Mount must be based upon the facts as they exist in Rocky Mount today. We must first identify our problems before we can move intelligently to solve them. The facts might be unpleasant, but we must face them squarely and honestly if we are to deal with them. What are some of the facts?

First, we must recognize that approximately 12,000 of the total population of 32,000 in Rocky Mount, or approximately 35 per cent are Negroes. Put another way, the ratio of Negro citizens to white citizens is better than one Negro to two whites. It is, therefore, readily seen that the welfare of this large minority of our citizens vitally affects the economic, social, cultural, and political welfare of our City and every individual therein. The rapid mechanization of agriculture in Eastern North Carolina will continue to release large numbers of agricultural workers from the farms and they will move to our City as well as to other cities.

Statistics show that North Carolina ranks 42nd among the states in per capita income and that Nash and Edgecombe counties rank low among the 100 counties in our State in this respect. Statistics also disclose the ugly fact that the income of Negro families in our section is less than half the income of whites. Recent statistics also show that the unemployment in Nash and Edgecombe County areas is above the average in the State and that the large percentage of unemployed is in the Negro race. Recent studies show that the rate of illiteracy, the number of babies born out of wedlock, and the cases of infectious diseases is much higher among our Negro group; that the percentage of school drop-outs is above the average in our section of the State and is highest among our Negro children; that housing conditions in Nash and Edgecombe counties are below national standards, and that housing for Negroes is in the bottom half of this low standard; and that juvenile delinquency and crime rate is highest among Negroes. It must be pointed out, however, in reference to the above statistics that sociologists relate socio-economic factors as being partially, if not wholly, responsible for their existence.

These facts assault the conscience of all thoughtful and civic-minded citizens, and they adversely affect the whole fabric of our community life. The individuals involved are, of course, the greatest and immediate sufferers, but beyond them the economic loss in reduced productivity and purchasing power on the part of these handicapped individuals and the heavy cost of welfare, health, and social service programs run the total cost to our taxpayers into millions of dollars.

The question presented to all of the people of Rocky Mount is, "How do we attack and solve these problems?" We recognize that many of these problems, or similar ones, have been with us since the beginning of time and that many of them, or new or similar ones, will be with us indefinitely. But we feel a sense of responsibility—in fact, we are charged with the responsibility of devising a plan to attack and solve these problems, at least as far as we as human beings can do so in the short span of our lives. To that end we therefore propose two separate but related programs for action, generally classified as:

A. Specific Plans and Programs for Immediate Action.

B. A Long-Range Basic Plan to Attack the Problems at Their Source and to Solve Them in the Future.

A. SPECIFIC PLANS AND PROGRAMS FOR IMMEDIATE ACTION.

(1) Employment Opportunities for Negroes.

Perhaps the greatest economic disadvantage suffered by the Negro race is the lack of job opportunities in our community. There are many reasons for this disadvantage. Among them is the hard fact that there is a scarcity of good job opportunities in our community. Next is the fact that many of our Negroes are not educated, trained, nor qualified to fill many jobs other than those requiring manual labor. This is due, however, to the fact that many have been denied the opportunity to qualify. And last, but not least, is the ugly fact that many Negroes are not employed because they are Negroes. In order to help meet this problem, the Good Neighbor Committee resolves to assist the Business Development Committee of the Rocky Mount Chamber of Commerce, the Business Development of the North Carolina Department of Conservation and Development, and all other appropriate agencies in promoting the industrial development of Rocky Mount in order to provide job opportunities for all. It further resolves to co-operate with the City School Board, the Industrial Training Centers, the State Board of Education, and all other educational agencies in educating, equipping, and training our people to fill existing and newly created jobs. In this connection we should request the Rocky Mount School Board to give immediate consideration to the establishment of a Distributive Educational Program in the Booker T. Washington Senior High School and request our business firms to co-operate with the School Board in this connection, as they are doing with white youth. We further resolve to encourage all businesses, stores, financial institutions, factories, plants, and industries in our City to open up and make available additional job opportunities to Negroes. We point with pride to the recent successful employment of some Negroes in our uptown businesses, and of many in our industrial plants and factories. We urge that this practice be continued and expanded. We emphasize, however, that individual Negroes seeking employment must be able to fill available jobs in as efficient a manner as other available employees. This would mean that pilot training programs would include Negroes so that employment standards can be met. Negroes should not be discriminated against, but they must not expect preferential treatment. We should always remember that gainfully employed Negroes provide additional payrolls to stimulate our economy. We suggest that employers give careful thought and study to the preparing of their present employees for the acceptance of Negro employees into their organizations. The experience of some employers in Rocky Mount in this regard will prove most helpful to others considering a change of policy in employment. We recommend that the Chamber of Commerce, the Rocky Mount Merchants' Association, and the Rocky Mount Voters and Improvement League take as a project the matter of helping to prepare employees for this transition. We recommend that the service of the Security Employment Commission be used to a greater extent than heretofore. We recommend that the Committee give consideration to the training of qualified domestic workers in special classes and vocational training programs and encourage their employment at adequate wages. We recommend that a special subcommittee be appointed to help put this recommendation into practice.

(2) Employment of Negroes by City Government and Appointment on Official Committees and Boards.

We feel that no discrimination on account of race should be made in employment of personnel by our city government, and that all Negro citizens should be given a fair and equal opportunity to qualify for city employment. We further feel that the Negro race should be represented by qualified individuals on all official governing boards, commissions, and committees. We are pleased that this policy is presently in practice to a great degree in our city government and we urge that it be continued and expanded. We feel that it is appropriate and proper that Negroes have representation on our city Council, elected in the normal course of democratic processes. We recommend that the city government seek out Negroes meeting employment standards to fill some positions in its several departments.

(3) Discrimination in Places of Public Accommodation.

The practice of discrimination or segregation practiced by many places of public accommodation in Rocky Mount is embarrassing and objectionable to Negroes in our City and we recommend that the owners, operators, and managers of all such establishments in Rocky Mount following this practice discontinue the same and accept the patronage of Negroes as they do other customers in the due course of business. We recognize the fact that owners and operators of private businesses have the legal right to pick and choose their customers, but we urge them in the interest of harmony and good will in our City and in accordance with the principles of moral justice and human dignity to consider accepting all citizens on an equal basis in the operation of their businesses. We also recommend that all signs on entrances, doors, and driveways indicating segregation of races in their places of business be removed. We recommend that a special subcommittee be appointed to help put this recommendation into practice.

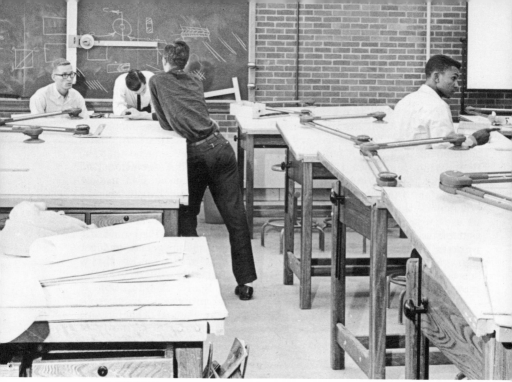

A BIRACIAL CLASS STUDIES AT AN INDUSTRIAL EDUCATION CENTER.

(4) Recreational Facilities.

There is a disproportionately large percentage of Negro children in our City, and due to housing and geographical conditions they have very few, if any, recreational facilities. Adequate recreational programs not only build healthy bodies and more contented minds, but help prevent juvenile delinquency. We, therefore, recommend that the City of Rocky Mount, through its Recreational Department, expand its recreational program and that the help and co-operation of all civic groups and organizations in Rocky Mount be enlisted in this effort. We are confident there is capable and willing volunteer help ready to respond to such a call. These recommendations apply to adult recreation as well as youth.

(5) Health and Welfare.

The ravages of disease and ill health still take a heavy toll in our community in terms of life, suffering, disability, reduction of productivity and income, and cost of medical care. We recommend that our City Health Department, working in close co-operation with county, State and federal agencies, rededicate itself to meeting problems. The privations resulting from exceptionally large numbers of children in many families prevent children in such families from getting adequate food, clothing, medical care, and educational advantages necessary to produce healthy, well-adjusted citizens. We, therefore, recommend that consideration be given to a program to assist such families in sensible planning for the number of children born under these circumstances.

(6) Rocky Mount Public Schools.

The educational system of our City is legally under the control of the Rocky Mount School Board, and we attempt in no way to meddle or interfere with its administration of our schools. We do wish to express, however, our concern over the tremendous loss resulting from school drop-outs. We know the school authorities are aware of this problem and we urge all children, parents, and citizens to co-operate with the School Board in every plan and program it proposes to meet the drop-out problem. We wish also to suggest to the Rocky Mount School Board that it consider applying for one of the "Pilot Reading, Writing, and Arithmetic Programs" that the Board of Education of North Carolina and the North Carolina Fund propose to sponsor in the State. We wish also to commend the Rocky Mount School Board on its acceptance this fall of a number of Negro children into previously all-white schools, and we hope that Board will continue this practice in conformity with law as now established.

(7) Publicity.

We feel that the success of "A Blueprint For Progress" will depend upon its acceptance by the people of our City, and we recommend that it be given full and repeated publicity through all news media and means of communication.

We can be justly proud of the progress we have made in the specific areas mentioned above, but perhaps our greatest and most significant accomplishment is the establishment of a clear and continuing line of communication between the races, and the development of a feeling of mutual confidence and respect. This line of communication and this faith and confidence in the good will of each group has helped us dispel many unfounded rumors and suspicions. When such a climate is actively sought demonstrations become unnecessary. The unfortunate experiences in other nearby cities have demonstrated to our people the wisdom of a sane and dispassionate approach to the problem. It is our hope and prayer that such an atmosphere will continue. We commend our Negro citizens for their restraint in a highly charged atmosphere and we promise to do all we can to see that their patience is rewarded with continued progress.

We appreciate the fact that we are dealing with a subject made sensitive by the change in customs and mores of our people which have been in existence for over a hundred years. For these reasons we strongly urge all of our citizens to act responsibly in making this transition. Approached in this manner, threats of violence, intimidation, or force of law will be unnecessary, and law and order will be maintained in our City. We hope and expect to gain our goals by appeal to a sense of fair play and justice. We feel that the vast majority of people of Rocky Mount share this feeling and will work in that spirit to accomplish our goals.

B. A Long-Range Basic Plan to Attack the Problems at the Source and to Solve Them in the Future.

The specific plans and programs for immediate action listed above will start us on the road to progress, but they, alone, however urgent, will not completely solve our basic problems. "A Blueprint for Progress" requires a hard look at these basic problems, concrete objectives for solving these problems, and a plan for action toward those objectives.

In the introduction we cited statistics to show that we have problems. In the midst of national prosperity and plenty we have too many families whose income is so low that daily susbsistence is often in doubt—too many men, women, and children who exist without the necessities of life. Too many of these families live in houses that are overcrowded and unsanitary. Too many parents lack the education or the skills of a rewarding job, even where they have the opportunity for work. Too many of their children are not getting the education essential for gainful employment today, both because they see no opportunity for the future and because their parents do not encourage them.

Eastern North Carolina is in the middle of an economic transition, and the tempo of change is speeding up. Peanuts, corn, and cotton farming have already been mechanized and this has displaced hundreds and thousands of people from our farms. Tobacco, our most profitable crop, will be next, and when the machine takes over the harvesting of tobacco, thousands more will be deprived of employment in agriculture. Thus, as our population grows, the number of jobs on the farm decreases and the migration from the farm to Rocky Mount and on to the cities of the North picks up momentum. Rocky Mount is the way-station for these people, most of them Negro, and most of them lacking the education and the skills needed for employment in factories and commercial establishments.

The decline in farm employment, the migration to the city, and the rising expectations of the Negro all combine to put pressure on Rocky Mount and other Eastern North Carolina cities. Those who once could find a satisfactory living on a farm with a small cash income now need a wage-paying job, and if they are to live up to the standards of living which all Americans strive for, they will need more than a minimum wage. We must provide more jobs with higher wages, and we must educate all of our people to fill these jobs to the best of their potential. And if we cannot provide the jobs in Rocky Mount, we should see that those who move on to other cities have the skills to compete for the jobs that are available there.

There is another development in this part of the State which further tends to strain our economy. Many adults, in the prime of life, have moved off the farm to the North and Middle West, and there find jobs. Because costs of living are higher, or for convenience, or a variety of reasons, many of them send their children back home to live with their relatives and grandparents. There are, as a result, an increasing number of children to be educated, as well as an increasing number of aged persons who cannot themselves earn a living, who depend on the schools and the welfare services of our community. In short, we in this section of the State must help support or educate a larger than average number of old people and children with a smaller than average number of wage earners.

We cannot escape these trends by pretending they do not exist. Neither can we just say that "the poor will always be with us," or that those with ability will by natural processes and ambition rise to the top. The evidence is overwhelming today that school drop-outs tend to be the children of drop-outs, that because of lack of opportunity and motivation children with basic intelligence and potential skills are leaving school and following the path of their parents into a marginal existence, accompanied by frustration and despair. When 50 of every 100 children who enter the public schools drop out of school without a high school diploma at a time when a high school diploma is almost a necessity for a living wage, and when it is found that a large proportion of those who drop out do so not because of lack of basic ability, but for a combination of other factors, we recognize that we must do something to make "the American dream" a reality for all, else all will suffer.

The long-range answer to these problems that infect our society can be summed up in two words—education and employment. To make this answer meaningful, we have an enormous task, some may say an impossible task, but we must undertake the impossible, if we are to prove the strength of our democracy.

1. We must go to work to bring all of our children through the public school system with a high school diploma and the desire and opportunity to go on for the technical or professional education that our society is demanding at all levels.

2. We must provide all our people with the opportunity for jobs that make the best use of their potential and offer a living wage—sufficient to house, feed, clothe, and educate a family at national standards.

These are the things we have not done, and their lack is part of the reason for the problems we face. But while we are looking a generation ahead for today's children, we must not forget those who have dropped out of school, who lack the skills and training necessary for employment, who are existing and raising families on a submarginal income and in unfit housing.

So we must add a third objective:

3. We must organize our community so that all our resources and community activities are committed to making an education and

NEGRO FAMILY INCOME

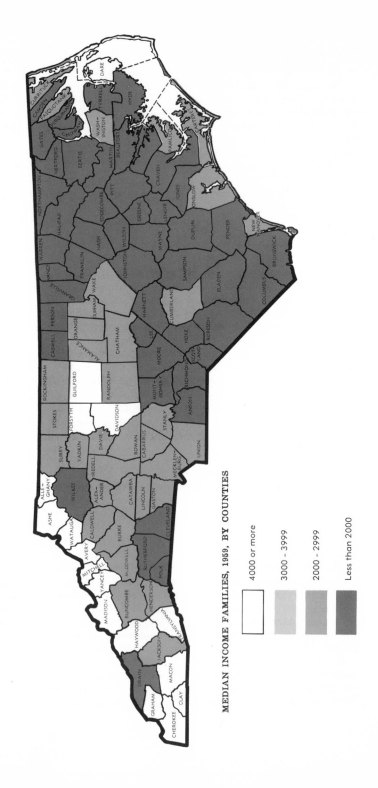

MEDIAN INCOME FAMILIES, 1959, BY COUNTIES

- 4000 or more
- 3000 - 3999
- 2000 - 2999
- Less than 2000

opportunity available to everyone in the community, whatever his present condition.

These goals must not be criticized as idealistic and impractical. They are the most practical we can devise. Behind each of them lies an individual—man, woman, or child—who today has no dream, no ability to be self-reliant, no way to contribute to the community. And because a quarter of our population lives in this condition, the entire community suffers. This is a condition which we cannot save with charity, though to remedy it may cost us an initial investment in money and effort.

If Rocky Mount is to approach this total problem with a total community effort, it must be prepared to think new ideas, experiment with new ways of approaching old problems, and not be afraid to throw over old precedents.

We must be willing to experiment in the public schools to find better ways of giving all our children an education, with emphasis on those who find school most difficult and unexciting today—those who come from homes where education is not a way of life and who therefore are slow to learn, and particularly slow to learn to read; those who see no future in a college preparatory course, but find no challenging alternative; those who find no motivation at home and find school a strange and alien world.

We must work to establish in this community a climate of opportunity for all, to continue the effort to provide new and better jobs for Negroes, so that Negro children will have a symbol of what can be achieved, to open up both jobs and a pattern of promotion in jobs, so that there will be incentive to work and produce.

We must use all our community resources to work constructively with those families, Negro and white alike, who, though unproductive today, can be helped. We must find jobs for those who are now illiterate, and the unemployable, and train them to fill those jobs; we must help parents provide healthier and more satisfactory homes through a higher level of community services; we must work toward better housing for all of our people by every means available.

While we have in this country, this State, and this· community a highly developed system of public and private services, the mechanism for bringing these resources to bear on our basic problems is unbelievably awkward and obsolete. We have specialized services, and specialized training for those who man these services, and a governmental structure to administer these services so specialized that no single agency or governmental unit can look at the problem as a whole. For example, if we are interested in the identification of jobs available in the community and the provision of training for persons who might become qualified for those jobs, we must deal with the City School Board, the industrial education center, the State employment service, and individual industries and businesses. If we are concerned with an understanding of a family in trouble, or whose children are in trouble, we must be concerned with the school system, the welfare and health departments, the law enforcement agencies, the juvenile court and the

223

probation officer, and on and on. We, therefore, are attacking our problems piecemeal, with different agencies responsible for different aspects of a single broad problem, but no agency or governmental unit able to co-ordinate all these efforts.

We are not saying anything new, nor are we criticizing the special programs, talents, and objectives of each of these agencies. But today communities throughout the country are finding, as we have, that they cannot deal with basic problems as they exist because the agencies whose co-operation is needed are responsible to so many different governmental units and private governing boards. The problem is more complicated than usual in Rocky Mount because the City lies in two counties.

If we, in Rocky Mount, are to achieve these necessary goals, we must act with imagination and commitment to work out a procedure under which leadership representative of the community and of the public and private governmental and service agencies in the community, can:

1. More specifically define these problems of education, employment, housing, income, and family services.

2. Define the kinds of programs which hold the greatest promise for constructive results, and in so doing canvass the country for the best new ideas and be willing to work out whatever intra-agency co-operation is needed to administer such programs.

3. Work with the city and the county governments, the state and federal governments, and with private community agencies to secure whatever financial support is needed to experiment with these programs.

4. Provide the leadership to make successful experiments an integral part of continuing community services and policy.

We are not so bold as to think we can propose a complete, foolproof, and final long-range blueprint for progress at this or any other time, but we do offer some suggestions.

1. We believe that this action program should be carried out at least for the present, by a new community-wide organization, representative of the community at large and having the participation, support, and commitment of the city government, the county government, and the city school system.

2. We believe that this organization should be able to call on the assistance and participation of governmental agencies and private community agencies in planning and carrying out its program.

3. We believe that it probably will be necessary at some time to employ a small, but highly-qualified staff to serve this organization, to provide continuing liaison with participating public and private

agencies, to help evaluate ideas for experimental programs, and to determine the success of the program.

4. We believe that this program should be financed through special appropriations from the city and county governments, through the aid of state and federal appropriations where available, through assistance from foundations where available, and through private subscription.

5. We believe that this organization should be established on the basis of a ten-year period. It will take that long for the success of the program to be judged, but we hope that during the life of the organization, ways of providing continuing leadership through a reorientation of the responsibilities of existing governmental units and agencies can be worked out.

It is important to note, at this stage, that the North Carolina Fund was recently established as a state-wide nonprofit corporation to give financial and other assistance to a limited number of communities in North Carolina for programs having objectives similar to those we have set forth here. If Rocky Mount can qualify as one of the communities to which the Fund will provide assistance for experimental programs, it may be that financial assistance to help launch the program we have set forth will be available. It is recommended that the Good Neighbor Committee invite the North Carolina Fund to send a representative to Rocky Mount to discuss with the Committee the possibilities of assistance from the Fund in supporting such a program.

The program we have recommended will not, by itself, solve our problem. We must continue our campaign for industrial development, to bring new jobs into Rocky Mount, and we have a feeling that the program we are recommending will complement our search for new industries by providing a more highly-trained labor force. We must continue our efforts to build a community which is attractive, convenient, and a pleasant place in which to live. But we must give new emphasis to the problems of our people. We must adopt as a goal a resolve that every child in this community shall have a chance to develop his full potential. And we must see that that child has the opportunity to use his talents and his skills in the best possible fashion, without regard to race, color, or creed.

Our Blueprint for Progress is to build in Rocky Mount the City of Opportunity.

IV

The Law and the Negro

When the United States Supreme Court decision in May, 1954, outlawed the policy of "separate but equal" school provisions by requiring integration of the public schools, the Honorable William B. Umstead, of Durham, was Governor of North Carolina. There was some violent reaction against the Court decision, but some North Carolinians advocated meeting the issue temperately and in prompt obedience. Some "token" integration did ensue promptly.

Many lawyers, including the state's senior United States Senator, Sam J. Ervin, Jr., contended that the Supreme Court had amended the Federal Constitution in an unlawful manner by abrogating a decision which had stood legal tests for sixty-seven years or longer. These lawyers contended that the Supreme Court had seized authority which it did not possess. They regarded the sixty-seven-year-old decision as actually a part of the Constitution and felt that if there were to be a change such as the Court decision made, it should be done by the prescribed methods of constitutional amendment.

Governor Umstead named a special committee of geographically representative citizens to study the problem of the Court decision as it affected this State. That committee reported in December, 1954, after Governor Umstead had died, November 9, and had been succeeded by the Honorable Luther H. Hodges, the Lieutenant Governor. Governor Hodges, who was re-elected for a full four-year term in November, 1956, inherited executive responsibility for dealing with the Court decision.

The committee that Governor Umstead had appointed expressed to the new governor the opinion that the General As-

LUTHER H. HODGES
GOVERNOR, 1954-1961.

WILLIAM B. UMSTEAD
GOVERNOR, 1953-1954.

sembly would not vote funds to support integrated schools and recommended that the General Assembly be called upon to decide what should be state policy to save the school in face of the emergency.

The committee appointed by Governor Umstead to make recommendations reported in part as follows:

The mixing of the races forthwith in the public schools throughout the State cannot be accomplished and should not be attempted. The schools of our State are so intimately related to the customs and feelings of the people of each community that their effective operation is impossible except in conformity with community attitudes. The committee feels that a compulsory mixing of the races in our schools on a state-wide basis and without regard to local conditions and assignment factors other than race would alienate public support of the schools to such an extent that they could not be operated successfully.

The General Assembly in 1955 endorsed this report and passed a resolution which noted that the Attorney General of the State, then the Honorable William B. Rodman, had filed a brief with the Supreme Court of the United States in the pending segregation cases before the Court, the resolution in part saying:

The people of North Carolina know the value of the public school, they also know the value of a social structure in which two distinct races can live together as separate groups, each proud of its own contributions to that society, and recognizing its dependence upon the other group. They have determined if possible to educate all of the children of the State. They are also determined to maintain their society as it now exists with separate and distinct racial groups in the North Carolina community.

The people of North Carolina firmly believe that the record of North Carolina in the field of education demonstrates the practicability of education of separate races in separate schools. They also believe that the achievements of the Negro people of North Carolina demonstrate that such an educational system has not instilled in them a sense of inferiority which handicaps them in their efforts to make lasting and substantial contributions to their State.

The General Assembly's resolution urged support of the Attorney General in the appeal to the Supreme Court, and approved the committee's opinion that the mixing of the races in the schools "within the State cannot be accomplished and, if attempted, would alienate public support of the schools to such an extent that they could not be operated successfully."

The General Assembly of 1955 commended the Umstead committee, enacted a law providing for assignment of students in a manner intended to evade the worst of the impact of the Court decision, and called for a new Advisory Committee on Education, of which the Honorable Thomas J. Pearsall of Rocky Mount became Chairman.

This Committee reported April 5, 1956, recommending a special session of the General Assembly to consider submitting an amendment of the State Constitution to a vote of the people and affirming its recognition of the necessity for adequate education of all of the people of the State. Governor Hodges called a special session for July 23, 1956, and that day addressed a joint meeting of the Senate and the House and advised action to amend the State Constitution.

Although declaring its opinion that the General Assembly would not support integrated schools, the special committee had included the following in its report:

> If the Negro children in North Carolina are to continue receiving public education, it will be as the result of the work and effort of the people of the white race. But that burden must be borne and must include a willingness to provide, at whatever cost, fully adequate schools and facilities for the Negro children of our State.
>
> North Carolina is already committed to an aggressive program of urging the provision of adequate facilities. That commitment must be performed, but the bearing of that burden is not entirely unselfish. If the State of North Carolina is to go forward, if the white race in North Carolina is to go forward, the Negro must go forward also. The advancement of our economy and the preservation of our democracy depend in large part upon the education, the understanding, and the morality of the Negro as well as the white. If there prevails ignorance in either race, servitude in either race, hatred in either race, our economy will stall, our society will seethe and our democracy will degenerate.

That Committee recommended to all school units, while awaiting further legislative action —

(1) To recognize that there is no law compelling the mixing of the races.

(2) To recognize that since the Supreme Court decision there can be no valid law compelling the separation of the races in public schools.

(3) To declare that the initial assignments to schools will be made in accordance with what the assigning unit or officer considers to be for the best interest of the child assigned, including in its consideration residence, school attended during the preceding year, availability of facilities, and all other local conditions bearing

upon the welfare of the child and the prospective effectiveness of the school.

(4) To see that initial assignments be made to permit transfers only upon application and hearing in due course and in accordance with the provisions of the 1955 Assignment Law.

The address that Governor Hodges made to the joint session of the General Assembly on the day it was called together was a strong recommendation for prompt and positive action, including the presentation of a constitutional amendment to the vote of the people. The special session did act promptly. The people had a vote on the amendment to the Constitution September 8, 1956, and overwhelmingly approved it.

The so-called Pearsall Plan, which included amendment of the Constitution and the statutes relative to student assignment, combined with the appeals from the Supreme Court decisions, prevented the brunt of the Negro discontent from falling heavily on the remainder of the Hodges administration. The discontent was manifest to the extent that, on one occasion when Governor Hodges addressed the student body at A. and T. College in Greensboro, he was booed by his audience because of his pronunciation of the word "Negro." Heat was increasing. Some limited integration of Negro applicants in a few white schools occurred, including the acceptance of several in formerly all-white schools in Greensboro.

The amendment to the State Constitution made under the Pearsall Plan is not reproduced in full in this book. However, the essence of it appears in Ralph Moody's contribution to the book which appears herein. Mr. Moody's article is a thorough analysis of the law in North Carolina affecting the race problem. There appears further discussion of the action of the General Assembly and its impact on the problem. A study of the Moody memorandum will give full information relative to both constitutional and statutory law in the State.

The third governor called upon to deal with the problem of Negro discontent came into office in January, 1961. This was Governor Terry Sanford, now serving the last of his four years in office.

Demonstrations by Negroes of their dissatisfaction with the slowness of integration, and with the denial to them of certain other civil rights, were intensified. The reaction to these demonstrations was less hostile as a rule than in some other southern states, but after a period of spreading Negro action, Governor Sanford, in a strong address, proposed to the Negro leadership that the kind of demonstrations that were being conducted were becoming counter-productive, alienating some of the Negroes' friends, and might lead to serious disorder and violence.

In this speech he urged the Negro leadership to find alternative methods to emphasize their petition for citizenship equality. He said the Negroes had succeeded in piercing the apathy of the State and suggested that education and negotiation were desirable substitutes for the demonstrations and should be adopted. He made it clear that he would not tolerate the breaking down of order in the State by mobs or demonstrations which could result in serious violence. While this statement by the Governor did not cause the Negroes to abandon their street demonstrations, there was a gradual reduction of them as the Governor began to discuss other methods with the Negro leadership.

LEGAL STATUS OF SEGREGATION IN NORTH CAROLINA — CONSTITUTION, STATUTES AND COURT DECISIONS*

This memorandum will attempt in a brief manner to outline the situation in North Carolina with respect to race segregation. The memorandum will deal briefly with constitutional provisions, statutory provisions, and court decisions with respect to public schools, parks and recreational systems supported by public funds, hospitals supported by public funds, public accommodations, civil rights as to criminal prosecutions and procedure, public buildings, and government facilities and transportation.

Since 1954, there have been so many judicial decisions on these problems we cannot discuss all the decisions in detail and will not attempt to do so, but we shall attempt to deal with our own state courts, district courts and decisions of the United States Court of Appeals for the Fourth Circuit.

CONSTITUTIONAL PROVISIONS

Article I, Section 17 of the Constitution of North Carolina, provides as follows: "No person ought to be taken, imprisoned, or dis-

---

* By Ralph Moody, Deputy Attorney General of North Carolina.

seized of his freehold, liberties or privileges, or outlawed or exiled, or in any manner deprived of his life, liberty or property, but by the law of the land." The phrase "law of the land" is equivalent to "due process of law," and also equivalent to "equal protection of the law" (*State v. Collins*, 169 N. C. 323; *State v. Crocker*, 239 N. C. 446; *Harriet Cotton Mills v. Local Union No. 578*, 251 N. C. 218).

Article XIV, Section 8 of the Constitution of North Carolina, provides as follows: "All marriages between a white person and a Negro, or between a white person and a person of Negro descent to the third generation, inclusive, are hereby forever prohibited." Therefore, a person who has one-eighth Negro blood in his veins is in the prohibitive degree set out in this section and also prohibited by G. S. 51-3 (*Cumulative Supplement of 1961*) which implements this provision. It should be pointed out that G. S. 51-3, *supra*, prohibits also marriage between a white person "or between a Cherokee Indian of Robeson County and a Negro, or between a Cherokee Indian of Robeson County and a person of Negro descent to the third generation, inclusive." The 1961 Amendment deleted the words "or Indian" formerly appearing after the word "Negro" four places in this section, and, therefore, it would appear that marriages between white persons and Indians are not prohibited.

The great source of litigation with respect to racial matters in the whole nation arises under the Fourteenth Amendment of the Constitution of the United States and more particularly under Section I of this Amendment and the particular clause which reads: ". . . nor shall any state deprive any person of life, liberty or property, without due process of law; nor deny to any person within its jurisdiction the equal protection of the laws." At this point we simply point out that the words "equal protection of the laws" have been very aptly said to mean "the protection of equal laws." It should be stressed also that the Amendment applies to action of the state and not to private action. State action includes action of any agency of the State whether through the legislature, through its courts, or through its executive or administrative officers. State action also includes acts under municipal ordinances and also acts under valid laws improperly enforced or administered and acts of state officers contrary to state law. State action may also include state inaction, and it also includes actions of lessees from the state. State action includes in certain instances action of private organizations receiving state aid, and it includes the action of private organizations that perform quasi-governmental functions such as political parties or the actions that result from privately owned or company towns (*Marsh v. Alabama*, 326 U. S. 501, 66 S. Ct. 276, 90 L. ed. 265).

Article IX, Section 2, provides the following: "The General Assembly, at its first session under this Constitution, shall provide by taxation and otherwise for a general and uniform system of public schools, wherein tuition shall be free of charge to all children of the State between the ages of six and twenty-one years. And the children of

GOVERNOR WILLIAM B. UMSTEAD READS THE 1954 OPINION OF THE UNITED STATES SUPREME COURT IN THE CASE OF *BROWN V. BOARD OF EDUCATION OF TOPEKA.*

the white race and the children of the colored race shall be taught in separate public schools; but there shall be no discrimination in favor of, or to the prejudice of, either race."

While the last clause in the above quoted provision still remains in our written Constitution, the Supreme Court of North Carolina has said that any constitutional provision of our Constitution or any of our statutes in conflict with the Brown Case (*Brown v. Board of Education of Topeka*, 347 U. S. 483, 98 L. ed. 873, 74 S. Ct. 683, 38 ALR 2d 1180; second case: *Brown v. Board of Education of Topeka*, 349 U. S. 294, 99 L. ed. 1083, 75 S. Ct. 753) must be deemed to be invalid because the Constitution of the United States as construed by the Supreme Court of the United States forbids segregation in schools and under Article VI, Section 2 of the Constitution of the United States, the Federal Constitution and the laws of the United States, which shall be made in pursuance thereof, shall be the supreme law of the land.

STATUTES OF NORTH CAROLINA

There are several statutes which are on the books of the *Code of North Carolina* which require segregation of races, but we have never thought that these statutes are now valid because of the holding of the Supreme Court of North Carolina in the Constantian Case (*Con-*

234

stantian v. Anson County, 244 N. C. 221, 93 S. E. 2d 163). It appears to us that all of the statutes (hereinafter referred to) have been declared to be invalid by our Supreme Court. The statutes in question are as follows:

(1) G.S. 122-3, 6, requires a racial separation of patients among the several institutions under the North Carolina Hospitals Board of Control.

(2) Article 13 of Chapter 116 of the *General Statutes* provides for colored orphanages.

(3) G.S. 116-109, 120, 124, provides for separation of the races in schools for the blind and deaf.

(4) G.S. 148-43 provides that white and colored prisoners shall not be confined together during eating or sleeping hours, "and at all other times separation of the two races shall be as complete as practicable." It should be added that it is still believed that this statute is valid as a matter of prison discipline. It is thought that the rights of convicted persons are somewhat curtailed and that for peace and good order this should be maintained.

(5) G.S. 134-79 and sections following, as well as G.S. 134-84.1 and sections following, establish training schools for Negro boys and Negro girls.

(6) G.S. 105-323 separates the races on the tax books of the State according to white, Negro, Indian and corporate taxpayers. It is thought that this is valid since this makes for convenience in tax collections and in locating taxpayers. The Bureau of the Census of the Department of Commerce of the United States in summarizing the population of the nation gives categories as to white, colored and persons of different races. It has consistently refused to alter its method of maintaining population statistics, although colored organizations have tried to make the Bureau omit the colored category.

(7) G.S. 65-38 provides that where property has heretofore been used as a burial ground for members of the Negro race, it shall remain and be established as a burial ground for the Negro race, and the same is true as to property which has heretofore been used exclusively for burial of members of the white race. This is dealing with property under the control of municipalities where the municipalities take possession of and continue the use of certain lands as cemeteries within the corporate limits. There are certain city ordinances regulating this question as well as the marking of graves.

(8) G.S. 90-212 provides that unclaimed bodies of white prisoners dying while in prison shall be equally distributed among the white funeral homes in Raleigh, and the bodies of Negro prisoners dying under similar conditions shall be equally distributed among the Negro funeral homes in Raleigh. Apparently there is no restriction of a racial nature as between white and Negro undertaking establishments.

(9) There also remains on the books of the State a statute requiring racial segregation on passenger trains and steamboats (G.S. 60-94 to 97).

(10) The Utilities Commission is directed by G.S. 62-44 and G.S. 62-127.71 to require separate waiting rooms.

(11) Street cars and motor buses are required by G.S. 60-135, 136, 137, to seat colored passengers in the rear of such vehicles and white passengers in the front portion (*Corporation Commission v. Transportation Committee*, 198 N. C. 317, *State v. Johnson*, 229 N. C. 701).

(12) Fraternal orders cannot do business in North Carolina if white and colored persons are members of the same lodge (G.S. 58-267).

(13) There have been on the books of some of the cities of the State various ordinances requiring segregation in taxicabs, carnivals, other places of amusement and restaurants. There are some city ordinances where Negro policemen are used which fix the territory in which the Negro policemen shall operate. It is thought that this type of ordinance in the administration of criminal laws is valid.

(14) There does not seem to be any law which requires the Director of the Department of Conservation and Development to enforce segregation in State parks and State-operated places of resort and amusement.

STATUTES REPEALED

So far as our research goes all statutes requiring segregation in public schools have been repealed.

Chapter 129 of the *Session Laws of 1963* repealed G.S. 127-6 and thus abolished segregation in the National Guard.

Chapter 1114 rewrote G.S. 95-48 and G.S. 95-49 and abolished racial separation in toilet facilities in manufacturing and other business establishments, but retained the separation of toilet facilities as to sex.

THE PEARSALL PLAN

The events leading up to the enactment of certain statutes which are commonly referred to as the "Pearsall Plan" are as follows:

The two Brown decisions (cited above) were handed down on May 17, 1954, and May 31, 1955.

Governor William B. Umstead, shortly before his death, appointed a Special Advisory Committee on Education to study the problems presented by the Brown decisions on the question of segregation in the public schools.

On becoming Governor, Luther H. Hodges re-commissioned this Committee, and this Committee filed its report with the Governor on December 30, 1954. The Report of this Committee, along with the Brief of the Attorney General of North Carolina, filed in the Supreme

Court of the United States in the then pending segregation cases, was approved by the General Assembly as a declaration of the policy of the State of North Carolina (see Resolution 29, *Session Laws of 1955*).

Resolution 29 of the *Session Laws of 1955* gave legal foundation to the Advisory Committee on Education which was thereafter known as the "Pearsall Committee" due to the fact that Thomas J. Pearsall was appointed Chairman of the Committee.

There is sent with this memorandum a copy of the Report of the North Carolina Advisory Committee on Education made on April 5, 1956, and also a copy of an Address by Governor Luther H. Hodges made before the Joint Session of the General Assembly of the Special Session of 1956, and on page 7 of this speech will be found the July, 1956, Report of this Advisory Committee.

There is also sent with this memorandum a copy of Resolution 29, a copy of an address by Governor Luther Hodges made on radio and television network on Monday, August 8, 1955, and we send you also *Summary of Statements and Actions by Governor Luther Hodges* issued on October 3, 1957, as well as copies of certain speeches made before the North Carolina State Bar on this subject by prominent lawyers, including the Honorable William B. Rodman, who was then Attorney General of the State.

The actions and studies of the Pearsall Committee resulted in the enactment by the General Assembly at the Extra Session of 1956 of an amendment to Article IX of the Constitution of North Carolina by adding Section 12 to this Article, which authorized the General Assembly to provide for education expense grants "for the private education of any child for whom no public school is available or for the private education of a child who is assigned against the wishes of his parents, or the person having control of such child, to a public school attended by a child of another race." This provided tuition expense grants which were to be made available "only for education in a non-sectarian school, and only when it was not reasonable and practicable to reassign such child to a public school not attended by a child of another race." The proposed constitutional amendment also authorized the General Assembly to provide a uniform system of local option whereby any local option unit, as defined by the General Assembly, could by majority vote of the qualified voters in the unit who vote on the question to suspend or authorize the suspension of the operation of one or more or all of the public schools in such unit. It was provided that no action taken would affect the obligation of the State or any political subdivision or agency thereof with respect to any indebtedness theretofore or thereafter created.

This constitutional amendment was submitted to the voters in a general election on September 8, 1956, and as a result Chapter 3 of the *Extra Session of 1956* and Chapter 4 of the *Extra Session of 1956*, went into full force and effect. Chapter 5 of the *Special Session of 1956* amended the Compulsory School Attendance Law so that it would accord with these other acts as to racial matters and Chapter 7 of the *Extra Session of 1956* amended and revised Article 21 of Chapter 115 of the *General Statutes* relating to assignment and enrollment of pupils in public schools. All of these acts will be found in the *Session Laws of North Carolina, Extra Session of 1956,* and they also appear in the *Public School Laws of North Carolina,* as follows: Assignment of Pupils Act appears as Article 21, Chapter 115 of the *General Statutes,* beginning with G.S. 115-176; the Local Option Act providing for elections to close schools appears as Article 34 of Chapter 115 of the *General Statutes,* beginning with G.S. 115-261; the Act providing Education Expense Grants appears as Article 35 in Chapter 115 of the *General Statutes,* beginning with G.S. 115-274; and the General Compulsory Attendance Law appears as Article 20 of Chapter 115 of the *General Statutes,* beginning with G.S. 115-166.

It is our thought that this constitutional amendment referred to above and the enactment and revision of these statutes represent the laws which are commonly referred to as the "Pearsall Plan."

We will not quote these statutes because it is our understanding that a complete copy of the *Public School Laws of North Carolina* as issued by the State Superintendent of Public Instruction and which contains all of these statutes, as well as the constitutional amendment, is available upon request.

SUMMARY AS TO STATUTES

The constitutional provision which prohibits intermarriage between white persons and Negroes, referred to above, in our opinion is still in force and effect and has not yet been invalidated by the Supreme Court of the United States.

It is believed that the statute providing for separate names on the tax books according to race is still valid for it was prompted by convenience and not discriminatory motives.

We believe that the statute which provides for the separation of the races in prisons is probably still valid for this is a matter of prison administration and was adopted to preserve peace and order in the prisons and to prevent prison riots.

All the other statutes above referred to, it would seem, are not valid, and, in fact, they are not being enforced at all. The General Statutes Commission will soon recommend repeal in order to get these statutes off the statute books.

The statutes that comprise the so-called "Pearsall Plan" have not been litigated as to their constitutionality except the article dealing with assignment and enrollment of pupils which has been found to be constitutional and valid and will be further discussed under the head of *Judicial Decisions.*

PUBLIC SCHOOL SYSTEM

In the first Brown Case, *supra,* the Supreme Court of the United States said:

We conclude that in the field of public education the doctrine of "separate but equal" has no place. Separate educational facilities are inherently unequal. Therefore, we hold that the plaintiffs and others similarly situated for whom the actions have been brought are, by reason of the segregation complained of, deprived of the equal protection of the laws guaranteed by the Fourteenth Amendment.

In the second Brown Case, *supra*, in which this office participated, the Supreme Court of the United States laid down certain principles for the implementation and enforcement of its decision in the first Brown Case. The Supreme Court of the United States said (349 U.S. 294, 99 L. ed. 1083, 75 S. Ct. 753):

The full implementation of these constitutional principles may require solution of varied local school problems. School authorities have the primary responsibility for elucidating, assessing, and solving these problems; courts will have to consider whether the action of school authorities constitutes good faith implementation of the governing constitutional principles.

But it should go without saying that the vitality of these constitutional principles cannot be allowed to yield simply because of disagreement with them.

It was in this opinion that the Court remanded certain of these cases to the district courts "to take such proceedings and enter such orders and decrees consistent with this opinion as are necessary and proper to admit to public schools on a racially non-discriminatory basis with all deliberate speed parties to these cases."

It was because of these decisions that North Carolina enacted the Assignment and Enrollment of Pupils Act (Article 21 of Chapter 115 of the *General Statutes,* beginning with G.S. 115-176). The Act has been held to be constitutional on its face (*Carson v. Warlick,* 238 F. 2d 724; *Holt v. Raleigh City Board of Education,* 265 F. 2d 95; *Covington v. Edwards,* 264 F. 2d 780). It has also been held by the United States Court of Appeals for the Fourth Circuit that the administrative remedy provided in the Assignment and Enrollment Act must be exhausted before instituting action in the Federal Courts (*Carson v. Board of Education,* 227 F. 2d 789; *Carson v. Warlick, supra; Holt v. Raleigh City Board of Education, supra; Joyner v. McDowell County Board of Education,* 244 N. C. 164). It has been held also that the plaintiff has the burden of proof to establish the exhaustion of administrative remedies (*McKissick v. Durham City Board of Education,* 176 F. Supp. 3), and that members of the State Board of Education are not proper parties in a segregation or integration case because they have no authority to control local school officials (*McKissick v. Durham City Board of Education, supra*).

It should be pointed out that although the Assignment and Enrollment Act has been held to be valid on its face, it can be conducted and administered in an unconstitutional manner and attention is called to the case of *Wheeler v. Durham City Board of Education,* 309 F. 2d 630, in which it was held that criteria for reassignment had to be the same for both races and that "resort to dual attendance area maps

'offends the constitutional rights of the plaintiffs.' " The Court further said: "It is an unconstitutional administration of the North Carolina Pupil Enrollment Act to assign pupils to schools according to racial factors."

In the Wheeler Case, *supra*, the Court said:

The injunction shall control all future assignment of pupils to schools unless and until the defendants submit to the District Court a suitable plan for ending the existing discrimination. "Any such plan, before being approved by the District Court should provide for immediate steps looking to the termination of discriminatory practices with all deliberate speed in accordance with a specified timetable."

In the case of *Jeffers v. Whitley*, 309 F. 2d 621, the case recites that the school board in question had disregarded the constitutional rights of Negro pupils and that where an administrative remedy respecting school assignments and transfers has in practice been employed principally as a means of perpetuation of discrimination, then a remedy so administered is inadequate and need not be exhausted or pursued before resort to the courts for enforcement of the protected rights. The conclusion is that the Assignment and Enrollment Act is apparently still valid if properly administered. There have been no decisions on the statute as to closing of schools or on the statute granting tuition expenses.

PARKS AND RECREATIONAL SYSTEMS

We do not spend any time on the cases as to parks and recreational systems for it is sufficient to say that if the State owns and operates such systems, they must be administered on a nondiscriminatory basis.

PUBLIC ACCOMMODATIONS

At the present time owners of restaurants, coffee shops and cafeterias, hotels and motels, and privately owned stores have a right to select their own customers and patrons, and the North Carolina Trespass Laws are still in force and have not been invalidated. Restaurants and cafeterias in our public buildings, either State, county or city, are required to be operated on a nondiscriminatory basis and a lease or concession to an individual or corporation requires that such lessee operate in a nondiscriminatory manner.

HOSPITALS

All public hospitals supported by tax funds must be operated in a nondiscriminatory manner, and this would appear to be so where the hospital has received Hill-Burton funds, although litigation in this respect has not ended. A private hospital still has a right to choose its own patrons and can practice discrimination if it so desires (*Eaton v. Board of Managers of James Walker Memorial Hospital*, 261 F. 2d 521, certiorari denied, 359 U. S. 984, 3 L. ed. 2d 934, 79 S. Ct. 941).

241

A 1949 DEMONSTRATION ON THE STATE CAPITOL SQUARE IN BEHALF OF BETTER LAW SCHOOL FACILITIES.

STREET DEMONSTRATIONS

You will find definitions of breach of the peace and of riots in the case of *State v. Cole*, 249 N. C. 733. It is thought that municipalities still have the right to regulate traffic and to preserve peace and order in the streets and to establish reasonable standards for the issuance of permits for parades and street demonstrations. This is established in the cases of *Cox v. New Hampshire*, 312 U. S. 569, and *Poulos v. New Hampshire*, 345 U. S. 395.

CRIMINAL PROCEDURE

It is a violation of the Fourteenth Amendment to obtain confessions from persons by means of brutality, long continued interrogation, or undue coercion. Generally speaking, indigent persons who are indicted for crimes are now entitled to counsel to be furnished by the State, and an indigent person is entitled to a transcript of the court record to perfect his appeal and is entitled to counsel on such appeal.

A RESUME OF THE CIVIL RIGHTS ACT OF 1964*

Title I of the Act does the following: It prohibits racial discrimination in qualification of voters for federal elections and does not allow any denial of voting rights in federal elections because of registration errors which are not material. Literacy tests as qualification for voting are not allowed unless administered in writing to all voters and a copy of the test a voter has taken, and the answers, are provided the voter requesting them within 25 days after such request. If a person has completed the sixth grade in school, he is presumed to have met the literacy requirements, but the contrary can be shown. The Attorney General of the United States, as well as a defendant in a voting case, can request a three-judge federal court to hear cases in which the Attorney General seeks a finding that a pattern or practice of discrimination exists with an appeal from a three-judge court directly to the Supreme Court of the United States.

Title II, briefly stated, does the following: Prohibits discrimination and segregation in places of public accommodation such as hotels, motels, restaurants, theaters, sports arenas, service stations, and concert halls if interstate commerce is affected. Interstate commerce is affected if a substantial portion of goods sold or exhibited move in interstate commerce or if the accommodations in question are on the premises of an establishment involved in interstate commerce such as a restaurant in a bus station or train station. There is exempted from this provision private clubs and rooming houses with no more than five rooms for hire when the proprietor is a resident. This provision also invalidates state and local laws permitting or requiring discrimination or segregation in places of public accommodation. An aggrieved person can seek protection of a federal court when there is reasonable ground to believe that a person is about to engage in acts prohibited under this

* This resume of H.R. 7152 (Eighty-Eighth Congress, Second Session) was prepared by Mr. Moody upon the passage of the Act to be cited as the "Civil Rights Act of 1964" and is attached as an addendum to this memorandum.

Title, and the Attorney General can seek court orders under this Title. Under this Title the court is permitted, in states where alleged discriminatory practices are not covered by local or state law, to defer civil and criminal action for as long as 120 days while the matter is referred to the Community Relations Service established by Title X of the Bill if the court believes there is a possibility of obtaining voluntary compliance. The Community Relations Service can conduct closed hearings unless all agree otherwise. The Attorney General can move for a temporary or permanent court order if he has reasonable cause to believe that any person or group is engaged in discriminatory practices covered by this Title and the Attorney General can ask for a three-judge court if the request is accompanied by a certificate saying that the case is of general public importance.

Title III does the following: Authorizes the Attorney General to file civil suits to end discrimination or segregation in facilities, except schools, owned by state or local governments if he believes the complaints have merit and the person making complaints cannot bear the costs of the suit or would be physically endangered or financially hurt by filing such suits.

Title IV does the following: The United States Commissioner of Education is to conduct a survey on the effects of discrimination and segregation on equal educational opportunity in public schools and report his findings to Congress and the President within two years. It authorizes the United States Commissioner of Education to provide technical assistance to states, school boards, and schools on problems in order to implement desegregation and to make federal funds available to facilitate training of teachers and administrators to cope with desegregation. If a person is refused admission to and removed from a public college or if a complaint is made that a school board has deprived children of the equal protection of the laws, the Attorney General can file a suit if in his opinion such persons cannot bear the costs of the suit or would be endangered by filing suit. Desegregation does not mean the assignment of students to public schools in order to overcome racial imbalance.

Title V does the following: It provides for a 30-day notice of hearings before the Civil Rights Commission. The Civil Rights Commission is a clearing house for information on denial of equal protection of the laws due to discrimination in any of the fields covered by the Act.

Title VI does the following: It bars discrimination in programs assisted by the federal government, excluding federal insurance and guaranty programs. It authorizes the assisting agency to order an end to discrimination in federally assisted projects with the order becoming effective upon the approval of the President. It authorizes termination of an assistance program in cases of noncompliance, but notice of termination and all pertinent facts of the case must be submitted by the head of the federal agency involved to the appropriate committees of the Senate and House of Representatives.

Title VII does the following: It applies to all employers and labor unions engaged in business affecting interstate commerce, but excludes employers who have less than 25 employees, private clubs, the United States Government, and religious organizations. This Title becomes effective one year from the date of its enactment and for one year thereafter, businesses having fewer than 100 employees shall not be covered by this Title; for the second year thereafter, businesses having fewer than 75 employees shall not be covered; and for the fourth year and thereafter, businesses having fewer than 25 employees shall not be covered. It prohibits discrimination and segregation in hiring practices, wage practices, labor union membership, or against an employee because he has opposed practices prohibited by this Title. It creates an equal employment opportunity commission which can investigate charges of employment discrimination. It empowers the commission to sue for compliance and permits the Attorney General of the United States to intervene. The Attorney General can also sue for compliance, ask for a three-judge court if the case is of public general importance with appeal directly to the Supreme Court of the United States. It requires employers covered by the Act to post notice of the fair-employment practice provisions of the Act.

Title VIII orders the Secretary of Commerce to compile voting and vote-registration statistics, including age and race data in areas recommended by the Civil Rights Commission.

Title IX authorizes the Attorney General to intervene in any civil suit for relief from denial of equal protection of the laws due to discrimination if he certifies the case of general public importance.

Title X establishes in the Department of Commerce the Community Relations Service which can provide conciliation assistance to communities and persons involved in discrimination disputes.

Title XI provides for $1,000 fine or six months imprisonment for a person found guilty of criminal contempt under Titles II, III, IV, V, VI, or VII of the Act and provides for jury trials if the defendant so requests.

EXAMPLES OF NORTH CAROLINA CITY ORDINANCES TO CONTROL DEMONSTRATIONS

Several cities and towns of North Carolina have various ordinances designed to control street demonstrations and picketing. Typical of these are the ordinances of Kinston which follow:

AN ORDINANCE TO AMEND THE CODE OF THE CITY OF KINSTON PERTAINING TO PUBLIC DISTURBANCES

BE IT, AND IT IS HEREBY ORDAINED, that the *Code of Ordinances of the City of Kinston, North Carolina,* be amended by adding a new Section 15-30 thereto, as follows:

Section 15-30—Creating a Public Disturbance
The gathering of any group upon the sidewalks or streets of the City of Kinston for the purpose of creating, or which creates, mechanical or vocal sound which is of such intensity or nature as to interfere with the rights of peaceful occupancy by property owners in the adjoining areas is unlawful and any individual who participates in, leads, directs, or encourages such actions shall be guilty of violating this section, provided, however, that nothing herein shall prevent the orderly expression of spectators at any regularly organized sport event or the peaceful assembly of any group for orderly expression or communication between those assembled.

This ordinance shall be in full force and effect from and after its adoption.

AN ORDINANCE TO AMEND THE CODE OF THE CITY OF KINSTON PERTAINING TO ISSUANCE OF PERMITS FOR PARADES OR DEMONSTRATIONS UPON THE CITY STREETS OR SIDEWALKS

BE IT, AND IT IS HEREBY ORDAINED, that the *Code of the City of Kinston, North Carolina,* be amended by adding a new Section 15-31 thereto as follows:

Section 15-31—Permits Required and General Regulations
(a) No parade, picket line or group demonstration is permitted on the sidewalks or streets of the City of Kinston unless a permit therefor has been issued by the City of Kinston, provided, however, that nothing herein shall be construed to prevent the peaceful assembly of any group for orderly expression or communication between those assembled.

(b) Wherever in this Code any regulation or enactment pertains to a parade, group demonstration or picket line the following definitions shall apply but shall not be exclusive as to coverage:

(1) "Parade" is any parade, march, ceremony, show, exhibition, or procession of any kind in or upon the public streets, sidewalks, parks or other public places.

(2) "Person" is any person, firm, partnership, association, company or organization of any kind.

(3) "Picket line" is any person or persons formed together for the purpose of making known any position or promotion of said person or persons or on behalf of any organization.

(4) "Group demonstrations" is any assembly together or concert of action between two or more persons for the purpose of protesting any matter or making known any position or thought of the group or of attracting attention to such demonstration.

(c) No person shall hamper, obstruct, impede or interfere with such activity or any person participating therein and the police force is authorized to establish lines for separation of the general public from such activity and it shall be unlawful to violate the provision of this section or to cross such lines.

(d) That upon violation of the terms of the permit by those participating the Chief of Police or such officer of the police force as may then be in charge, is authorized to then revoke the permit and direct those participating to disperse. That no such parade, picket line, or group demonstration is permitted within any public building or structure.

(e) **Exceptions.** This section shall not apply to:

1. Funeral processions.

2. Students going to and from school classes or participating in educational activities where such activity is under the immediate supervision and direction of proper school authorities.

3. A governmental agency acting within the scope of its functions.

(f) **Appeal Procedure.**

Any person aggrieved by the denial of a permit, as herein provided shall have a right of appeal to the City Council, but such appeal notice must be given five (5) days thereafter and the appeal upon such notice will be heard by the Council at its next regular meeting or at any special called meeting the Council may set.

This ordinance shall be in full force and effect from and after its adoption.

AN ORDINANCE TO AMEND THE CODE OF THE CITY OF KINSTON PERTAINING TO THE REQUIREMENTS FOR PERMITS FOR PARADES, PICKET LINES, OR GROUP DEMONSTRATIONS

BE IT, AND IT IS HEREBY ORDAINED, that the *Code of Ordinances of the City of Kinston, North Carolina,* be amended by adding a new Section 15-32 thereto, as follows:

Section 15-32—Requirements for Permits

The Chief of Police, or, in his absence, the next highest ranking officer of the Kinston Police Force, is authorized to issue permits as required in Section 15-31 and in the issuance thereof shall:

(a) Require a written application therefor to be filed twenty-four (24) hours in advance of such parade, picket line or group demonstration on a form prescribed by said department and which shall require the application to be signed by the person or persons filing such application, and the applicant shall therein state the proposed place, time, purpose and size of such parade, picket line, or group demonstration, and whether or not any minors below the age of eighteen (18) years shall participate.

(b) Refuse to issue such permit when the activity or purpose stated in the application would violate any ordinance of the City of Kinston or statute of the State of North Carolina, or when the activity or purpose would endanger the public health or safety, or hinder or prevent the orderly movement of pedestrian or vehicular traffic on the sidewalks or streets of the City of Kinston.

(c) Specify in the permit whether or not minors below the age of eighteen (18) years will be permitted to participate. That the Chief of Police, or, in his absence, the next highest ranking police officer of the City of Kinston on duty, shall pass upon whether or not minors below the age of eighteen (18) years shall be permitted to participate in the parade, picket line or group demonstration, and shall base his determination upon whether or not the purpose or time or place of the participation will be detrimental to or endanger the health, welfare or safety of said minors.

(d) The permit may set the starting time and duration of such parade, demonstration or picket line and may set the speed of its travel, the space between persons or vehicles, the portions or areas of the streets and sidewalks to be used, the length of the parade, group or line, and such other requirements as the Chief of Police or other designated officer may include in the permit for the control of free movement of traffic upon the streets and sidewalks, or for the health, safety and property rights of the participants and general public. Failure to comply with such requirements, as set forth in the permit, shall be unlawful.

(e) The applicant for permit shall specify and the permit shall designate, the person in charge of the parade, group demonstration and picket line and such person in charge shall accompany such parade, demonstration or picket line and shall carry such permit with him at that time.

(f) The Chief of Police or other designated officer in considering the issuance of a permit shall, among other considerations provided, consider and find as a requisite for issuance that:

1. The activity will not require excessive diversion of police from other necessary duties.

2. The activity will not interfere with the right of property owners in the area to enjoy peaceful occupancy and use of their property.

3. The activity can be conducted without unreasonable interference with normal vehicular or pedestrian traffic in the area and will not prevent normal police or fire protection to the public and will not be likely to cause injury to persons or property or provoke disorderly conduct or create a public disturbance.

This ordinance shall be in full force and effect from and after its adoption.

AN ORDINANCE TO AMEND THE CODE OF THE CITY OF KINSTON PERTAINING TO THE REQUIREMENTS FOR PERMITS FOR PARADES, PICKET LINES, OR GROUP DEMONSTRATIONS

BE IT, AND IT IS HEREBY ORDAINED, that the *Code of Ordinances of the City of Kinston, North Carolina,* be amended by adding a new Section 15-33 thereto, as follows:

Section 15-33—Limitations on Parades, Picket Lines and Group Demonstrations

(a) In any parade, picket line or group demonstration, it shall be unlawful:

(1) For any minor below the age of eighteen (18) years to participate or be allowed to participate, and any person encouraging, leading, or allowing such minor to so participate, unless a permit therefor has been issued, shall be guilty of a violation of this section.

(2) For any person to lead, guide, participate in, or in any way support or encourage such parade, picket line, or group demonstration when a minor below the age of eighteen (18) years is participating therein, unless a permit for such participation by such minor has been issued.

(3) For any parent to knowingly permit any minor child of such parent under eighteen (18) years of age to participate in such parade, picket line, or group demonstrations, unless a permit for such participation by such minor has been issued.

(4) To cause, participate in, lead, or encourage any parade, picket line, or group demonstration to deviate in any manner from the authority therefor specified in the permit.

(b) That any picket line or group demonstration which participates in any area subject to normally heavy pedestrian or vehicular traffic may be limited in the permit issued to a concentration of not more than six (6) persons participating within any designated area of the street or sidewalk. Provided, that the officer issuing the permit may specify a larger number in the designated area wherein his judgment conditions permit a higher concentration. A designated area is defined as the entire width of said street or sidewalk within a distance measured along its length for 100 feet.

This ordinance shall be in full force and effect from and after its adoption.

AN ORDINANCE TO AMEND THE CODE OF THE CITY OF KINSTON PERTAINING TO USE OF THE STREETS AND SIDEWALKS

BE IT, AND IT IS HEREBY ORDAINED, that Section 20-2 of the *Code of Ordinances of the City of Kinston, North Carolina,* be amended by adding to the end of said section the following:

It shall be unlawful to obstruct or block the sidewalks or streets of the City of Kinston by any exhibition, demonstration, picket line or commercial venture, so as to prevent the normal flow of pedestrian or vehicular traffic except that special permit may be granted by the Chief of Police, or next highest ranking officer, of the City of Kinston for temporary and peaceful occupancy of a limited portion thereof for purposes other than hostile demonstration or commercial gain. That participation in such illegal exhibition, demonstration, or picket line, by any individual through leadership, organization or physical participation therein, is unlawful.

This ordinance shall be in full force and effect from and after its adoption.

THE NEGRO AND THE LAW WHEN THE NATION WAS FOUNDED

The Director of Columbia University's Conservation of Human Resources Project, Dr. Eli Ginzberg,* in an article published by *The New York Times,* contends that the so-called Negro problem is also the white man's problem and he says that for "three hundred fifty years white America has stood the

---

* Excerpts from "The Negro's Problem Is the White's" by Dr. Eli Ginzberg (c) 1964 by The New York Times Company. Reprinted by permission.

Negro off. Why it did so and with what consequences, are lessons we should study carefully."

Dr. Ginzberg points out that the Constitution was not written with a view to protection of the Negro's right as a citizen. The following is a quotation from this article:

The Constitution—the basic law of the land—dealt with the Negro in three ways: first, it stipulated that Congress could put an end to the slave trade but not before 1808; second, it authorized the Federal Government to return runaway slaves to their owners; and third, it provided that a slave would be counted as three-fifths of a man in determining the basis of representation in the House of Representatives—hardly the type of legislation to justify Myrdal's belief that we had a democratic commitment to the Negro. A further piece of evidence is that no President of the United States from George Washington to William Howard Taft had any answer to the problem presented by Negroes in white America except to suggest, in one way or another, that they leave the country.

The second historical fact is that although the Negro has mostly lived in the South, the North and the West have also been, and remain, generally hostile to him. Even today, the Administration is finding it difficult to persuade Republicians from states where there are few Negroes to agree to the passage of a broad civil-rights bill.

The South has never had the determining voice. The destiny of the Negro in America has always been shaped primarily by the attitudes and actions of white citizens in the North and West, who were not interested in the Negro and made no commitments to him. As early as the drafting of the Constitution, and many times thereafter, the North said to the South: "We will not interfere in your relationships with the Negro if you will not interfere with some of our basic economic policies."

The third conclusion from history is that such gains as Negroes have been able to make usually came when whites did not have to pay for them—and when they wanted something from the Negro or from each other. Negro slaves had a chance to win their freedom during the Revolutionary War when the British offered to free all those who would fight for them. George Washington, who had at first refused to take Negroes into the army, then permitted them to enlist. Later, when North and South engaged in fratricidal war, Lincoln himself said that he would settle the war gladly even if he could not free a single Negro. He believed his primary responsibility as Chief Executive was to settle the war; emancipation was merely a military expedient.

It is only since 1940, when the North needed and wanted Negro labor in pursuit of the defense effort and of economic growth, that the Negro has begun to make significant gains. When the country finally needed Negro man-power, Negroes were able to advance as citizens.

Editors' comment: Not until the Thirteenth, Fourteenth, and Fifteenth Amendments to the Constitution were adopted were full civil rights for Negroes given constitutional backing and the Negro insists that these amendments have been ignored for one hundred years following his technical emancipation. For sixty-seven years the United States Supreme Court supported the proposition that the Constitution was being honored when "separate but equal" provisions for the education of the two races were established. A reversal of this opinion is the most radical action that has been taken in the interest of the Negroes' plea for equal rights and equal opportunities. He now is urging not only unequivocal acceptance of that decree, but full citizenship rights in other particulars.

Dr. Ginzberg may be exactly correct in his statement that no President of the United States from Washington through William Howard Taft had any better suggestion for solution of the race problem in the United States than the emigration of the Negro portion of our citizenship; but it is also true that one of the greatest of our Presidents, the philosopher who wrote the Declaration of Independence, Thomas Jefferson, changed his mind about the potential of the Negro citizen and expressed himself clearly. It was in 1809 that Jefferson wrote as follows:

Be assured that no person living wishes more sincerely than I do to see a complete refutation of the doubts I have myself entertained and expressed on the grade of understanding allotted to them by nature and to find that in this respect they are on a par with ourselves. My doubts were the result of personal observation on the limited sphere of my own State where the opportunities for the development of their genius were not favorable and those of exercising it still less so. I expressed them, therefore, with great hesitation; but whatever be their degree of talent is no measure of their rights.

V

Sanford's Constructive Program

Governor Sanford recognized that the Negroes' petition for a change of customs to improve their citizenship status in North Carolina was just. He has proceeded to take steps to correct some of the disadvantages under which the Negro portion of the state's population lives. This section of the book is devoted to the report by the Chairman of the State Good Neighbor Council which was established by the Governor. It reflects a large portion of the economic progress that has been accomplished since the present Governor took the leadership in dealing with the petitions of the Negroes at the state level.

This report and the individual municipal reports which are incorporated herein show the advancement that has been made in promoting civil rights for the Negro in North Carolina. Whether a Congressional statute guaranteeing the Negro equal service at places of public accommodation is enacted or not, an objective in North Carolina, expressed by the Governor and by the groups formed under local city and town governments, is to create an atmosphere in this State in which civil rights for the Negroes can be assured.

Inspired by Governor Sanford's challenge to the Negroes to substitute education for some of their demonstration methods, North Carolina's Negro college and university students formally organized themselves into the North Carolina Intercollegiate Council for Human Rights, Tuesday afternoon, February 25, 1964. The new organization elected officers and adopted two major programs.

The purpose of the new organization is to promote human rights for all citizens of North Carolina through the use of any medium which holds promise of "relieving human indignities and of securing adjustments in a segregated society."

The first program proposed is a documentary television series depicting "Why the Negro Demonstrates." This series is being prepared by some of the State's Negro student leaders in response to Governor Sanford's challenge.

Governor Sanford: "The Negroes' mass demonstrations are not effective in getting across to the public the reasons for the protest and dissatisfaction. In the long run these demonstrations create ill will at a time when we must seek more good will. The time has now come when we should attempt to find a more constructive substitute for the protests by street demonstrators. It is time to turn toward civic enterprise, time to translate physical action into intelligible dialogue."

The documentary television series will attempt to show the future of the Negro college graduate. It will picture the extent to which poverty hinders Negroes' personal and community improvement. It will set forth the Negroes' concern for the transcendent problems of the world and his desire to help solve those problems.

THE NORTH CAROLINA INTERCOLLEGIATE COUNCIL FOR HUMAN RIGHTS PLANS A FILM SERIES. SEATED CLOCKWISE AROUND THE TABLE ARE: AURELIA L. YOUNG, WILLIS McLEOD, JAMES ROBINSON, ULYSSES RALPH LEE, JR., WILLIAM T. PARKER, PAMELA PFAFF, JESSE L. JACKSON, *CHAIRMAN*, JAMES ANDERSON, JR., JOANE EDWARDS, MARY TREADWELL, HORACE J. CHAPMAN, JOHN C. BROOKS, JUNE RYAN, NORRIS E. FRANCIS, JR., ALICE WALKER, AND PATRICIA SPELLEN.

The television series will include an evaluation of the quality of education in the state's Negro schools. It will survey Negro academic standards. It will discuss civic responsibility and the Negroes' role in a changing and increasingly complex society.

One documentary film will deal with the Negroes' contribution to North Carolina's history and will attempt to define the Negroes' role in cultural and intellectual affairs.

Governor Sanford: "This appears to be a far more intelligent way of expressing the aspirations and ambitions of the Negro citizens of North Carolina than do the methods which are being employed at present. I hope that this program will be developed, programmed, and accepted in the same spirit of good will which prompted its establishment."

The second program approved by the new Council for Human Rights is a high school advisory and tutoring service. This program is designed to assist faltering high school students with their academic work with a view toward discouraging their dropping out of school and of encouraging their college enrollment. The aim is to provide personal help for students who are unable to acquire it on a regular basis from their overworked teachers.

*THE NORTH CAROLINA GOOD NEIGHBOR COUNCIL**

On January 18, 1963, Governor Sanford, speaking before the North Carolina Press Institute, said, "Reluctance to accept the Negro in employment is the greatest single block to his continued progress and to the full use of the human potential of the nation and its states."

In that same eloquent speech, the Governor announced the establishment of a 24-member North Carolina Good Neighbor Council. This Council has a two-fold mission: (1) to encourage the employment of qualified people without regard to race, and (2) to encourage youth to become better trained and qualified for employment.

In making this announcement, the Governor said:

(1) In North Carolina we will attempt to provide the leadership for the kind of understanding America needs today.

---

* By D. S. Coltrane, Chairman.

(2) We are asking all mayors and chairmen of county commissioners to establish local good neighbor councils.

(3) We have issued a memorandum to heads of state agencies, departments, and institutions, asking them, if they have not already done so, to examine and formulate policies which do not exclude from employment qualified people because of race.

(4) We call on church leaders, pastors, civic organizations, to support the objectives of the good neighbor councils in their own effective ways.

In the statement announcing the establishment of the Good Neighbor Council, the Governor further said:

The American Negro was freed from slavery one hundred years ago. In this century he has made much progress, educating his children, building churches, entering into the community and civic life of the nation. Now is a time not merely to look back to freedom, but forward to the fulfillment of its meaning. Despite great progress, the Negro's opportunity to obtain a good job has not been achieved in most places across the country.

The time has come for American citizens to quit unfair discriminations and to give the Negro a full chance to earn a decent living for his family and to contribute to higher standards for himself and all men.

We can do this, we should do this, we will do it because we are concerned with the problems and welfare of our neighbors. We will do it because our economy cannot afford to have so many people fully or partially unproductive. We will do it because it is honest and fair for us to give all men and women their best chance in life. We are just going to have to open up jobs for all people on the basis of ability and training, and promotions on the basis of performance. I do not intend to try to force anybody. I do not believe in force. In fact, this is a voluntary, low-pressure program. I do believe the conscience of North Carolinians will get the job done.

THE PROGRAM IN PERSPECTIVE

With the establishment of the North Carolina Good Neighbor Council, the State launched a bold, constructive program to secure equal job opportunities for all citizens. The program was applauded by more than 50 newspapers across the State and nation. Since the inception of this program, noticeable progress has been made. A wide range of activities has been initiated. Twenty-six members of the State Council have been appointed by the Governor. These 26 members have been selected from all walks of life and from all sections of the State, from Edenton in the east to Asheville in the west. Meetings of the Council have been held in Raleigh, Charlotte, Wilson, and Greensboro.

LOCAL GOOD NEIGHBOR COUNCILS

On the local level, "Good Neighbor" groups have been formed, or subcommittees of human relations councils, biracial committees, or similar groups have been designated to expand educational programs and employment opportunities in the following cities, towns, and communities: Alamance County, Albemarle, Asheville, Chapel Hill, Charlotte, Dunn, Durham, Elizabeth City, Fayetteville, Gastonia, Goldsboro, Greensboro, Greenville, Hickory, High Point, Kinston, Laurinburg, Lexington, Mooresville, Mount Airy, Oxford, Raleigh, Rockingham, Roxboro, Rocky Mount, Salisbury, Sanford, Shelby, Smithfield, Thomasville, Wadesboro, Warrenton, Whiteville, Wilmington, Williamston, Winston-Salem, and Wilson.

ACTIVITIES OF THE STATE COUNCIL

The activities of the State Council are carried on through the office of the Chairman, D. S. Coltrane, with assistance from its Vice-Chairman, Dr. James T. Taylor, employment services representative of the Employment Security Commission, and Mrs. Sarah W. Herbin, employment services representative of the Good Neighbor Council.

In its activities, the Council employs the methods of persuasion, education, conferences, fact-finding, research, and negotiation. To date the following steps have been taken by employees of the Council or by Council members:

(1) Through communications, visits, and speeches, assistance has been given in the formation of local groups or subcommittees in practically all of the communities heretofore mentioned. Hundreds of letters and memoranda concerning formation of local groups have been mailed from the office of the Chairman.

(2) Letters have been sent to all directors of state departments, institutions, and agencies calling their attention to Governor Sanford's pledge to end discrimination in state jobs and urging assistance and co-operation.

(3) The Council has alerted Negro leaders in several communities to the increasing number of job openings in the follow-

D. S. COLTRANE, *CHAIRMAN*, PRESIDES OVER A QUARTERLY MEETING OF THE
NORTH CAROLINA GOOD NEIGHBOR COUNCIL IN GREENSBORO. PICTURED FROM
LEFT TO RIGHT: FIRST ROW: DR. JOHN R. LARKINS, *RECORDING SECRETARY*,
DR. JAMES T. TAYLOR, *VICE-CHAIRMAN*, MRS. HOWARD MARSH, JOHN S.
STEWART, CLARK S. BROWN, AND J. W. JEFFRIES. SECOND ROW: ROBERT J.
BROWN, THOMPSON GREENWOOD, HARRY D. GORE, MARSHALL A. RAUCH, AND
DR. G. K. BUTTERFIELD. THIRD ROW: JEFF D. BATTS, J. MARSE GRANT, ERNEST
ROSS, JAMES A. NELSON, JOHN W. WINTERS, AND EDWARD LOEWENSTEIN.
ABSENT MEMBERS ARE: MRS. GENEVA J. BOW, DR. REGINALD A. HAWKINS,
JOHN E. JERVIS, BRUCE F. JONES, J. P. STROTHER, JOHN H. WHEELER, AND
E. R. ZANE.

ing state agencies: Department of Mental Health, Prison Department, Board of Paroles, Probation Commission, Board of Public Welfare, Board of Juvenile Correction, and Memorial Hospital at Chapel Hill. Many requests from Negroes for employment have been answered through the council office.

(4) Links of communication have been established with several large industries throughout the State concerning employment practices and problems.

(5) Contacts have been made with many schools throughout the State, questioning them on the activities of Negro graduates and advising administrative leaders and students of some of the opportunities that are open for Negroes.

(6) Warm support for the Good Neighbor program has been received from the press and from church leaders throughout the State. Pertinent facts relative to the Good Neighbor program were sent to more than 1,100 ministers during 1963.

EDUCATION— THE TRAINING OF
YOUTH FOR EMPLOYMENT

During the 18-month existence of the North Carolina Good Neighbor Council, no point has been realized more keenly than the importance of better trained and qualified people for employment. The Good Neighbor Council has endeavored to impress upon Negro youth that one of the most important additions to North Carolina's educational program in recent years is a far-reaching system of 20 Industrial Education Centers located throughout the State. In these centers courses are designed to give youth and adults job-preparatory training, upgrading, updating, related instruction for apprentices, and supervisory development training.

Emphasis has been made of the fact that these 20 Industrial Education Centers are all integrated and that the program is broad and inexpensive.

BROCHURE ON VOCATIONAL EDUCATION

The Good Neighbor Council early in its existence realized that Negro youth and many of the school counselors and teachers were not familiar with the vocational training opportunities offered by the State of North Carolina. Therefore, a 95-page brochure was published in October, 1963. Contained in this brochure are descriptions of the major vocational training programs offered in North Carolina. This brochure is serving as a guide for local councils and committees seeking to improve the educational and economic conditions of the State. It has been in great demand as more than 1,300 copies have been distributed through local councils and school people. Copies are available by writing The North Carolina Good Neighbor Council, Box 584, Raleigh, North Carolina.

An extensive campaign has been launched to encourage more co-operation between local councils and people responsible for the educational programs, especially the vocational educational programs. Greater understanding of high school counselors and improvement in Career Day programs seem quite necessary.

In Rocky Mount, an eastern North Carolina town, the local Good Neighbor Council promoted a program in the Negro high school to screen promising juniors and seniors who are not planning a college career to interest them in secretarial and clerical training and to prepare them for trades by enrolling in the Industrial Educational Centers. This kind of program can be of tremendous value in placing persons in jobs available, but now hard to fill.

ECONOMIC STATUS OF NEGROES

North Carolina has perhaps done more to raise the economic status of the Negro than any other southern state. It has, for instance, provided better schools, particularly on the level of higher education, expanding college attendance and participation in government and civic affairs. However, employment opportunities have not been expanded rapidly enough. Unquestionably jobs with a good financial future have been limited.

For whites, in North Carolina the median income per family is $4,588, whereas for Negroes it is only $1,922. Thus we see that the average Negro income is a little less than four-tenths as much as the income for white people in this State. This poverty and insecurity are particularly appalling to the Negro, who sees the white society that surrounds him grow increasingly affluent while he remains tied to his slum. The future is even bleaker than the present because automation, new management techniques, and many other changes are all reducing the demand for unskilled and semiskilled labor. More people are now being employed as professional, technical, office, and sales workers than as manual workers. We have shifted from a blue-collar to a white-collar society. North Carolina is rapidly changing from an agricultural economy, where Negroes have been employed, to an industrial economy, where competition is keen and where well-trained personnel is demanded.

All local Good Neighbor Councils and similar groups should take cognizance of the employment situation; otherwise, more and more people will be placed on the welfare rolls.

PROGRESS IN EMPLOYMENT OF NEGROES

Negroes are being employed in many job categories that were closed to them eight to ten years ago. They are being employed in industrial plants throughout the State on a nondiscriminatory basis. The greatest progress has been made by many of the largest industries in the Piedmont area, including some of the largest manufacturers in the tobacco, textiles, electronics, and aircraft industries. One electronics company with plants in three or four cities of the State employs Negroes as engineers, draftsmen, chemists, clerk-typists, electricians, technicians, librarians, and bench workers. Reynolds Tobacco Company, large manufacturer of cigarettes, has a number of Negroes in administrative, supervisory, and clerical positions. This company's operations have been integrated to such an extent that *The New York Times* carried a feature story in regard to the company's policy and program.

The Charlotte Division of the Douglas Aircraft Company adheres to the general policy of the company which guarantees equal economic and employment opportunity to each of the 72,000 men and women on its payroll. Negroes are employed by the Douglas Company in personnel, clerical, planning, drafting, and graduate engineering jobs. The company cafeteria and other facilities are all integrated.

In Greensboro where there are 75,000 employees, 50 per cent of all jobs are controlled by employers who have racially equal employment policies.

Rocky Mount reports: "In the industrial area, ten industrial concerns six months ago had 157 Negro employees and are presently employing 244 Negroes, which represents a 56 per cent increase."

A garment factory in Wilson is now employing 40 Negro women, whereas a year ago they were not employing any Negro women.

EMPLOYMENT OF NEGROES BY
THE MERCANTILE INDUSTRY

The North Carolina Merchants' Association reports that many retail stores are training and hiring Negro salespeople. One manager of a large variety store reports: "We have asked our managers to adopt a tolerant and understanding attitude on this matter and to seek the opportunity to employ Negroes when good applications are received. Also, it was suggested that they counsel with school principals and other leaders. To date, we have three persons employed as salespeople. They have been well received among other personnel and by our customers." This is typical of the reports from most retail sales stores.

We believe that considerable progress was made during 1963 in upgrading present Negro employees, plus employment of new Negro help. Several of the larger stores have upgraded those who are qualified. Some few banks and savings and loan associations have given Negroes who are qualified jobs in teller and clerical positions. Many merchants have employed or promoted Negroes in jobs that were formerly held only by white employees. These include department stores, shoe stores, grocery super markets, furniture stores, hardware stores, drugstores. The reports from managers are most encouraging. The Negroes are making good employees and there has been practically no objection to them by the consumers. We are hopeful this trend will increase without either race being embarrassed.

A large chain store which operates in North Carolina reports that there are 542 Negroes on the payroll in North Carolina—27 are in full customer contact jobs and six in supervisory jobs. A key store in Winston-Salem reports that 12 per cent of its employees are Negroes, an increase of about 15 per cent over a year ago. Fayetteville reports that in the retail sales, clerical, bookkeeping and teller areas, nine firms are currently employing one to three Negro employees each, as compared to no employees in this area one year ago.

Many merchants who have adopted an equal employment policy have not had any openings for additional personnel and do not feel inclined to replace long-time, capable employees just for the sake of employing Negroes. Then, too, many merchants have been unable to locate Negro personnel with training in merchandising. The Good Neighbor Council has carried on a campaign urging Negro youth to take courses offered in distributive education. It is the consensus of the Council that any Negro girl who finishes a course of this kind will readily find employment.

EMPLOYMENT OF NEGROES BY COUNTY AND MUNICIPAL GOVERNMENT

By and large county and municipal governments throughout North Carolina have adopted an equal or merit employment policy. In many instances application forms for employment contain no reference to race.

Cumberland County and the City of Fayetteville are used as examples to denote progress in the area of employment.

Cumberland County — The sheriff's office employs 42 people, three of whom are Negroes—two deputies and one employee in the county jail. The County Board of Health operates under the state merit system. It has four Negroes employed, two nurses, one assistant and one janitor, out of the total of 30 employees. The Welfare Department operates under the state merit system. Out of the total of 49 employees, four are Negroes—two caseworkers, one homemaker, and one janitor. The other county offices have adopted an equal employment policy. However, no Negroes to date have been employed.

City of Fayetteville — Employment by the city is open to all on the basis of merit. Positions in the police and fire departments are open by examination by the Civil Service Committee. Cape Fear Valley Hospital is integrated in service, facilities, employment, and membership on the Board of Trustees. Out of a total of 365 employees, 75 are Negroes. There are three Negro physicians on the hospital staff.

Another eastern North Carolina city reports that in the area of city government the percentage of Negroes employed is estimated to be 38 per cent. A report from this same city says this report would be incomplete without emphasizing the climate which now exists in the city which appears to be healthy in every respect. Whites and Negroes are working out a long-range program which should be helpful to both races and to the overall economy of the community.

MUNICIPAL GOVERNMENT

Winston-Salem, a large city in the Piedmont Section of the State, reports there are 682 Negroes employed out of a total of 1,738. Of this number 25 are at the secretarial level, 62 are at the graduate nurse level. There are nine Negro librarians, nine firemen, two fire sergeants, two fire captains, and one first lieutenant. There are two Negro detectives. Negroes are employed by this City at eight different levels, and the City has an upgrading policy.

In Greensboro there are a number of Negroes employed in the post office department.

REPORT FROM AN EASTERN NORTH CAROLINA TOWN

The chairman of the employment committee of the Biracial Council of Goldsboro, an eastern North Carolina town, has reported as follows:

NONDISCRIMINATORY EMPLOYMENT IS SOUGHT BY STREET MARCHERS.

At our initial subcommittee meeting we classified the firms of employment in our area and noted those hiring Negroes above the unskilled level. The "employment picture" revealed that many large industries were discriminating in their hiring policies and that we should make personal contact with the managers in an effort to have them adopt a fair hiring policy based on merit.

Realizing the enormous job we had undertaken, we asked the chairman of our council to grant us the privilege of adding workers to our subcommittee. Our request was granted and five additional people were added as "advisers to the subcommittee." Since our original committee was composed of three Negroes and two whites, we added two Negroes and three whites to form five contact teams with a Negro and a white on each. We asked our council chairman to send a letter to the firms prior to our visit.

After talking with managers and personnel directors, we knew that eventually we would have calls for qualified workers in areas previously denied Negroes. We recognized the need for additional help in recruiting trainees and setting up training programs. To this end the principal, assistant principal, distributive education co-ordinator, guidance counselor, counselor from the Employment Security Commission, and the director of the Industrial Education Center met with the subcommittee and advisers. We divided ourselves into two groups—one to work with a survey and determine the number and job classifications of Negroes and the other to set up a training program.

Through the news media we requested persons interested in training or retraining to meet at a designated time and place. The director of our Industrial Education Center addressed the 76 people who came and reviewed the many courses offered at the center. Those who wished registered for employment and/or training.

At another meeting a representative of the Employment Security Commission administered aptitude tests to the 32 registrants. From these tests we know we have people with aptitudes for most jobs in our area. Some of these people are presently enrolled in classes at the Industrial Education Center. Some placements have been made from our group; however, there are three openings (stenographer-typist, secretary, and television repairman) that we have been unable to fill. The managers in all cases have promised to consider all eligible applicants when these jobs or other jobs are open in their firms.

A survey with the retail stores and other downtown businesses revealed that there are 100 Negroes working in retail stores in our city with 26 holding jobs previously held by whites (full-time salespeople, supervisors, and foremen). Every manager interviewed stated that the work of the Negroes had been very satisfactory and their reception had been good with other employees and the public.

Our city government has announced a fair hiring policy based on merit and is presently hiring 92 Negroes, three of whom are policemen. Fair hiring policies have been made by some departments of our county government. A Negro caseworker and a Negro deputy sheriff have been added recently. The Health Department has had a Negro public health nurse for many years. In our city there are 14 Negroes working in the post office and at the Social Security Board. Ten of these are in competitive civil service.

NEGRO EMPLOYMENT IN STATE GOVERNMENT

State government is North Carolina's largest employer, with over 36,000 regular employees, excluding teachers, working in over 1,500 types of classified jobs. As of May, 1963, Negroes employed in state government totaled 5,061. Of this number, 2,693 were in maintenance and operations; 1,386 in administrative and clerical; and 712, faculty.

Not included in the figures above are the following Negro public school employees: teachers, principals, and supervisors, totaling 11,994; janitors and maids, 3,672; mechanics for school buses, 42; clerical workers and property cost clerks, 514; school bus drivers, 2,604.

The attached table shows by departments, institutions, and agencies the total number of Negro employees in three major occupational categories: faculty, administrative and clerical, and maintenance and operations.

Figures are not available for the number of Negro employees currently in nontraditional positions. While many are employed in such positions, the majority of these are in segregated institutions or agencies.

Since July 1, 1963, however, Negroes have been employed in the following positions: draftsmen, park ranger, counselor, factory inspector, tax auditor, parole and probation officers, stenographers, dental technician, prison guards, accounting clerk, duplicating machine operator, and maintenance mechanic.

It is our hope that in the future Negroes will be employed in a wider range of jobs available in state government agencies.

GOOD NEIGHBOR GOALS

The goal of the North Carolina Good Neighbor Program will be reached only when employees all over North Carolina are judged on the basis of merit and not on ancestry. During the past year, we have made progress toward this goal, but we would not be honest if we failed to recognize that we have just begun and that this is a long-range program. It is perhaps needless to say that in many cases Negroes are not being used to their fullest capacity because of racial discrimination and lack of education.

There is a great deal that all of us working together can do. With the proper co-operation from business, government, and labor; from city, town, and community leaders; from church leaders and forward-looking citizens, we can make the next decade the greatest ever in our desire for an equal employment program. Working together we can achieve the goal of equal opportunity for all. An increasing number of people are thinking positively in North Carolina. People are beginning to realize that for moral, patriotic, and economic reasons, we must strive for greater equality of opportunity for all our citizens.

NEGRO EMPLOYEES IN STATE GOVERNMENT BY
DEPARTMENTS AND JOB CATEGORIES
MAY, 1963

DEPARTMENTS	FACULTY	ADMINIS-TRATIVE AND CLERICAL	MAINTE-NANCE AND OPERA-TIONS	TOTALS
General Government	——	2	103	105
Public Safety and Regulation	——	13	10	23
Correction and Training	51	105	69	225
Public Welfare	7	3	35	45
Education	587	551	1,256	2,394
Highways	——	——	336	336
Health and Hospitals	31	702	1,084	1,817
Non-Highway Transportation	——	——	——	——
Natural Resources and Recreation	——	5	20	25
Agriculture	——	4	40	44
Employment Security Commission	36	——	10	46
Retirement and Pensions	——	1	——	1
TOTALS	712	1,386	2,963	5,061

WOMEN AND TEEN-AGERS ARE HELPING

What is regarded as a development of special importance in the efforts in North Carolina to effect adjustment of racial discontent in justice and good will is the new role women are assuming. First in High Point and next in Goldsboro the women enlisted for direct action in promoting the kind of group discussion designed to promote understanding. These groups are encouraging teen-agers to take a stand for racial fairness and friendship, and great improvement in human relations in the State is expected to come from these special forces.

The Good Will Committee of the City of High Point was formed by women in July, 1963. The Chairman of the High Point Biracial Committee recommended that the women of the community become directly involved in dealing with the problem of race relations. Acting as individuals, but through appeals to existing church and civic organizations, a group of women leaders met and accepted the civic service challenge.

The two women members, one Negro and one white, of the Biracial Committee undertook to promote action on the assignment. A steering committee of two Negro and eight white women, including the two members of the Biracial Committee,

GENERAL CAPUS M. WAYNICK INTRODUCES MRS. HOWARD MARSH, CHAIRMAN OF THE HIGH POINT WOMEN'S GOOD WILL COMMITTEE, TO THE NORTH CAROLINA GOOD NEIGHBOR COUNCIL. FROM *LEFT TO RIGHT:* J. E. SMITH, MRS. ELSIE W. PITTS, MRS. MARSH, GENERAL WAYNICK, DR. JOHN R. LARKINS, DAVID SCHENCK, HUGH M. RAPER, DR. VIVIAN W. HENDERSON, DR. JAMES T. TAYLOR, AND D. S. COLTRANE.

were chosen to determine the area of service to be undertaken. Individuals, who were representative of the total community, were selected because of their outstanding leadership experience.

It was stated that the purpose of this Women's Good Will Committee of High Point would be "To work through public discussion and dissemination of information toward increased understanding in relations between the races, as well as among those of the same race with different views" about the problem presented by the Negro petition for citizenship equality.

The Mayor of High Point officially endorsed the Women's Good Will Committee and its relationship to the whole civic movement.

In September, 1963, a "dutch-treat" luncheon meeting was held. Invitations were sent to 150 civic and church organizations of women, both Negro and white, requesting that at least one representative be present at the luncheon. This meeting was attended by 165 people representing 80 organizations. Capus Waynick addressed the group as special representative of Governor Terry Sanford.

The Chairman of the Good Will Committee presented the plan of offering the services of discussion leaders from the committee for programming on race relations, moral obligation, and civic responsibility. These discussion leaders were trained in three workshop sessions. The topics included the following: information on the various organizations working in the area of race

268

relations, discussion techniques, and consideration of questions to be presented for discussions. In the ensuing weeks the response was encouraging as church groups, YWCA, service clubs, Association of American University Women, and college alumnae groups were scheduled for programs. A biracial team of discussion leaders was requested by some groups.

The steering committee of the High Point Women's Good Will Committee began holding regular biweekly meetings. The role of the churches, schools, and other organizations, and the current progress in race relations are among the subjects presented by local people in these specialized fields. Interested women are invited to take part in these "round-table" discussion meetings.

Teen-agers were enlisted and some results of the Youth Good Will Committee of this group follow:

(1) The white Y-Teens and the teen-agers from the Negro YWCA (Mary Bethune Branch) agreed to join in community projects. Their first project was the packaging of materials to be sent to Algeria.

(2) An interracial tennis tournament took place in High Point.

(3) The swimming pool at the white YWCA was opened to Negroes without incident. Swimming instructions were given to one Negro Girl Scout Troop by the white staff at the YWCA.

(4) The Negro and white high school students formed a Youth Council, holding their meetings at the white YWCA.

In November, 1963, the Goldsboro Biracial Committee formed a Women's Good Will Committee following the procedure established in High Point. Mrs. Howard Marsh and Mrs. Matt Wall, Co-chairmen of the High Point group, went to Goldsboro on invitation and aided that city's movement by discussing methods and results.

When the High Point Biracial Committee was replaced by the Human Relations Commission which was made directly responsible to the Mayor and the City Council, it was decided that the organization of women and teen-agers could serve more appropriately as a High Point ally of the State Good Neighbor Council set up by the Governor with D. S. Coltrane as Chairman.

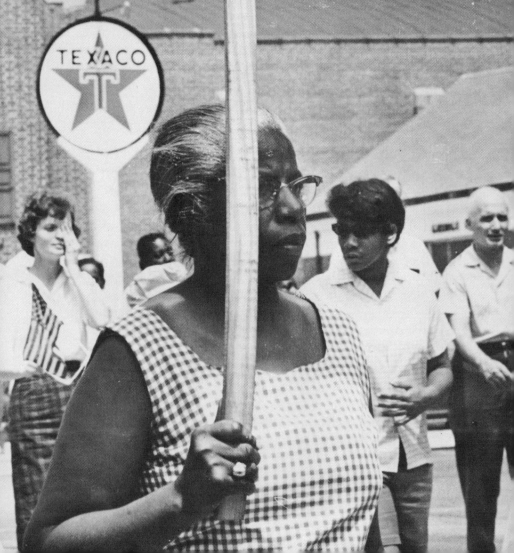

VI

Bibliography

A wealth of material has been compiled and published on race relations during recent years. Without attempting to set forth an exhaustive list below, the editors have selected a number of books and articles which they believe may be of particular use to the readers of this book. In order to present the material in a useful form the bibliography is arranged in groups according to the publications' general subject matter. The books are further annotated in some cases to furnish the reader additional insight into the contents of cited works.

Books

BASIC BACKGROUND MATERIAL

RACE, PREJUDICE, AND HARMONY

Allport, Gordon W. *The Nature of Prejudice.* Cambridge, Massachusetts: Addison-Wesley Press, 1954.
   This is a psychological approach to prejudice and stereotypes.

Benedict, Ruth and Weltfish, Gene. *The Races of Mankind.* New York: Public Affairs Committee, Inc., n.p. (First Edition, 1943), 1947.
   A general discussion of what anthropologists mean by "race," including the role of heredity, environment, and the social implications.

Buck, Paul H. *The Road to Reunion: 1865-1959.* New York: Knopf (Vintage K72), 1959.

Chase, Stuart. *Roads to Agreement: Successful Methods in the Science of Human Relations.* New York: Harper and Brothers, 1951.

Clark, Kenneth B. *Prejudice and Your Child*. Boston: Beacon Press, 1955.

Coon, Carleton S. *The Origin of Races*. New York: Alfred A. Knopf, Inc., 1962.
This presents a controversial thesis that the five major races of man evolved separately and at different times.

Daniel, Bradford. ed. *Black, White and Gray: Twenty-one Points of View on the Race Question*. New York: Sheed and Ward, 1964.

Dykeman, Wilma and Stokely, James. *Neither Black Nor White*. New York: Rinehart, 1957.
Two Southerners explore the unity and variation in the South—its change and continuity, the patterns of a section "neither black nor white," uncertain of the relations between the two.

Griffin, John H. *Black Like Me*. Boston: Houghton Mifflin Company, 1961.
This story of a white man who underwent all the agony of seeing discrimination from the brunt end is a challenge to any sensitive person. By a chemical process the author slowly darkened his skin; he describes the progressive stages of discrimination and rejection in New Orleans.

Lewis, Hylan. *Blackways of Kent*. Chapel Hill: The University of North Carolina Press, 1955.
This important source book for race relations tells the substance and meaning of a subculture in a southern town.

Mason, Philip. *Common Sense About Race*. New York: Macmillan, 1961.

Montagu, Ashley. *Man's Most Dangerous Myth: The Fallacy of Race*. New York: Harper and Brothers (First Edition, 1942), 1953.
The author tries to expose the false ideas of race, presenting the biological, psychological, and cultural aspects of the race question.

Myrdal, Gunnar. *An American Dilemma: The Negro Problem and Modern Democracy*. Revised edition. New York: Harper and Row, 1962.

This book has become the classic study of the Negro and racial problem in American life. It is still the best composite analysis of the larger social issues.

Putnam, Carleton. *Race and Reason, A Yankee View*. Washington: Public Affairs Press, 1961.
A defense of segregation, this attack on Boas' concept of anthropological equalitarianism asserts that the Negro is a "younger brother" who must be brought along. W. C. George supplements the author's biological views.

Record, Wilson. *Race and Radicalism: the NAACP and the Communist Party in Conflict*. Ithaca, New York: Cornell University Press, 1964.

Sabiston, Dothory and Hiller, Margaret. *Toward Better Race Relations*. Department of Data and Trends, National Board of the YWCA. New York: Women's Press, 1949.
This story of 17 local YWCAs in the community effort to improve race relations can be a helpful guide.

Smith, Lillian E. *Killers of the Dream*. Garden City, New York: Doubleday. Revised and enlarged edition, 1963.
The author poignantly portrays the South's tragic loss of creative social values, killed by the schizophrenic etiquette of white supremacy.

Stanton, William R. *The Leopard's Spots: Scientific Attitudes Toward Race in America, 1915-1959*. Chicago: University of Chicago Press, 1960.

Tumin, Melvin M. *Desegregation: Resistance and Readiness*. Princeton, New Jersey: Princeton University Press, 1958.
This valuable social science study of attitudes toward race relations and desegregation examines the factors of education, exposure to mass media and occupational status that influence such attitudes.

Woodward, C. Vann. *The Strange Career of Jim Crow*. New York: Oxford University Press. New and revised edition, 1957.
This history of Jim Crow reveals its social origins in the late nineteenth century.

SOUTHERN PERSPECTIVES

Ashmore, Harry. *An Epitaph for Dixie.* New York: W. W. Norton and Company, 1958.
   The former editor of the *Arkansas Gazette* expresses his views on the necessity and fact of change in the South.

Blair, Lewis H. *A Southern Prophecy: The Prosperity of the South Dependent Upon the Elevation of the Negro.* Edited with an Introduction by C. Vann Woodward. Boston: Little, Brown and Company, 1964.
   Published first in 1889, before the rise of Jim Crow, the book contains the view of a Richmond patrician that the economic well-being of the South rests on the elevation of the Negro to full equality.

Boyle, Sarah Patton. *The Desegregated Heart: A Virginian's Stand in Time of Transition.* New York: William Morrow and Company, 1962.
   This story is an account of the experiences that led a southern white woman to take a stand for Negro integration.

Cable, George F. *The Negro Queston: A Selection of Writings on Civil Rights in the South.* Edited by Arlin Turner. Garden City, New York: Doubleday, 1958.

Carter, Hodding, III. *The South Strikes Back.* Garden City, New York: Doubleday and Company, 1959.
   This book reveals the beginning of the Citizen's Councils, their increasing power through economic boycotts and keeping alive the specter of miscegenation.

Cash, W. J. *The Mind of the South.* New York: Alfred A. Knopf, 1941.
   This classic is still considered the most perceptive presentation of the development of the southern mind and attitudes.

Civil Rights and the South: A Symposium. Special Edition. *North Carolina Law Review,* Volume 42, No. 1, Fall, 1963. Chapel Hill, North Carolina.
   This is a reasoned and balanced monograph that includes an article by Senator Sam J. Ervin, Jr., and a preface by Attorney General Robert F. Kennedy.

Cook, James Graham. *The Segregationists*. New York: Appleton-Century-Crofts, 1962.

The author presents a cynical description of the segregationists and outlines an integration plan that will take 7,288 years, using 1962 calculations of integrated pupils.

Dabbs, James McBride. *The Southern Heritage*. New York: Alfred A. Knopf, 1958.

From concepts developed during a lifetime as a South Carolina planter and centered on the integrity and unity of the individual personality, the president of the Southern Regional Council expresses his views of the southern heritage and its transition.

Dollard, John. *Caste and Class in a Southern Town*. Garden City, New York: Doubleday (Third Edition), 1957.

This is another sociological classic of social conditions, culture, Negro subculture and a white attitude that forces Negroes into a caste system. First published in 1937.

Edmonds, Helen G. *The Negro and Fusion Politics in North Carolina, 1894-1901*. Chapel Hill: The University of North Carolina Press, 1951.

Equal Protection of the Laws in North Carolina. Report of the North Carolina Advisory Committee to the United States Commission on Civil Rights, 1959-1962. Washington: United States Government Printing Office, 1962.

Fitzhugh, George and Helper, Hinton R. *Ante-bellum: Writings of George Fitzhugh and Hinton Rowan Helper on Slavery*. Edited by Harvey Wish. New York: G. P. Putnam's Sons, 1960.

Fitzhugh was a prolific propagandist for slavery. A Virginian, he developed a Hobbesian "sociology for the South" that justified slavery as an integral part of that society.

Helper, a North Carolinian, fled the State after publishing a statistical and economic tract that criticized slavery as ruinous *(The Impending Crisis of the South)*.

Golden, Harry. *Mr. Kennedy and the Negroes*. Cleveland and New York: World Publishing Company, 1964.

This is a microcosm of the entire racial situation in the South.

Hays, Brooks. *A Southern Moderate Speaks*. Chapel Hill: The University of North Carolina Press, 1959.

Key, Valdimer O., Jr. *Southern Politics in State and Nation*. New York: Alfred A. Knopf, 1949.

Lewinson, Paul. *Race, Class and Party: A History of the Negro Suffrage and White Politics in the South*. New York: Russell and Russell, Inc., 1963.

McGill, Ralph E. *A Church, A School*. New York and Nashville: Abingdon Press, 1959.
In a series of brief essays, Editor McGill deplores the bombing of churches and schools. He believes these were the harvest of hate sown by defiance of law and order and calls for consecrated effort to face the necessities of our present situation.

McKean, Keith F. *Cross Currents in the South*. Denver: A. Swallow, 1960.

Nicholls, William H. *Southern Tradition and Regional Progress*. Chapel Hill: The University of North Carolina Press, 1960.
The author goads the South toward the better life as an integral part of the nation, seeing the problems of race and agrarian life as the core of the region's problems.

Norris, Hoke (ed.). *We Dissent*. New York: St. Martin's Press, 1962.
This is a selection of essays written by eminent southerners. It is a stirring voice of native opposition ("dissent from") to the rabid segregationists. All are white, Protestant, born and reared in the South, including Paul Green, Lenoir Chambers, and Hodding Carter III.

Peters, William. *The Southern Temper*. Garden City, New York: Doubleday and Company, 1959.
A report on the progress of desegregation in the Deep South reveals that there are church women, businessmen, labor leaders and responsible politicians (the "silent South") working to bring about an harmonious end to segregation.

Rowan, Carl T. *Go South to Sorrow*. New York: Random House, 1957.
The new director of USIA presents a touching analysis of the racial problem in America.

Sellers, Charles Grier (ed.). *The Southerner as American.* Chapel Hill: The University of North Carolina Press, 1960.
Nine southerners contribute an attempt to show some of the misinterpretations of southern history and differences between the South and the rest of the nation.

Silver, James W. *Mississippi: The Closed Society.* New York: Harcourt, Brace and World, Inc., 1964.

Warren, Robert Penn. *Segregation: The Inner Conflict in the South.* New York: Random House, 1956.
The author records sensitively conversations across Kentucky, Tennessee, Mississippi, and Louisiana, encompassing all aspects of the racial question in the South.

Wynes, Charles E. *Race Relations in Virginia, 1870-1902.* Charlottesville: The University of Virginia Press, 1961.

EDUCATION

Ashmore, Harry S. *The Negro and the Schools.* Chapel Hill: The University of North Carolina Press, Second edition, 1954.

Blossom, Virgil T. *It Has Happened Here.* New York: Harper and Brothers, 1959.
The tragic story of Little Rock stands as a warning.

Campbell, Ernest Q. *When A City Closes Its Schools.* Chapel Hill: The University of North Carolina, Institute for Research in Social Science, 1960.
This survey of the September, 1958, closing of the Norfolk public schools reveals the far-reaching effects of such action.

Carmichael, Omer and James, Weldon. *The Louisville Story.* New York: Simon and Schuster, 1957.

Coates, Albert and Paul, James C. W. *The School Segregation Decision.* Chapel Hill: The University of North Carolina, The Institute of Government, 1954.

Edwards, Newton. *The Courts and the Public Schools: The Legal Basis of School Organization and Administration.* Chicago: University of Chicago Press, Revised edition, 1955.

Green, Reginald H. (ed.). *The College Student and the Changing South.* Report of the Southwide Student Human Relations

Conference, 1958. Philadelphia: United States National Student Association, 1959.

Harlan, Louis R. *Separate and Unequal: Public School Campaigns and Racism in the Southern Seaboard States, 1901-1915*. Chapel Hill: The University of North Carolina Press, 1958.

Kilpatrick, James J. *The Southern Case for School Segregation*. Riverside, New Jersey: Crowell, Collier Press, 1962.

A prominent Virginian presents the conservative point of view. For his purposes, "the South" is the white South with an attitude on race relations derived from the old South. It is an apologia for a system that has disappeared now that every southern state has accepted some desegregation.

Muse, Benjamin. *Virginia's Massive Resistance*. Bloomington, Indiana: Indiana University Press, 1961.

Shoemaker, Don C. (ed.). *With All Deliberate Speed: Segregation-Desegregation in Southern Schools*. New York: Harper and Brothers, 1957.

This is the summary by the Southern Education Reporting Service of the first three years' developments after the 1954 decision.

Trillin, Calvin. *An Education in Georgia: The Integration of Charlayne Hunter and Hamilton Holmes*. New York: The Viking Press, 1963.

Wey, Herbert and Corey, John. *Action Patterns in School Desegregation: A Guidebook. Commission on the Study of Educational Policies and Programs in Relation to Desegregation*. Bloomington, Indiana: Phi Delta Kappa, 1959.

This is a guidebook that details the procedures and approaches that have been effective and ineffective and the accommodations and problems that have faced school desegregation.

Williams, Robin M., Jr. and Ryan, Margaret W. (eds.). *Schools in Transition: Community Experiences in Desegregation*. Chapel Hill: The University of North Carolina Press, 1954.

The authors report some of the experiences of 24 communities bordering the South as they moved toward desegregated schools, with stress on the role of law in the patterns of racial separation and integration in American school systems.

THE LAW AND RACE

Blaustein, Albert P. and Ferguson, Clarence C., Jr. *Desegregation and the Law: The Meaning and Effect of the School Segregation Cases*. New Brunswick, New Jersey: Rutgers University Press, 1957.

Gellhorn, Walter. *American Rights: The Constitution in Action*. New York: The Macmillan Company, 1960.

Greenberg, Jack. *Race Relations and American Law*. New York: Columbia University Press, 1959.

Harris, Robert J. *The Quest for Equality: The Constitution, Congress, and the Supreme Court*. Baton Rouge: Louisiana State University Press, 1960.
    This first complete synthesis of American political theory, constitutional history, and law with regard to equal protection presents in highly readable form the struggle for equality in this country.

McKean, Dayton David. *The Integrated Bar*. Boston: Houghton Mifflin Company, 1963.

Murray, Pauli. *State's Laws on Race and Color, and Appendices Containing International Documents, Federal Laws and Regulations, Local Ordinances and Charts*. Cincinnati: Woman's Division of Christian Service, Board of Missions and Church Extension. Methodist Church, 1951.

Peltason, Jack W. *Fifty-Eight Lonely Men: Southern Federal Judges and School Desegregation*. New York: Harcourt, Brace and World, Inc., 1961.
    This is the story of the pressures, threats and isolation of 58 federal district judges, all southerners, whose duty it was to uphold and apply the national law in desegregation cases.

Ziegler, Benjamin Munn (ed.). *Desegregation and the Supreme Court*. Boston: D. C. Heath and Company, 1958.

NEGRO CULTURE, HISTORY, LIFE, AND WORK

Baldwin, James. *Nobody Knows My Name: More Notes of a Native Son*. New York: The Dial Press, 1961.

——————. *Notes of a Native Son.* Boston: Beacon Press, 1955.

Bardolph, Richard. *The Negro Vanguard.* New York: Rinehart and Company, 1959.

This study of Negro leadership, its source and qualities, in the United States presents the history of the struggle for a full realization of our democracy. The author teaches at the University of North Carolina at Greensboro.

Booker, Simeon. *Black Man's America.* Englewood, New Jersey: Prentice-Hall, Inc., 1964.

Burgess, Margaret E. *Negro Leadership in a Southern City.* Chapel Hill: The University of North Carolina Press, 1962.

This sociological study of Negro leadership in "Crescent City" (Durham, N. C.) deals with the three phenomena of power, desegregation and the structure of the Negro sub-community.

Butcher, Margaret Just. *The Negro in American Culture.* New York: Alfred A. Knopf, Inc., 1956.

David, R. E. *The American Negroes' Dilemma.* New York: Philosophical Library, 1954.

This is a brief, objective portrayal of the Negro as he fits into the politcial, social, economic, fraternal, and religious parts of American society.

Ellison, Ralph. *Invisible Man.* New York: Random House, 1952.

Essien-Udom, E. U. *Black Nationalism: A Search for an Identity in Amercia.* Chicago: University of Chicago Press, 1962.

Franklin, John Hope. *From Slavery to Freedom: A History of American Negroes.* New York: Alfred A. Knopf, Inc., 1956.

This is a new edition of a work that relates Negro history to other forces in the American heritage.

Frazier, Edward Franklin. *Black Bourgeoisie.* Glencoe, Illinois: The Free Press of Glencoe, 1957.

——————. *The Negro in the United States.* Revised edition. New York: The Macmillan Company, 1957.

Originally published in 1932, this book is almost a classic as a comprehensive study of the life of the Negro; especially pertinent to problems in industrial areas.

Ginzberg, Eli. *The Negro Potential.* New York: Columbia University Press, 1956.
The author traces the economic gains made by Negroes between 1940 and 1956 and the challenges yet to be faced before the country can fully utilize the latent potential of the Negro race.

Humphrey, Hubert H. ed. *Integration vs. Segregation.* New York: Thomas Y. Crowell Company, 1964.

Johnson, James Weldon. *Black Manhattan.* New York: A. A. Knopf, 1930.
The book describes the rediscovery of the Negro intellectual and the Negro renaissance of art in the late 1920s.

Karon, Bertram P. *The Negro Personality: A Rigorous Investigation of the Effects of Culture.* New York: Springer Publishing Company, 1958.

Lincoln, Eric. C. *The Black Muslims in America.* Boston: Beacon Press, 1961.

Logan, Frenise A. *The Negro in North Carolina 1876-1894.* Chapel Hill: The University of North Carolina Press, 1964.

Meier, August. *Negro Thought in America, 1880-1915.* Ann Arbor: University of Michigan Press, 1963.

Moon, Henry Lee. *Balance of Power: The Negro Vote.* Garden City, New York: Doubleday and Company, 1948.

National Planning Association. *Selected Studies of Negro Employment in the South: Four Studies of Negro Employment in the Upper South.* Chapel Hill: Prepared for the National Planning Association Committee of the South, 1955.

Nichols, Lee. *Breakthrough on the Color Front.* New York: Random House, 1954.
This account reveals the impact of the integration of the Negro into the Armed Forces upon military efficiency, foreign relations, and social change at home.

Redding, J. Saunders. *The Lonesome Road: The Story of the Negro's Part in America.* New York: Doubleday and Company, 1958.

Starkey, Marion L. *Striving to Make It My Home: The Story of Americans From Africa.* New York: W. W. Norton and Company, Inc., 1964.

Thompson, Daniel C. *The Negro Leadership Class.* Englewood Cliffs, New Jersey: Prentice-Hall, 1963.
This is a case study of Negro leadership tactics and strategy in New Orleans.

Weaver, Robert C. *The Negro Ghetto.* New York: Harcourt, Brace and Company, 1948.

THE NEGRO AND SOCIAL MOVEMENTS

Albany. Atlanta: Southern Regional Council, Winter, 1962.

Brink, William and Harris, Louis. *The Negro Revolution in America.* New York: Simon and Schuster, 1964.
This is the book form of the classic *Newsweek* article, enlarged and elaborated.

The Freedom Rides. Atlanta: Southern Regional Council, May, 1961.

Garfinkel, Herbert. *When Negroes March: The March on Washington Movement in the Organizational Politics for F.E.P.C.* Glencoe, Illinois: The Free Press, 1959.

Hayden, Tom. *Revolution in Mississippi.* New York: Students for a Democratic Society, 1962.

Johns, Major. *It Happened in Baton Rouge, USA.* New York: Congress of Racial Equality, 1962.

Kahn, Tom. *Unfinished Revolution.* New York: Students for a Democratic Society, 1960.
This is a comprehensive and detailed report on the Southern sit-in struggle, with additional chapters on the Negro in labor and politics.

King, Martin Luther, Jr. *Letter from Birmingham Jail.* Philadelphia: American Friends Service Committee, 1963.

—————————. *Stride Toward Freedom.* New York: Harper and Brothers, 1958.
This book tells of the victory of passive resistance in the

Montgomery bus boycott and is an excellent documentary and an important reference on the current situation in the South.

——————. *Why We Can't Wait.* New York, Evanston, and London: Harper and Row, 1963.

Lomax, Louis E. *The Negro Revolt.* New York: Harper and Row, 1962.
 The author presents the current Negro revolt as a continued episode of the American revolution. The book is an excellent study of the rise of the more active civil rights organizations and their challenge to the Negro leadership in the established ones such as NAACP.

The Negro Protest. James Baldwin, Malcolm X, Martin Luther King, Jr. talk with Kenneth B. Clark. Boston: Beacon Press, 1963.

Patrick, Clarence H. *Lunch-Counter Desegregation in Winston-Salem, North Carolina.* A Report of the Mayor's Good Will Committee, 1963.

Peck, James. *Freedom Ride.* New York: Simon and Schuster, 1962.

Proudfoot, Merrill. *Diary of a Sit-In.* Chapel Hill: The University of North Carolina Press, 1962.

Record, Wilson. *The Negro and the Communist Party.* Chapel Hill: The University of North Carolina Press, 1951.

Silberman, Charles E. *Crisis in Black and White.* New York: Random House, 1964.

Steps Toward Equality. A Report on Desegregation in the United States. Philadelphia: United States National Student Association, July, 1961.

The Student Protest Movement. Atlanta: Southern Regional Council, 1960.

Wakefield, Dan. *Revolt in the South.* New York: Grove Press (Evergreen), 1960.

RELIGION AND RACE

Haselden, Kyle. *The Racial Problem in Christian Perspective.* New York: Harper and Brothers, 1959.

—————. *The Bible and Race*. Nashville: The Broadman Press, 1959.

Maston, Thomas Bufford. *Segregation and Desegregation: A Christian Approach*. New York: The Macmillan Company, 1959.

Pettigrew, Thomas F. and Campbell, Ernest Q. *Christians in the Racial Crisis: A Study of Little Rock's Ministry*. Washington: Public Affairs Press, 1959.
    This study of the Little Rock ministry is a scientific analysis of factors bearing on the role of ministers and churches in the racial issue.

Richardson, Harry Van Buren. *Dark Glory, A Picture of the Church Among Negroes in the Rural South*. New York: The Friendship Press, Published for Home Missions Council of North American and Phelps-Stokes Fund, 1947.
    This study deals with the history and setting of the Negro church in the South.

Sellers, James E. *The South and Christian Ethics*. New York: Association Press, 1962.

Tilson, Charles Everett. *Segregation and the Bible*. New York: Abingdon Press, 1958.

Articles

"As Trouble Spreads: Ten Years of Mixed Schools," *U.S. News and World Report*, September 16, 1963, pp. 33-35.

Bickel, Alexander M. "Beyond Tokenism: The Civil Rights Task That Looms Ahead," *The New Republic*, January 4, 1964, pp. 11-14.

Brooks, Tom. "Negro Militants, Jewish Liberals, and the Unions," *Commentary*, September, 1961, pp. 209-216.

Carter, Barbara. "The Fifteenth Amendment Comes to Mississippi," *The Reporter*, XXVIII (January 17, 1963), pp. 20-24.

Carter, Hodding, III. "Desegregation Does Not Mean Integration," *The New York Times Magazine*, February 11, 1962, pp. 21, 71-72.

Chapin, Thomas T. "When Negro Child Meets White," A Special Report in *The Christian Century*, October 30, 1963, pp. 1333-1334.

"The Civil Rights Movement," *Current*, October, 1963, pp. 35-55.

Clark, Dennis. "Racism in the North," *Commonweal*, March 27, 1959, pp. 663-665.

Coles, Robert. "In the South These Children Prophesy," *The Atlantic Monthly*, CCXI, March, 1963, pp. 111-116.

Courtenay, Walter R. "Can Laws Make Men Equal? — A Minister's Answer," *U.S. News and World Report*, November 18, 1963, pp. 113-116.

Dugan, Kieran. "The Race Question: One View," *America*, February 20, 1960, pp. 606-607.

Dunbar, Ernest. "The Negro in America Today," *Look*, April 10, 1962, pp. 26-36.

Elfin, Mel. "Why Pick on New Rochelle?" *The Reporter*, December 8, 1960, pp. 28-30.

Fisher, J. E. "Leadership, Education and Our Racial Predicament," *The South Atlantic Quarterly*, LXII, 1963, pp. 532-538.

Friedrich, Carl J. "Rights, Liberties, Freedoms: A Reappraisal," *The American Political Science Review*, Volume 57, No. 4, December, 1963, pp. 841-854.

Gruenberg, Robert. "Dixie Hate in Yankee Suburb," *The Nation*, January 16, 1960, pp. 47-50.

Harrington, Michael. "Harlem Today," *Dissent*, Summer, 1961, pp. 371-377.

"How Whites Feel About Negroes: A Painful Dilemma," *Newsweek*, October 21, 1963, pp. 44-57.

Johnson, Gerald W. "To Live and Die in Dixie," *The Atlantic Monthly*, Volume 206, No. 1, July, 1960, pp. 29-34.

King, Martin Luther, Jr. "Report on Civil Rights: Fumbling on the New Frontier," *The Nation,* March 3, 1962, pp. 190-193.

Lee, J. O. "Racism: Effects, Origins, Remedies," *The Christian Century*, LXXX, July 17, 1963, pp. 907-909.

Lomax, Almena. "Journey to the Beginning: A Northern Negro Moves to Dixie," *The Nation*, March 25, 1961, pp. 249-256.

Magner, Thomas A. "The Race Question: Another View; Negroes Next Door," *America*, February 20, 1960, pp. 608-609.

Matthews, Donald R. and Prothro, James W. "Political Factors and Negro Voter Registration in the South," *The American Political Science Review*, Volume 57, June, 1963, pp. 355-367.

Meyer, Agnes E. "Middle-Class Negroes Should Assume More Responsibility," Text of Letter to *The New York Times*, June 29, 1963, *U.S. News and World Report*, July 15, 1963, p. 61.

Moon, Henry Lee. "The Negro Voter," *The Nation*, September 17, 1960, pp. 155-157.
    This now classic article on the 1963 summer protest of the American Negro is required reading for everyone.

"The Negro's Future in the South: Interview with Governor Barnett of Mississippi," *U.S. News and World Report*, June 3, 1963, pp. 60-64.
    An exclusive interview with Governor Ross Barnett.

Podhoretz, Norman (Moderator). "Liberalism and the Negro: A Round-Table Discussion," by James Baldwin, Nathan Glazer, Sidney Hook, and Gunnar Myrdal, *Commentary*, March, 1964, pp. 25-42.

——————————. "My Negro Problem—And Ours," *Commentary*, February, 1963, pp. 93-101.

Russell, Richard B. "The South States Its Case," *U.S. News and World Report*, June 24, 1963, p. 78.
    Full text of a statement by Senator Richard B. Russell, June 12, 1963.

Samuels, Gertrude. "Little Rock Revisited, Tokenism Plus," *The New York Times Magazine*, June 2, 1963, p. 13, 57-58, 60.

Silberman, Charles E. "The Businessman and the Negro," *Fortune*, LXVIII, No. 3, September, 1963, pp. 97 ff.

Stringfellow, William. "Race, Religion and Revenge: Negroes in New York's Harlem," *The Christian Century*, February 14, 1962, pp. 192-194.

"Tokenism Frustrates Negro Hopes," *The Christian Century,* LXXX, March, 1963, p. 357.

"What New Turn in Negro Drive Means," *U. S. News and World Report,* June 17, 1963, pp. 40-47.

"Where The Color Bars Are Quietly Dropping," *U.S. News and World Report,* June 24, 1963, pp. 42-43.
    This is a good report on voluntary desegregation in Durham, Winston-Salem, and Greensboro that may be a pattern for the South.

Woodward, C. Vann. "A Southerner's Answer to the Negro Question," *The Reporter,* February 27, 1964, pp. 39-44.

Yinger, J. Milton. "Desegregation in American Society: The Record of a Generation of Change," *Sociology and Social Research,* XLVIII, July, 1963, pp. 428-445.

VIEWS OF THE AUGUST 28, 1963, MARCH ON WASHINGTON.

VII

Index

case cited, 238; second case cited, 234, 239.

Bullard, William Robert, III, sentenced, 49.

Burlington, Alamance County Committee of Civic Affairs is active Negro organization, Alamance Voters League operates there, 27; "Burlington Plan" recommended in Lexington, 125; CORE has active chapter there, municipal report of, NAACP has active chapter there, Negro organizations there, cited, 27.

Burlington Industries, Mooresville, practices "equal employment," 131.

Butterfield, G. K., picture of, 258.

C

Camp Lejeune, officers of, visit Jacksonville Mayor to discuss contents of Navy Directive, 114.

Campbell, Joe G., serves on Goldsboro Biracial Committee, 86.

Capitol Square, picture of group demonstrating there, 241.

Carey, Gordon, calls 1960 Shaw University meeting, 1.

Carr, George Watts, Jr., serves as chairman, Durham Interim Committee, Durham, 67.

Carson v. Board of Education, cited, 239.

Carson v. Warlick, cited, 239.

Carver, George Washington, picture of, 13.

Celebrezze, Anthony J., speaks at Greenville, 100.

Chadwick, W. C., his report of Biracial Committee, New Bern, 201-205; mentioned, 191; serves as chairman, Biracial Committee, New Bern, 133.

Chapel Hill, Board of Aldermen of: amends picketing ordinance, 38; fails to vote, public accommodations ordinance, 35; lacks authority for ordinance, 43; meets with Human Relations Committee, 41; Church of God there (Carrboro), demonstrators leave, 37; Citizens' United for Racial Equality and Dignity (CURED) of, replace Committee for Open Business, 33; civil rights cases of, transferred to Orange County Superior Court, 36; civil rights

cases of, tried, 51; Committee for Open Business (COB) of, organizes, 30; Committee of Concerned Citizens of, picket four establishments, 41; "Committee of 100," there, mentioned, 39; CORE chapter of, organizes demonstrations, demonstrators there arrested, 37; Durham NAACP-CORE chapter sponsors demonstration, 29; First Baptist Church of: destination of Durham-Chapel Hill "walk," 35, rally there, 42; first "freedom ride" passes through, 1; Freedom Committee of, holds fast, 42; Freedom Movement there, stages march, 37; Human Relations Committee of, biracial organization, 29; Institute of Government, mentioned, 46; Ku Klux Klan, holds meeting there, 42; Lincoln High School stages walkout, 39; Mayor's Committee on Integration of, organizes, 43; Mayor's Mediation Committee of: activities of, inaugurated, 47, meets with Human Relations Committee, 41; Merchants' Association of, requests dropping of charges against demonstrators, 33; municipal report of, 29-52; NAACP of, organizes demonstrations, 37; North Carolina Memorial Hospital, limited segregation there, protested, 29; North Carolina Council of Human Rights, adopts resolution, 47; Peace Union of, organizes demonstrations, 37; picture of Board of Aldermen of, 44; picture of demonstrators there, 38; picture of fast at Post Office, 42; picture of parking lot demonstration, 50; picture of pro-civil rights letters being mailed there, 28; picture of sit-down demonstration there, 39; picture of street demonstration there, 34; picture of Sunday "walk" to, 32; proposed public accommodations ordinance of, 45-47; public accommodations ordinance introduced there, 3; St. Joseph Methodist Church: protest demonstration begins there, 43, COB meets there, 31; Student Conference Educational Fund of, organizes demonstrations, 37; Student Non-violent Co-ordinat-

with Mayor's Biracial Committee, 82, has active chapter, 80,
Negotiating Committee of, meets
with Mayor, 82, sponsors student demonstrations, 81; Greensboro chapter of, directs demonstration, 89; Greenville, sponsors Emancipation Proclamation
Day, 93; High Point: chapter of,
cited, 107, seeks objectives, 109;
Jacksonville, committee of, visits store managers in quest of
additional job opportunities for
Negroes, 115; Juniors, Goldsboro, establish "Study In" program, 87; Kinston, Adult and
Youth chapters of, active, 116;
Laurinburg, has active chapter,
121; Mount Airy, meets with
Board of Commissioners to authorize biracial committee, 132;
Raleigh, has active chapter, 138;
Reidsville, chapter of: has youth
and young adult branches, petitions for reforms, 144; Rockingham County, has active chapter,
144; Surry County, has active
membership, 131; Tarboro, requests organization of Community Relations Committee, 160;
Warren County, chapter of, se-
cures injunction against Warrenton school board, 163; Warrenton, has active chapter, 163;
Whiteville, chapter there, 165;
Wilmington, chapter of, active
there, 176.
"Negro and the Law When the
Nation was Founded, The,"
249-250.
Negro Exodus from North Carolina, The, picture of, 4.
Negroes, discrimination against,
discussed, 9; economic status of,
discussed, 260; map of potential
voters registered in State, 196;
map showing distribution of, in
North Carolina, 8; map showing family income of, 222; number of employed in State Government, 265-267; petition of, for
equality, 10-11; population per
cent, 10; population statistics of,
4-5; slaves, origin of, 7; table
showing number of, employed in
State Government, 267.
Nelms, John K., selected as chairman, Oxford Biracial Committee, 137.
Nelson, James A., picture of, 258.
New Bern, Biracial Committee of,

biracial organization, 133; municipal report of, 133-134; report
of Biracial Committee there, 191,
201-205.
New Hanover County, Board of
Commissioners of, appoints Biracial Committee, 176; citizens
urged to adopt fair policies, 177;
Wilmington-New Hanover County Biracial Committee of, biracial organization, 176.
New York Times, The, carries feature on Reynolds Tobacco Company, 261; publishes articles by
Eli Ginzberg, 249; reports David Schenck's statement, 194.
Newport, Biracial Committee of,
biracial organization, Cherry
Point Mutual Veterans Housing
Association segregates park facilities there, municipal report
of, 135.
Noble, Cecil W., serves as chairman, Hickory Community Relations Council, Hickory, 104.
Norfleet, Roscoe C., serves as
chairman, Progressive Citizens
Council, Greenville, 93.
North Carolina, "Constructive
Creed" for Negro Citizens, outlined, 11-13; State Government
of, employs Negroes, 265-267,
table of employees in State Government, 267.
North Carolina College, Durham,
scene of sympathy demonstrations, 64; students of, arrested,
36.
North Carolina Council of Human
Rights, adopts resolution, Chapel
Hill, 47.
North Carolina Good Neighbor
Council, activities of, discussed,
257-258; deals with economic aspects of race problem, 3; emphasizes education, 258-259;
Good Neighbor Program, goal
of, cited, 266; has brochure
available, 259; picture of, 258;
purposes of, 255.
"North Carolina Good Neighbor
Council, The," report on, 255-
266.
North Carolina Fund, mentioned,
225, proposed program of, men-
tioned, 219; selects Rockingham-
Richmond County area, 148.
North Carolina Intercollegiate
Council for Human Rights, approves second program, 255; or-

ganized by Negro students, 253; picture of, 254.

North Carolina Joint Council on Health and Citizenship, Andrew A. Best serves as chairman of, 93, discussed, 99-101; listed, 93; organized, 99.

North Carolina Merchants' Association, reports on Negro employment, 261-262.

North Carolina Performing Arts School, Winston-Salem, mentioned, 185.

North Carolina Press Institute, addressed by Terry Sanford, 255.

North Carolina State (of the University of North Carolina at Raleigh), students of, implement street marches, 139.

North Carolina Mayors' Co-operating Committee, opinion of, 189; picture of, 190; results from Mayors meeting, Greensboro, varies method of settling race problems, 3.

O

Orange County Superior Court, adjournment of, 43; cases transferred there, 37; civil rights cases tried, 36, 37, 39, 47; closes after five special weeks, 51; discussed, 48; gains jurisdiction in civil rights cases, 49; sentences given by, protested, 43.

Ordinances, examples of, to control street demonstrations and picketing, 245-249; one creating biracial council, Greensboro, 194-198.

Ottaway, Richard N., serves as chairman, Pitt County Interracial Committee, Greenville, 93.

Oxford, Biracial Commission of: biracial organization, 135, organized to supersede Biracial Committee, 137; Biracial Committee of, Negroes request organization of, 137; Good Neighbor Council of: biracial organization, 135, Negroes request organization of, 137; Granville County Co-ordinating Committee, Negroes request organization of, 137; municipal report of, 135-138.

P

Page, Joe, picture of, 44.

Parker, Clarence, elected co-chairman, COB, 31.

Parker, Kellis, leads demonstrations sponsored by CORE, Kinston, 116.

Parker, William T., picture of, 254.

Parks, North Carolina, mentioned, 236; relevant laws discussed by Moody, 240; see Municipal Reports.

Pate, J. W., Jr., mentioned, 210; serves as chairman, Mayor's Biracial Committee, Fayetteville, 80.

Peck, Robert H., picture of, 44.

Penn, Mrs. Nannie N., meets with Mount Airy Board of Commissioners to discuss Negro representation on Board of Education and employment problems, 131.

Perry, Dan E., attends first meeting, Mayor's Biracial Committee, 117; serves as chairman, Mayor's Biracial Committee, Kinston, 116.

Pearsall, Thomas J., appointed as chairman, Special Advisory Committee on Education, 237; serves as chairman, 230.

Pearsall Committee, see Special Advisory Committee on Education.

Pearsall Plan, includes amendment of State Constitution, 231; mentioned, 238; prevents major Negro discontent, 231; statutes of, cited, 236-238.

Peterson v. City of Greenville, cited, 70; Earl Warren speaks for Supreme Court, 67.

Petitioners, picture of, for desegregation, 204; picture of, in friendship circle, 212; picture of, on State Capitol steps, 142; picture of, picketing segregated theater, 90.

Pfaff, Pamela, picture of, 254.

Phillips, G. Vic, serves as Mayor, Gastonia, 84.

Picketers, for equal employment, picture of, 264; picture of, at eating establishment, 188; picture of, demonstrating against unequal employment, 126; picture of, petitioning for open accommodations, 75.

Picketing, Kinston, ordinances pertaining to, 245-249.

Piephoff, Zachary T., Jr., serves as chairman, Human Relations Committee, Asheboro, 20; picture of, 21.

Pierce, Sterling B., serves as Mayor, Weldon, 165.
Pitt County, Pitt County Interracial Committee, Greenville, work of, 99; work of, discussed, 95-99, *passim;* United Pitt County Citizens' Council there, presents Negro viewpoint, United Pitt County Citizens' League, oldest group, presents Negro viewpoint, 93.
Pitts, Mrs. Elsie W., picture of, 268.
Plaster, Hubert S., serves as Mayor, Shelby, 155.
Population, that of Negroes in North Carolina, map showing, 8.
Poulos v. New Hampshire, cited, 242.
Powell, Junius K. serves as Mayor, Whiteville, 165.
Pray-in, picture of, in High Point, 108.
Proctor, Samuel D., speaks at Greenville, 100.
Public accommodations, picture of demonstrators protesting segregation of, 118; picture of picketers petitioning for, 75; proposed Chapel Hill ordinance for, 45-47; relevant laws discussed by Moody, 240; *see* Municipal Reports.
Public accommodations ordinance, picture of Chapel Hill Board of Aldermen meeting on, 44; pictures of demonstration for, 40.
Public disturbances, Kinston, ordinance pertaining to, 245-249.
Public school system, relevant laws discussed by Moody, 238-240; *see* Municipal Reports; *see* Pearsall Plan.
Public School Laws of North Carolina, cited, 238.

R

Raleigh, "Committee of One Hundred," deals with problems caused by demonstrations, 139; Community Relations Committee of, biracial organization, 138; CORE chapter of, active there, 138; Mayor's Community Relations Committee of: appointed by Mayor, 139, issues "Statement of Purpose," 140-141; Mechanic's Committee of "Committee of One Hundred," aids in

gradual desegregation, 139; mentioned, 202; municipal report of, 138-143; NAACP chapter of, active there, 138; North Carolina State, students of, implement street marches, 139; picture of demonstrators there, 136; picture of marchers there, 170; plans "Community Relations Week," 142; Raleigh Citizens Association of, encourages Negro registration and seeks Negro job opportunities, 138; St. Augustine's College there, major Negro college, 139; Shaw University there: major Negro college, 138, 139, site of 1960 meeting of CORE leaders, 1.
Raper, Hugh M., picture of, 268.
Rauch, Marshall A., picture of, 258; serves as chairman, Human Relations Committee, Gastonia, 84.
Ray, Moses, serves as chairman, East Tarboro Citizens Council, Tarboro, 160.
Recreation, relevant laws discussed by Moody, 240; *see* Municipal Reports.
Redding, Mrs. W. F., Jr., picture of, 21.
Reese, R. L., serves as Mayor, Asheboro, 20.
Reid, A. B., picture of, 86.
Reid, James W., picture of, iii; serves as Mayor, Raleigh, 138; serves on Mayors' Co-operating Committee, 190.
Reidsville, American Tobacco Company there: desegregates facilities and adopts fair employment practices, 146, Negro labor union of, aids in leadership of Negro movement, 143; has informal biracial conference, 143; municipal report of, 143-147; NAACP chapter of, petitions for reforms, 144; Rockingham County has NAACP chapters, 144.
Reynolds Tobacco Company, Winston-Salem, featured in *The New York Times,* 261; offers equal employment to Negroes, 260-261.
Revolutionary War, Negro slaves who serve for British, have chance at freedom, 250.
Rice, Joe S., appointment as chairman, Good Neighbor Council, Winston-Salem, 184; serves as chairman, Good Neighbor Council, 180; serves as chairman,

Warrenton, 163.

Strause, Nathan P., Jr., serves as chairman, Biracial Committee, Henderson, 101.

Street demonstration, Kinston, ordinances pertaining to, 245-249; relevant laws discussed by Moody, 242.

Strother, J. P., serves on North Carolina Good Neighbor Council, 258.

Strowd, Gene, picture of, 44.

Student Non-violent Co-ordinating Committee (SNCC), organizes in Nashville, Tennessee, 1; organizes demonstrations, Chapel Hill, 37.

Suddreth, Henry C., serves as chairman, Good Neighbor Council, Kinston, 116, 117.

Summary of Statements and Actions by Governor Luther Hodges, mentioned, 237.

Surry County, has active NAACP chapter, 131.

Swann, Melvin C., picture of, 65.

T

Taft, William Howard, mentioned, 250.

Talton, Hugh C., serves as Mayor, Smithfield, 156.

Tarboro, Community Relations Committee of: biracial organization, subcommittee of, confers with representative of Industrial Educational Center, Wilson, 160; East Tarboro Citizens Council of: plans adult education program, supports Community Relations Committee, 160; facemask ordinance of, aimed at Ku Klux Klan, 161; municipal report of, 160-161; NAACP there, requests organization of Community Relations Committee, 160; Negro citizens there, form East Tarboro Citizens Council, 160.

Taylor, Mrs. Bettye, picture of, 21.

Taylor, Mrs. George, serves as chairman, Human Relations Committee, Chapel Hill, 29.

Taylor, James T., picture of, 258, 268; serves as vice-chairman, North Carolina Good Neighbor Council, 257.

Taylor, Lavert, picture of, 42.

Theaters, picture of picketers at segregated one, 90.

Thomasville, Biracial Committee of, biracial organization, municipal report of, shares industrial school with Lexington, 162.

Tieger, Joseph "Buddy," sentenced, 51.

Treadwell, Mary, picture of, 254.

U

Umstead, William B., appoints Special Advisory Committee on Education, 236; committee appointed by, reports on school desegregation policy, 229; committee of, commended by General Assembly, 1955, 229; death of, 227; names committee to study school integration problem, 3; names committee to study Supreme Court decision, 227; picture of, 228, 234; receives report, committee studying Supreme Court decision, 229; serves as Governor, 227.

United States, Supreme Court of, decisions of, in Brown cases, 238-239; May, 1954, decision of, cited, 3; resolution supporting appeal to, 229; school desegregation decision called unlawful, 227; supports "separate but equal" provisions, 251; Umstead committee report to, on school desegregation decision, 229; Umstead committee studies school desegregation decision, 227; William B. Rodman files brief with, 229.

United States Circuit Court of Appeals, Fifth Circuit, hears cases, 171.

United States District Court, Eastern District, cases moved to, from Martin County, 169; Middle District: permits free assignment of Negro pupils, Durham, 69, mentioned, 48, rules on the Orange County Superior Court verdicts, 49.

University of North Carolina, Chapel Hill, faculty members of, march, 39; Floyd B. McKissick, first Negro student of, 37; Institute of Government, memorandum of, prepared by George H. Esser, Jr., 46; NAACP chapter there, co-operates with Durham NAACP, 29; professor of, tried, 48; student of, leads Kin-

to United States District Court, 169; desegregated Easter Service there, 175; E. J. Hayes School, students of, organize boycott, 171; files petitions for remanding cases to Martin County Superior Court, 171; "Freedom Rallies" held nightly there, 171; Martin County: Board of Commissioners there, votes to discontinue participation in federal surplus food program, 174, Courthouse there, scene of mass arrest, 169, Sheriff's Department of, provides protection for demonstrators there, 168, Superior Court of, hears action instituted by demonstrators against Town, 169, Welfare Department of, furnishes food and clothing to persons there, 174; municipal report of, 166-174; needy families of, helped by trust fund, 174; Negroes send "Freedom Choir" to Boston, Massachusetts, 171; picture of Greene Memorial Christian Church there, 167; picture of leaders there, 167; Police Department of, provides protection for demonstrators, 168; Southern Christian Leadership Conference: leads peaceful demonstrations, there, 167, sends representative to work with local unit, there, 172; United States Circuit Court of Appeals, Fifth Circuit, hears cases, 171.

Wilmington, Biracial Committee appointed, 176; citizens of, urged to adopt fair policies, 177; CORE, chapter of, active there, 176; Industrial Education Center there, desegregated, 178; municipal report of, 176-178; NAACP has active chapter, 176; Wilmington-New Hanover County Biracial Committee of: aims of, 176-177, biracial organization, 176, confidence expressed in, 177.

Wilson, Citizens Committee of: biracial organization, makes survey, 178; City and County Boards of Commissioners of, hear recommendations, 179; Darden High School there, prepares students for trades, 179; equal employment policies there, 261; Good Neighbor Council of: biracial organization, 178, formation of, 179; Industrial Education Center of: cited, 160, prepares students for trades, 179; munici-

pal report of, 178-180.
Wilson, A. R., reviews Assistant Attorney General's opinion, 70.
Wilson, Fred M., serves as Mayor, Monroe, 129.
Wilson, John D., serves as Mayor, Wilson, 178.
Wilson, Kenneth B., named first chairman, Mount Airy Human Relations Council, 132; serves as chairman, Human Relations Council, 131.
Winston-Salem, employment statistics of, 263; equal employment opportunities urged there, 185; Good Neighbor Council of: biracial organization, 180, has never met, 184; Governor's School there, mentioned, 185; Mayor's Good Will Committee of: biracial organization, 180, members appointed, purpose of, 183; municipal report of, 180-185; North Carolina Performing Arts School there, 185; Reynolds Tobacco Company there: featured in *The New York Times*, 261, offers equal employment to Negroes, 260-261; Rockefeller Foundation, General Education Board of, finances Winston-Salem race relations survey, 180-181; Salem College there: concerts open to public, 184, desegregated, 185; survey made of reaction to desegregated eating places, 182; Urban League of: biracial organization, 180, mentioned, 184, work discussed, 181; Wake Forest College there: concerts open to public, 184, desegregated, 185.
Winters, John W., picture of, 258.
Woltz, William K., serves as chairman, Employment Activities Committee, Chamber of Commerce, Mount Airy, 131.
Women's Good Will Committee, High Point, copied by women of Goldsboro, 87.
Woolly, Donald, picture of, 21.
Woolworth, lunch counter of, Durham, desegregates, 75.

Y

Young, Aurelia L., picture of, 254.

Z

Zane, E. R., serves on North Carolina Good Neighbor Council, 258.

"The dogmas of the quiet past are inadequate to the stormy present . . . We must think anew and act anew."

ABRAHAM LINCOLN

DATE DUE

NOV 5 '86			
NOV 19 '86			
DEC 3 '86			
NOV 10 '87			

PRINTED IN U.S.A.